Landscape in Lavender

Landscape in Lavender

Brooks Kolb

SHE WRITES PRESS

Published in 2026 by
SparkPress, an imprint of The Stable Book Group

1569 Solano Ave #546
Berkeley, CA 94707
https://shewritespress.com

Library of Congress Control Number: 2026904473
ISBN: 979-8-89636-380-4
eISBN: 979-8-89636-381-1

Interior Designer: Andrea Reider
Interior illustrations by Brooks Kolb

Printed in the United States

This book is memoir. It reflects the author's present recollections of experiences over time. Names and identifying characteristics have been changed to protect the privacy of certain individuals.

Dedicated to the memory of James Colles Draper
(December 1, 1956–September 30, 1993)

*May this story take the place of the panel in the
AIDS Memorial Quilt that you were never granted*

And dedicated to the memory of my grandfather Percy F. Kolb,
who once told me, "If all else fails, you might try writing."

TABLE OF CONTENTS

PART 1: Open the Closet Door

PART 2: Open Your Golden Gate

City Hall from Benjamin Franklin Parkway, Philadelphia

PART 1

Open the Closet Door

Consult the genius of the place in all.

—Alexander Pope, "Epistle IV to Richard Boyle,
Earl of Burlington"

1   URBAN COWBOY

"NOBODY'S COMING," my beautiful blonde housemate said.

"Good," I said. "Now, on the count of three!"

Grunting, we hoisted the heavy, broken-down couch over the open windowsill and gleefully shoved it out the fourth-floor kitchen window. The loud thud it made when it hit the ground and splintered was most satisfying.

"I don't think we have to clean it up, do you?" asked Birgyte.

"Of course not!" I said, as we high-fived.

Returning to the living room, we gazed back toward the kitchen, equally revolted by the sight of peeling, yellow paint and patchy, linoleum floor tiles. I popped open a bottle of champagne and clinked glasses with Birgyte.

"Here's to our graduation!" I said.

Laughing at our sordid surroundings, we enthusiastically toasted our imminent departure from the crumbling, off-campus apartment we had shared for the last three years.

Then I hugged Birgyte goodbye and escorted her down four flights of stairs. Outside, her blue MGB convertible waited at the curb.

"Goodbye, Ducky!" I yelled.

Birgyte gave a quick wave and hopped in the car. The engine revved and screeched as she zoomed off, disappearing around the corner. While I was destined to stay in Philadelphia to start my job at the city's most up-and-coming landscape architectural firm, she was already on her way to a new life in California.

Momentarily saddened by Birgyte's sudden departure, I grabbed the newspaper and checked the want ads for rentals. I couldn't wait to move away from the University of Pennsylvania campus to Center City, the beating heart of Philadelphia, where the races mixed and you could walk everywhere you needed to go. My new life in the business world promised time to explore my long-suppressed sexuality. I had always assumed I was straight, but I had never had a girlfriend, and now I was no longer sure. Mostly, I tried not to think about it.

Unable to afford an apartment in the perfectly restored Society Hill neighborhood, I headed for South Street, which had recently blossomed into the hippest avenue in Philly. Populated by a blend of traditional, working-class residents with the yuppie, upwardly mobile white colonizers that *Philadelphia* magazine had recently dubbed "urban adventurers," it boasted a serious art-movie theater, a crunchy-granola organic grocery store, and several trendy bars and restaurants.

On one brick-lined corner stood an ancient, tiny bridal shop. Like a lonely tableau in an Edward Hopper painting, its sole mannequin glanced out the dirty, plate-glass window, pointing a finger toward Kater Street, where I found a third-floor studio apartment. Her dusty wedding gown stubbornly trumpeted the fashions of a bygone era, proclaiming, "You want urban grit? Step right up, I've got it!"

No more than a narrow lane, Kater Street occupied a no-man's-land between cosmopolitan South Street and the gigantic, all-Italian neighborhood of South Philly. Weedy ailanthus saplings sprang up randomly in pavement cracks along the front stoops of the undistinguished brick buildings.

Soon after I moved in, an elderly Italian American lady, dressed in black, approached me on the sidewalk.

"Good afternoon," I said.

She fixed me with a contemptuous, black-eyed stare, then continued wordlessly down the street. I blinked and froze, fighting to assure myself that she had not cursed me with the Italian "evil eye." Her gesture could not have been more clear: Young Anglo gentrifiers were not welcome in the border zone.

In spite of my joy at moving to Center City, the incident left me lonely and bereft, familiar emotions that I naively assumed I had left behind on the Penn campus. I had carried them everywhere with me for the last nine years, having said goodbye to my mother, father, and brother while I moved away from Seattle to study, first in Paris, then in Philly.

The year was 1980, and John Travolta's new movie, *Urban Cowboy*, had recently caused a sensation, compelling thousands of young men to don western gear. On my frequent trips to New York to visit undergraduate friends who had moved there, I kept passing myriad cowboy boutiques that had sprung up on the Upper West Side as suddenly as wildflowers in a meadow, each one stocked floor-to-ceiling with shelf upon shelf of pointed-toe, high-heeled Noconas and Tony Lamas. The boots came in all the colors of the rainbow, and the salesclerks relied on wooden library ladders to reach the highest shelves. The shops were veritable leather candy stores, and the more often I passed them, the more obsessed I became. I had to have those boots! I wanted a different pair for every night of the week.

Fashionable cowboy boutiques had yet to infiltrate staid old Philly, but the windows of a menswear store on Chestnut Street had recently been dressed in a western theme. When I entered the store, ranks of tables covered with the usual boring corduroy pants rose up to insult me. Where was the cowboy gear? Cursing myself for not having bought my hat and boots in New York, I negotiated the maze of aisles until at last I spied one or two in a distant corner. Just as I reached out to stroke the soft velvet of a Stetson, hypnotized by its sensuousness, a salesman sidled up. Dressed in a cheap suit, an Oxford button-down shirt, and a loosely knotted tie, he broke the spell with a high-pitched lisp that made me wince.

"May I help you?"

"I'm . . . just . . . loo- looking. Where's the dressing room?"

The preppy salesman waved a limp hand toward a nearby hallway with a row of cubicles.

"Thanks." A cloud of cologne lingered in the air while I quickly grabbed the closest hat and boots and headed off.

Drawing the dressing-room curtain tight, I sighed with relief at my newfound privacy. After stroking the boots with reverence, I pulled one on, then the other. In the full-length mirror, I kicked one foot back, the better to admire my new heels. Then I put on the hat, slowly lifting my head until I met my own eyes under the shadow of its brim. Adopting my most smoldering expression, I stared at myself for as long as I dared. At last, in a state of excitement, I nodded to myself. I looked great in my perfect new cowboy outfit. I hastened out of the dressing room, ready to pay for my new identity.

"I'll wear these out the door," I told the salesman as I reached into my wallet.

"Of course, sir," he replied, ever the nelly faithful servant. But when I strutted out onto Chestnut Street, traffic whizzed by in a cacophony of horns, shattering my fantasy of the wide-open plains. What did the "urban" in urban cowboy mean? I wasn't sure. Would a cowboy hail a cab? I was fairly certain he wouldn't.

Suddenly, a childhood memory came to me in a jolt. Although the scene was now frozen in amber, more like the memory of a memory, I still remembered how on my second birthday, my father had unexpectedly lifted me up and placed me on top of a tall bookshelf. Leaning against the wall in Dad's arms, I felt as if I were perched on a cliff. All at once, Dad placed a large box on my lap, opened the lid, and pushed away the flaps of white tissue. Inside, I beheld a beautiful cowboy hat, a tiny pair of boots, a red kerchief, and suede chaps.

I instantly adored my new cowboy suit, but just as Dad started pulling the boots on my feet, I heard him saying, "Of course, you're not a real cowboy. Real cowboys ride horses but they're ignorant and spit. And they rope calves—do you know how to rope a calf?"

"No," I said in my shyest little-boy voice.

Boorish as they may have been, according to my dad, I already dimly knew that cowboys were heroes who could do exciting, manly things that I could not. The message I got, now firmly implanted in my psyche, was that I was not a real man . . . maybe not even a real boy.

As much as I wanted to dress up in the outfit, Dad's belittling words made me feel phony. Like my mother, I had a truthful disposition and couldn't begin to fake it. Dreading to be unmasked as an imposter, I was too shy to put on the suit, so it went back into its box, never to reemerge.

Now I was reliving that painful drama in the busy traffic of Chestnut Street. Didn't sporting the hat and boots mean that the world would see me exactly the way I viewed the salesman—as a pathetic sissy? With my vivid and overactive imagination, he felt like a red flag in my path. Wasn't he a warning that if I ever dared to consider coming out of the closet, I would turn into a limp-wristed, lisping old homo as surely as Cinderella's coach turned into a pumpkin at midnight? Also, why had I bought a brown hat? Clearly, a black one was much cooler. Even in my desire to sport a theatrical new outfit, I had opted for the less flashy headgear.

South Street was a vibrant fashion boulevard, tailor-made for sporting a cowboy suit with pride, but so deep was my shame at not being a real cowboy that I didn't dare face the glances of its hip and stylish pedestrians. Afraid of being mocked, I detoured two blocks south to Bainbridge Street, in the no-man's land between Center City and South Philly, where I was much less likely to be seen and scrutinized. Night had fallen, and when I turned the corner into the shadows of Bainbridge, I hung my head as I clip-clopped toward my apartment.

In a flash, two young Black men ran toward me from out of nowhere and flanked me on both sides. Before I had a chance to look at their faces in the dim light of one far-off streetlamp, they grabbed my wrists.

"Give us your money!"

I could almost feel their hearts beating as I hastily reached into my pocket to pull out my wallet. Roughly shoving me, they ran off without another word, disappearing as suddenly as they had appeared. They didn't threaten me with knives or, worse yet, pull out a gun. They didn't have to, because, in my panic, I was so quick to hand over my wallet.

I was panting now, adrenaline coursing through my veins. Patting my chest and empty pockets to confirm that I was still all in one piece, I hurried home. Was this what the Italian lady's evil eye had dialed up for me?

Never had I felt so vulnerable and dejected, but somehow I couldn't be angry with the two youths, so intensely did I absorb their fear while they accosted me. Although nothing had betrayed their emotions, I was convinced they were as scared of robbing me as I was afraid that they might stab me. The main thing I felt was more shame—shame that I hadn't tried to defend myself and shame for wearing a hat I hadn't earned. More than anything, my failure to fight back proved once and for all that Dad was right—I was no more than a fake cowboy.

Back in my dark, forlorn apartment, I pulled the window shade down and brooded. Donning boots and a cowboy hat made me feel like I was in drag, but that didn't mean I was consigned to wear them without pride. That was my choice, and it had turned out to be a bad one. If only I had assumed the role of a proud cowboy, holding my head high and parading down South Street as nonchalantly as if I were wearing a business suit, I never would have been held up.

Shaking off my reverie, I called the police. I assumed they would be bored by this latest routine crime in one of America's most crime-ridden cities, but to my surprise, the cop listened to my story with relish. No more than ten minutes later, a police van idled noisily in the narrow street outside my apartment, siren wailing. Banging loudly on my door, a burly white cop led me downstairs to identify my assailants.

Out on the street, I was nearly blinded by the flashing red lights on the van's roof. The double back doors opened, and down a metal ramp came five slim young Black men in handcuffs, roughly jostled by the cop's partner, who shoved them into a line. No older than eighteen or twenty, all five stood before me shaking in fear. Dressed in tank-tops and backward baseball caps, I saw them for the kids they were.

"Are any of these the guys who assaulted you?" asked the first cop.

"Um, no, I can't be sure," I said, squinting in the bright-red light as my voice trailed off. Two of them might have been, but it was equally possible that none of them were. They had surrounded me so quickly that I never got a chance to look at their faces.

The first cop glared at me with pure contempt while his partner frowned and folded his arms.

"Sorry." My voice cracked. I didn't know what else to say, so I watched as the two men reluctantly herded the boys back into the van, slammed the doors shut, and drove off.

In my confusion, I couldn't understand why the cops were so hostile, but when I returned to the forced solitude of my apartment and closed the door, it dawned on me that both officers were angry that I had squandered their perfect opportunity to shove two young Black men in jail. Although nobody spoke of "white privilege" in those days, I got the distinct impression that not only did I possess it, but the cops were counting on me to exploit it, no matter how indiscriminately. My failure to please them rattled me even more than the holdup, almost as if I were the one who had committed the crime. Nor did I feel any calmer when, turning on the lights, I realized that the five suspects now knew where I lived.

Reflecting on this incident in the weeks to come, I ruminated about how cut off I was from Philadelphia's vast Black population. Everywhere except in Center City the races were kept strictly apart, as if separated by an invisible fence. Philly's very urban geography had been arranged to segregate the races. South Philly was dominated by Italian Americans, but North Philly was almost entirely Black. City Hall Tower marked the exact center of the city. Beginning there, the long, grand, and leafy Benjamin Franklin Parkway cut a wide swath, radiating out from City Hall toward the distant acropolis crowned by the Greek Revival temple of the Philadelphia Art Museum. Another tree-lined boulevard circumnavigated the museum, skirting the riverfront of giant, verdant Fairmount Park, as if expressly designed to rush Center City's Anglo workers home to the equally leafy, lily-white suburbs beyond.

During my long years of college and graduate school I had been surrounded almost entirely by white strivers and academic stars, yet I had always yearned to step out of my bubble and make friends from diverse backgrounds. Now, in spite of, or perhaps because of the mugging incident, I hungered to make a connection across the racial divide. Could the rousing rhythm and blues that I overheard jumping and pulsing out of boomboxes all over town help me find common ground with my Black neighbors?

On my weekend strolls, I discovered several small record shops that had sprouted up along the east end of Market Street. Venturing in, I browsed records by young African American singers who were completely unfamiliar to me. The colorful album covers burst into life with photographs of glamorous divas like Stephanie Mills, who had recently starred on Broadway in *The*

Wiz. Every now and then, I bought an album just to try it out, entranced to discover a new musical style fusing soul, jazz, and disco.

Now a bona-fide Philadelphian, no longer a mere student, I rejoiced in this vicarious way of joining the broader, integrated life of the city, no matter how tenuous my connection to it. Although the joyful sounds of Stephanie Mills and Rick James could not quite pierce through my sexual confusion, at least in some mysterious way they promised to unlock the deeper, hitherto unexplored part of myself that lay beyond my career ambition.

2   LOW-RISE NORTH

MY INTERRACIAL aspirations had begun eight years earlier, when I first arrived on the Penn campus as a sophomore transfer student. Exiting baggage claim at sundown in Philly, I immediately got swept up in the hectic round of arriving and departing cars, all so much faster-paced than in my hometown of Seattle. This was the urban vibrance I craved. However, when my taxi dropped me off on the edge of campus, the sight of all the dilapidated old brick row houses dismayed me.

Trekking across the windy, scruffy lawns of Superblock, the high-rise urban renewal project on the west end of campus, I headed for Low-Rise North. The long, four-story brick dorm appeared to enclose the high-rise towers like a barrier, as if to wall them off from the crumbling buildings across the street in what I soon learned was a largely Black neighborhood.

I dimly knew that Philadelphia's neighborhoods were segregated, but I had no sense for what that would feel like on the ground. Seattle was pretty much lily-white, and my only exposure to race relations came when our family gathered around to watch the *CBS Evening News.* In his authoritative but reassuring voice, Walter Cronkite filed regular reports on Martin Luther King Jr.'s marches, the civil rights struggle in the South, and the race riots in the North. Grainy images of young Black kids crowding onto stools at white lunch counters. Close-ups of Dr. King declaiming one of his resounding, inspirational speeches, juxtaposed against blurry shots of Alabama governor George Wallace in his wheelchair, yelling hate-filled taunts against "Nigras."

All this was on my mind when I entered the lobby of Low-Rise North. It was deserted except for a slim, young African American man who sat behind a heavy table against the back wall, nose down in a book. Assuming that he was either the building manager or a student on work-study duty as a receptionist, I approached him.

"Hi, my name's Brooks. I've been assigned to Room 312," I said. There I paused, thinking he might ask for my ID.

Momentarily glancing up, the young man said, "I'm Alonzo. Your room is upstairs." This was in a gruff monotone, and after pointing to the stairway on the left, he quickly lowered his eyes back to his book. With his little black goatee and short Afro, he was undeniably handsome, and I decided that Alonzo was the sexiest name I had ever heard. I wanted very much for him to like me and become my friend, but his pinched expression told me that wasn't going to happen. I sighed, realizing that he had no good reason to trust me—to him I was probably just another obnoxious white boy sent over from central casting to harass him. Still, I wished he could be more welcoming.

Casting one more wistful glance in his direction, I mounted the staircase, from which I heard Alonzo greeting a Black comrade who had come into the lobby, laughing and joking with gusto. I already envied that young man—Alonzo was a completely different person with him, all friendly and relaxed.

Entering my room, I encountered a tidy, bare-bones studio with a single bed, utilitarian cinder-block walls and a small sliding window overlooking Walnut Street. When I opened it, the urgent roar of rushing traffic filled the little room. Throwing my bags on the linoleum floor, I sat on the bed and sighed again. This wasn't exactly the university welcome wagon I had anticipated, but I steeled myself, being well-accustomed to loneliness after spending the previous year as a freshman at the American College in Paris. *It has to be easier to make friends here than it was in Paris*, I told myself. How could I forget my American classmates there, military brats who had lived all over the world and whose idea of a treat was to buy Oreo cookies at the American embassy? For them, Paris was not Paris, it was just another place they had accidentally washed up in, like so much flotsam and jetsam on a random beach.

The next day, I met my fellow third-floor Penn transfer students. Linda had long, straight, dark-blonde hair, large blue-green eyes, and an oval face that tapered to a narrow chin. I found it easy to talk and joke with her, smiling at how she viewed the world through a prism of amused but sympathetic irony. She had smuggled her boyfriend, Jim, into the dorm, and they appeared to be joined at the hip, which made me feel awkward and lonely.

Across the hall from Linda lived stocky, wall-eyed Samantha, whose dark-brown hair was pulled back in a tight, no-nonsense ponytail, secured with a proletarian rubber band. She was a student militant, always on the front lines of the latest cause from the pages of *Mother Jones*.

Even more memorable was a tall and statuesque young woman whose classical face could have been sculpted by Michelangelo. Hailing from New Orleans, Susan was full of colorful, southern similes, not unlike Molly Ivins's memorable phrase, "drunker than a hog in a peach orchard." Her nickname, Bruisin' Susan, came from her love of partying, which had already bestowed her with an adorable round beer belly, as if she were in the first trimester of a pregnancy.

One day, after Samantha marched off to a rally, fist raised defiantly in the air, Linda emerged from her room and tapped me on the shoulder. "Brooks," she said, "what do you think she's protesting about today? Are they dropping more toxic chemicals in the Cuyahoga River or something? Should we get down there right away and form a blockade, or can I get back to *Moby-Dick*?"

"I think it's safe to stay away," I chuckled.

Linda regarded Samantha with the same mixture of respect and bemusement that I did, and we bonded over our shared commitment to art and literature at the expense of the 1970s' protest movements. If the main thing we wanted was to demonstrate, we didn't have to go to college to do it.

One night, Susan and I went to eat dinner at a greasy, little hoagie shop a block from the dorm, where there was at least a fifty-fifty chance they wouldn't card us.

"This place sure ain't New Orleans," Susan said. "Where are the parties? Philly's got nothing on Bourbon Street!"

"It's not Seattle, either. I miss the mountains and Puget Sound."

"Come on now, I haven't been to Seattle, but I don't guess it's got anything like Bourbon Street either!" As usual, Susan's southern yarns made me laugh, and I basked in the glow of her attention. However, as soon as we sat down next to a window, a cloud came over her face.

"I have to call Dakota in New York," she said, rising from her chair and heading for the door. As I bit into my meatball sandwich on a Kaiser roll, I could see her standing at an open-air pay phone under a streetlamp, the metal cord wrapped tensely around her wrist. Moths fluttered around her face as she leaned, frowning, against the light pole, crossing her long, graceful legs.

Like a small child, I reexperienced the intense impatience I had felt when my mother was on the phone too long. Okay, so she liked her boyfriend, Dakota, a trader in pork-belly futures on Wall Street, but everyone on the third floor knew he was a cad who treated her badly. Didn't she enjoy my company too? Her interminable phone call reminded me of how alone I was.

While I gazed at Susan brooding and tapping her foot, I felt more and more abandoned. Then I remembered that a cute acquaintance of ours lived across the street, and I began fantasizing about him. The unusually named Horatio Holbrook was a handsome young man with a black moustache, a goatee, and curtains of lustrous, evenly parted black hair. He was so cool and grown-up that instead of rooming in the dorms, he lived in an off-campus apartment. The most amazing thing about him, though, was that I had met him the year before at the American College in Paris, where I had painted and studied art history. Somehow, he had surprised me by turning up at Penn. Since he didn't have a girlfriend, I found myself wondering whether he might be interested in me.

Interrupting my reverie, Susan came back in, her smile restored. "Let's go over and drink beer with Horatio," she said.

"Yeah, great idea!" I replied.

In a flash, he buzzed us in, and we climbed the rickety stairway to his apartment, where strips of steak sizzled in a skillet with peppers and onions—the makings of a Philly cheesesteak. Horatio stood at the stove listening to a piano concerto.

"Don't you just love Rachmaninoff?" he asked.

"Love him!" I lied, having never really listened to Rachmaninoff before.

As we listened to the bravura piano, backed by orchestral swells and moody chords, we settled down to have a few Rolling Rocks.

"I had more country cousins at Tulane than whores in the French Quarter," Susan said. "And here I don't know anybody!"

"I know what you mean," Horatio said. "I have a big family in Kentucky, and the buildings in Louisville aren't all falling down like the ones here."

He seemed to like her, but he wasn't making a move on her, which confused me. Did it mean he was gay, that he wasn't into her, or just that he respected her relationship with Dakota enough to keep his distance? I didn't have a clue.

Witnessing them bonding so easily, it seemed impossible to pull him aside to find out whether he liked me. As usual, I took the easy way out by trying to be as engaging as I could, straining not to reveal any cards about my sexual orientation. In truth, I scarcely showed those cards to myself. As far as I was concerned, I was straight, and that was that. It was the story I told myself every day.

When Susan and I shared pitchers of beer at a little deli-tavern on the edge of campus, the songs on the jukebox introduced me to soul music for the first time—it was a genre completely missing from Seattle's FM stations. Listening to Marvin Gaye's "What's Going On" for the first time was a revelation. Marvin's instrumentals, his lyrics pleading for peace, and especially the background soundtrack of people partying and getting down, moved me in a way that no other pop song previously had, making me at once sad and joyful. As a civil rights anthem and an antiwar protest song, it offered a heartbreaking expression of what was going on in the vast world beyond the confines of the Penn campus. Walter Cronkite never failed to remind us that American soldiers were still being mowed down by the thousands in Vietnam, while angry parents and school boards bitterly fought school busing programs across the country.

Marvin's song had a way of bringing us all together in Low-Rise North, softening Samantha's activism, validating Linda and Jim's romantic love, and giving voice to the struggles of the Black students, who had recently won the right to a home of their own on campus. By now I had learned the reason for Alonzo's near hostility on my first day. The Black student union had petitioned the university to grant them a place to live together. In response, the administration had bequeathed the lower two floors of Low-Rise North to them. Now union members were on a mission to annex the top two floors, and rumors went up and down our hall that by spring semester all of us on the third floor were to be dispersed, like so many birds on the wing, to the nearby high-rise dorms.

Ignorant of the heavy burden of racism the Black students endured, it bewildered me that they were actively countering Dr. King's gains for integration by petitioning for segregated housing. I had scarcely given a thought to racism, but when I did consider it, I naively believed that the North was an accepting realm where true integration, as opposed to forced integration, had won the day. In my ignorance, I assumed that Philadelphia welcomed its Black citizens. The idea that it could still be hostile toward them was as alien to me as the unknown fact that George Washington had owned slaves in Philadelphia when he attended the Constitutional Convention, or that slavery did not end in New York until 1827.

Going down to the lobby one day on my way to class, I watched as a group of Black students gathered to celebrate the expansion of the newly rechristened W.E.B. Du Bois House. Spotting Alonzo off to one side, laughing and joking with three or four comrades, I wanted so much to join in, but I knew that I was not invited. I sighed, wishing I could wave a magic wand and make America's ugly racism just disappear. Then, maybe Alonzo and I could be friends. Maybe we could be more than friends.

But, as usual, I quickly suppressed the thought.

3   INVISIBLE DRAGONS

WHY DID it take me so long to come out of the closet? Growing up in an upwardly mobile white family, I knew I was different, but I didn't have a name for my difference, only a vague sense that I didn't belong. Our house was not ruled by a judgmental deity or narrow-minded politics; both my parents were liberal and secular. People at church reminded Mom and Dad of the small-town pettiness they had escaped by moving to Seattle from Bozeman, Montana, so we didn't belong to any congregation and rarely went to services. Nobody ever told me I would burn in hell if I kissed a boy, yet I learned, as if through electrical currents in the air, that it was not okay to be gay. If I hoped to uncover my true identity, I would have to find a way to slay those invisible dragons. Just because they were invisible didn't mean they weren't real.

My father, Keith Kolb, cast a long shadow, not only over our family, but over the entire architectural community of Seattle. Before becoming a professor at the University of Washington, he had received his architecture degree there, but it was his postgraduate studies at Harvard under Walter Gropius, the former head of the world-renowned Bauhaus School of Design, that turned Dad into a strict Modernist. Nothing pleased him more than sharing his passion for modern architecture with any captive audience, and no audience was more captive than my brother and me.

One day at breakfast, Dad paused his architectural monologue long enough to clear his throat. Dad's impressive throat clearing was one of the principal weapons he deployed to establish his professorial authority. As usual, my mind wandered. I was eight years old, sitting at the kitchen table with Mom, Dad, and my younger brother, Bliss. The table was a white, round, pedestal-mount sculpture designed by Eero Saarinen, surrounded by matching white, swoopy swiveling chairs. I loved how the table and chairs reminded me of *The Jetsons*.

"If you bush hammer a concrete wall, you'll achieve a highly desirable pebbly finish with a coarser texture than if you merely sandblast it," I heard Dad saying, snapping out of my reverie.

"What's sandblasting?" Bliss asked.

"Shh, don't ask him anything," I whispered. "You know Dad will go on and on, and when he finally finishes talking, we still won't understand what sandblasting is."

"Okay," Bliss whispered back, lowering his eyelids, but Dad was already clearing his throat again.

"Sandblasting is when you force air and sand at high pressure through a big hose and spray it against a concrete surface, but you have to be careful to . . ." Dad began, but I had already tuned him out again.

Dad always complained that Bliss and I ate our meals too fast, but while we reached for the toast, we watched his fork hover in midair over his plate, knowing that he would not take the next bite until he came to the end of his speech. Was it any wonder that we finished our breakfasts first?

The central event of my childhood was the construction of the house Dad designed for our family of four. The first time he drove us to see the vacant lot in Seattle's Laurelhurst neighborhood, I stared out the window, dumbfounded at the towering cedars and birches framing the majestic, pretentious houses on their curving, bucolic streets. Even at my tender age, I realized it was a swank neighborhood.

"Dad, how can you pay for it?" I asked, from the back seat.

"Well, I can use the architectural drawings as collateral on a construction loan because the bank knows how much more valuable the land will be once the house is built on it," Dad explained.

I rubbed my nose against the car window, watching the trees rush by. As usual, I had no idea what he was talking about. It was nice that he treated my brother and me like adults, but most of what he said was as impenetrable as the multiplication tables I was trying to learn in school.

"What's collateral?" I asked.

"It's when you tell the bank that you'll give them something valuable if you can't pay your loan back."

"Oh," I said, still not understanding.

As our white, wood-and-glass house rose above mounds of dirt flanking the basement-level garage excavation, it became the first Modernist house on the block. A two-story glass window-wall ran the length of the street facade, culminating in a white tower that concealed the stair hall behind it. A narrow, horizontal window topped the tower, whose roof cantilevered so far out toward the street that I thought of it as a diving board. On the dazzling white terrazzo floor in "the high space" behind the window-wall, Dad set up a low table that Bliss and I shared for our incessant art projects. I sat facing south; Bliss faced north. People constantly drove by, gawking at us as we sat completely exposed behind the windows. We loved to witness the shocked expressions on their faces when we surprised them by proudly waving back.

Bliss and I spent many hours at our shared table, drawing, painting, and making models from our fertile imaginations. Art was our shared passion, and I was never happier than when immersed in my latest creation. I always yearned to finish it as quickly as possible, so that I could wave my artistic triumph in front of Mom. Nothing gave me satisfaction like the instant gratification of finishing a drawing that pleased her. Less concerned with pleasing Mom, Bliss took longer to finish his creations, and it showed in the finesse of his more exacting technique.

In grade school, our classmates called Bliss and me "the kids from the glass house," which to them made us different and weird. It was not rare for us to wake up at night to the sound of a great splat. In the morning, we looked out to spy long yellow trails of egg yolk streaking down the glass. I could never be sure if the schoolkids who bullied me for being a sissy threw the eggs to prove they knew where I lived or whether other kids did it for a lark just because they could. It didn't occur to me that Bliss might also have been the object of their scorn.

One day, I found myself standing in front of our new house with two or three boys from the neighborhood. Still at the age when kids find the opposite sex icky, one of the boys exclaimed, "Eeuuw, girls! I will never get married."

The other two quickly agreed, but I said, "You're wrong. All of you will get married, but I won't." I have no idea where my conviction came from, but it must have risen from some mysterious place deep inside. I knew there was something different about me, something that would probably keep me from getting married. I just didn't know exactly what it was.

Actually, there was one girl that nine-year-old me did want to marry. When I saw *The Wizard of Oz* for the first time at a sleepover with family friends, I fell in love with Dorothy before the end of the first chorus of "Somewhere Over the Rainbow."

"I'm going to marry Dorothy," I told Mom the next day, although truthfully, I didn't know if I liked Dorothy better than Mom.

"Oh, darling," Mom said. "Dorothy is an imaginary person played by an actress. Her name is Judy Garland and she's all grown up—she's twenty-one years older than she was when the movie was made."

"Really? She is?" Not only was I heartbroken, but my young mind couldn't grasp the conundrum that the moving images I saw with my own eyes could be lying. The idea that Dorothy was actually much older than she appeared in the movie seemed like black magic. I felt betrayed; now I could never marry her.

Like every other kid, I wanted to please my parents, and I felt a strong pull to fit in. Apart from my artistic talents, the only thing that kept me from being a perfect little conformist was the mysterious something that made me different. It was something missing, something that when I became a teenager drove me time and again to look in the mirror and say "I hate myself." I didn't hate myself because I was gay—that I had not yet grasped, let alone admitted to myself. Unready to understand the source of my discomfort, I thought I hated myself simply because I was awkward, uncoordinated, and bad at sports.

As I was walking home from grade school one day, two or three of the Laurelhurst boys came from behind, ganged up on me, punched me in the nose, and knocked me to the ground, scornfully calling me a sissy.

As I picked myself up, bruised and tearful, they turned and spat on me, yelling "You're a sissy!"

"Sissy" was a word I heard regularly at school, but it applied to any kid who was weak or unable to defend himself. The bullies didn't call me "faggot," a word I had never heard, because no doubt they hadn't heard it either.

Afterward, I did the sissy thing—I went to the principal's office and registered a formal complaint. He was a kindly gentleman and assured me that he would put an end to it, but there was nothing he could do, so Dad decided to teach me how to fistfight. Beckoning me out onto the driveway at my grandparents' house, he stood next to the garage door and raised his fists like a boxer.

"Go ahead, hit me," he said, bouncing on the balls of his feet.

I stood frozen, hands in my pockets. "No, I can't!" I said. My words sounded as feeble as my body felt.

"Come on, hit me!" he repeated.

But the whole situation felt ridiculous. I loved my father, so why would I want to hit him? Also, what was the point? He was so much bigger and stronger than I, and there was no doubt that he would whup me. I froze. Then I put up my fists and pointed them toward Dad, but I froze again, unable to move.

"I can't hit you—I can't!" I exclaimed.

In the end, Dad gave up, and I never learned how to fight. Instead, I thought of myself as a sort of pacifist.

Apart from the bullying incidents, I'm not sure how I first became aware of homophobia and racial prejudice—it was as if both pathologies were floating on the breeze or rushing out with the water every time someone turned on a faucet. No matter how it started, two specific incidents were imprinted on me.

The first happened on a family road trip to San Francisco when I was thirteen years old. Bliss and I were in the back seat of our Chevy station wagon when Dad turned up a steep street on Russian Hill. Near the top of the sidewalk on the left side, we spotted two middle-aged men slowly strolling hand in hand toward the summit. Dad rolled down the window and pointed at them.

"Look, there are two homosexuals," he said. "How sad."

That was the first time I ever heard the word "homosexual." I took a closer look at them, and I thought I knew what Dad meant. There was something lonely about them, something that branded them as outcasts. Nobody else was out walking on that block, and they appeared isolated from the rest of the world. My first thought was I certainly did not want to be like them.

Not long afterward, my impression was further cemented when I learned that homosexuality had been classified as an official form of mental illness by the American Psychiatric Association.

On the second occasion, we were in the car again, this time on a family errand in Seattle. Just as Dad turned into the Washington Park Arboretum, he slowed to let a young woman cross the street in front of us.

"Now there's a handsome Negress," Dad said.

I was horrified. I knew nothing about racism, but I was beginning to have some rudimentary ability to detect racist speech. Why did she have to be "handsome," when that word was usually reserved for men, and why was she a "Negress?" It seemed to imply she was some sort of impressive zoo animal.

"Dad," I said. "Why can't you just say, 'There's a beautiful woman?'" The color of her skin was so obvious as to be redundant.

Dad didn't have an answer because he didn't know there was anything wrong with what he had said. The incident disturbed me because it revealed two conflicting truths: Dad was prejudiced but he was innocent because his prejudice was unintentional. He was simply unaware of it, just as he was unaware of his homophobia.

Around the time I told Mom that I wanted to marry Dorothy, Dad took me to see the Seattle World's Fair construction site. Holding my hand, he pointed at the giraffe-like legs of the Space Needle rising naked against the sky before its flying-saucer top flew in to land on them. Nearby, he showed me the vast excavation for the International Fountain, a deep concrete pit with bare steel rebar sticking up everywhere and construction workers hopping around like ants.

I had no idea what I was looking at, but as he explained it to me, I was almost awed by his confidence, his seeming command of the complex construction operation, even though it was not one of his own projects. The experience stimulated my growing interest in design, but it didn't make me feel like becoming an architect. Despite my passion for drawing, I couldn't picture myself churning out the reams of technical drawings that I saw piled high on the three long tables that lined Dad's window-walled studio on the top floor of our house. When I looked at the plans, I failed to observe a manifestation of the creative energy I craved to unleash. All I could see were ranks upon ranks of tiny bathrooms and closets, each door swing carefully arranged so that no door bumped into another.

As I grew up, the more I needed Dad to be a mentor or a guide, the more cryptic or evasive he became, losing interest if I asked him about any career besides architecture. He repeatedly told Bliss and me, "You can be anything you want—but if you want to be an architect, you have to . . ." and then he would list, step by tedious step, all the things we had to accomplish to become an architect.

The message we both received was unequivocal: "You can be anything you want, but if you want me to love you, you will become an architect." Unconsciously imprinted, I never outgrew the thought that I would let him down if I didn't become an architect. No matter how much I wanted to please him, though, I wanted more to excel at something of my own.

DOWN THE street lived Dad's mentor and architecture professor, Lionel "Spike" Pries, whose life was documented in Jeffrey Ochsner's book *Lionel N. Pries, Architect, Artist, Educator*. Spike's house announced itself with a wooden garage door bearing Northwest Indian art motifs that Spike had painted in hues of red, green, and white. From there, an imposing exterior stairway led up over the garage roof, through dense shrubbery, to the front door. Inside the house, a terrazzo staircase continued upward, lined with built-in vitrines displaying Spike's unparalleled collection of pre-Columbian sculptures and pottery. At the top, more Northwest Indian patterns graced the living room ceiling.

Spike clearly had no qualms appropriating an art form that rightfully belonged to the great tribes of coastal British Columbia, but this social justice distinction was lost on me. Instead, I marveled at a floor-to-ceiling bookcase that filled one wall of the dining room. Periodically, an invisible door in the bookshelves swung open to allow Spike's white-aproned cook to pass through, briefly revealing the small galley kitchen beyond. Fascinated by this magic trick, it was only years later that I unlocked the mystery. When no one was looking, I examined the bookshelf closely enough to discern that Spike had sliced a bunch of books, gluing their severed spines to the door. Here was a clever design riff that appealed to my sense of drama, my desire for artistic expression.

Spike often entertained his students and colleagues at serious Sunday afternoon salons. When I was allowed to attend, he sat stiffly in a throne-like chair, his back to the fireplace. Conforming to his expectations, Dad sat cross-legged with all the other architects in a semicircle on the floor, listening spellbound as Spike held forth in a rarefied air. The pearls of architectural and cultural wisdom that he dispensed were meaningless to me, sending me into daydreams as quickly as Dad's lectures. As I grew older, I began to think of him as a sort of cult leader passing the torch of the god "Design" down to Dad and all the other acolytes. Perhaps one day Dad would hand it to me, but I was reluctant to receive it. The torch felt more like a rigid manifesto than a dancing flame of inspiration. Until then, it merely fascinated me that Spike's last name was Pries, and I privately dubbed his followers the "Pries'hood."

As a child, I had no idea that Spike had suddenly and unexpectedly resigned from his faculty position at the University of Washington. It was a complete mystery why he had taken a lowly draftsman's position at one of Seattle's largest architectural firms.

Years later, after Spike's death, Dad finally learned what had happened, and even then he was sworn to secrecy. Many more years passed before he shared the secret with me: Spike had been arrested for cruising in a park in Los Angeles. The LAPD had immediately called the University of Washington to inform them that Spike had been picked up on a morals charge, explaining that it was their lawful duty to report the incident.

Despite being the most eminent professor in the architecture department, he was immediately forced to resign and banished forever from the university. This man my father emulated, whose artistic flair and erudition I hoped to acquire one day, was simply discarded, thrown away, as if all his contributions to teaching, art, and architecture counted for nothing. Of all the invisible dragons in my childhood warning me about the dangers of homosexuality, Spike's case ranked the highest, and I didn't even know it.

Like every other kid, I felt a strong pull to fit in, without ever succeeding. My sense of alienation reached a peak at the end of the tenth grade, when I went on a summer camping trip to a wild part of Washington's Pacific Coast with over a dozen classmates chaperoned by someone's parents. As we hiked around Lake Ozette on our way to the ocean, I reveled in the camaraderie and group spirit I so often felt with my high school friends. After a long walk through a thick forest carpeted with sword ferns, we suddenly burst through a dense canopy of tall firs onto a rocky beach where layers and layers of driftwood lay piled high in a long crescent, as far as the eye could see. Rays of sun pierced thick ranks of damp gray clouds, spotlighting the smooth, silvery logs, which stood out against the distant, jagged edge of dark green forest. My classmates and I jumped onto the logs and trekked along them, spreading our arms for balance.

"Let's see how far we can get without touching the ground," one of them said, and it became a fun game to hop from log to log without slipping.

While I calculated my next step, one of the boys clasped hands with a girl, then another boy joined hands with another girl, and so it went down the line. Soon it looked like all my comrades had found partners and coupled up. That night we set up camp in secret cubbyholes among the logs, spreading tarps over two or three pieces of driftwood to make a roof. I watched as Sue and Paul burrowed into one nest and John and Jill climbed into another.

In my innocence, this appeared to have happened spontaneously, as if it were the first time that each boy and girl had selected one another in this way. Then, all at once I realized that they must have already had crushes on each other; I had simply never witnessed it. Could it be that I was the only one without a girlfriend? There was no girl left for me, nor did I even want one. All I wanted was for the other kids to stop coupling, so that we could return to our team spirit. Then, once again, I could feel like I belonged.

When I turned seventeen, my awkward relationship with Dad came to a head. That year, I was required to register for the military draft, which terrified me. I dreaded being conscripted into the army, where I assumed I would die in Vietnam at the first sign of combat. I couldn't get out of it by claiming to have poor vision, a bad heart, or a clubfoot, and the idea of telling the sergeants I was gay never occurred to me because I lacked a vocabulary for what I was.

That night at dinner, Dad and I got into a big argument. When I told him I would sooner move to Canada than go off to the Vietnam War, he blew up.

"No son of mine is going off to Canada," he said. "If you're drafted, you will serve your country. Yours is not to question why, yours is but to do or die," he concluded, quoting a refrain popular with his World War II comrades-in-arms. We had already had several arguments about Vietnam, and I knew what Dad thought about it—as far as he was concerned, he had helped America win World War II, and by God, we would win in Vietnam too, no matter how long it took and how many lives were lost.

"But Dad," I said, "Vietnam is not like World War II. The people don't want us there, and it's not even a stalemate. We're losing."

This insubordination provoked new yelling from Dad. Nothing I said could change his conviction that the war was righteous and that all of us young lads should go off and fight proudly for their country. I looked over to Mom for support. Bliss frowned, lowered his head, and stared into his bowl of soup.

"Keith, listen to Brooks. He has a good point," she said, but I could tell she was unwilling to take my side unequivocally. A natural peacemaker, she tried her best to remain neutral. No matter how unrealistic it was, she wanted to bring Dad and me into some sort of consensus.

Fortunately, by the time I turned eighteen and was eligible to serve, President Nixon put an end to the draft. I didn't have to move to Canada or claim conscientious-objector status, and Dad and I never had a serious falling-out. Instead, I admired and loved him, resented him, and felt alienated from him all at once. I wanted so much for him to show me how to become a fully formed adult—to become a whole person on my own terms—but now I wasn't sure if he had my best interests at heart or if I could ever trust him again. I desperately needed a mentor, but I now realized I would have to look beyond Dad to find one.

When I thought about how I might disappoint him by not becoming an architect, I didn't consider that I might let him down even more by being gay. I knew that Dad expected me to marry a woman, and despite what I had said to the neighborhood boys as a child, I assumed that eventually I would find the right girl. More than becoming an architect, marrying meant acceptance into respectable adult society, a future I felt entitled to and had never truly questioned.

In the fall of my junior year, a senior invited me to join the annual yearbook staff, where for the first time I experienced the joy of being a team player, part of a fun group creating something meaningful. Then in my senior year, one of the staffers asked me to design the cover of *Strenuous Life*, since I was known around school as a talented artist. That was a great honor, and I couldn't wait to work on the cover. Picturing students' faces in my mind's eye, I began doodling until I eventually produced a slightly abstracted, black line-drawing of a young man's face inscribed in a triangle against a yellow-ochre background.

The boy was nobody in particular; his was an imaginary face, but gazing at him, I felt that he was undeniably handsome. At first, I told myself I was creating an idealized self-portrait, but my sub-conscious mind knew better. I was actually drawing the imaginary boy I was most attracted to. His hair was short and flat on top of his head. Could it be that he was Black? I didn't know, but if I had thought about it, I would have noticed that he looked a lot like the handful of African American students who were bused into our oh-so-white school from Seattle's Central District.

Going home from high school every day, I got off one bus in the University District and transferred to the Laurelhurst bus. On University Way, known as "The Ave," hordes of sexy college men flowed continually past the bookstores and coffee shops. Behind them, a pretty girl with giant blue eyes and long, flowing hair hawked copies of *The Helix*, a free underground newspaper that advertised local rock concerts and head shops in those trendy, puffy, 1960s-style, psychedelic letters that were almost unreadable. Although I noticed the girl, I was in awe of the men: how tall and beautiful they were, how confidently they moved, how fully they possessed their bodies. But when I watched them, my brain blocked any overt perception that I was attracted to them. All I allowed myself to think was how much I wanted to *be* like them, to look like them, to act like them. That was as close as my mind came to telling me what my body already knew.

Why was I sublimating, blocking my true feelings? Maybe because gay boys and men were invisible. I had never met one, had never seen one, even on TV. If something was that deeply buried, did it even exist?

5   PARIS CALLING

"I FEEL LIKE an old crrust behind a trrunk in the attic," Manie said in her charming French accent, taking a deep drag on her Camel cigarette.

Manie was my beloved French grandmother, but she was always following my poor mother around like a helpless puppy, complaining of being left out of the family activities. In turn, her miniature poodle, Demi, tracked her step for step, whining hysterically the instant she left the house. Manie had married my grandfather, Dr. Floyd Jump, a man twenty years her senior, and after he died suddenly of a heart attack in 1945, she never dated or remarried. Instead, she focused a laser beam of neediness on her daughter.

Bliss and I adored Manie for nurturing our artistic natures, encouraging our creativity in an unstructured way completely unlike Dad's lecturing and rules. When I was nine years old, she unexpectedly took a set of pastels from her desk, flourished one as if it were a cigarette, and began to draw bright-green lily pads against the dark-blue background of a piece of construction paper. I watched, astonished at how she added the white highlights of the flowers, magically transforming the paper into a lily pond.

"Herre, now *you* do it," she said, as if I were a budding Monet. Taking a pastel in hand, I copied her triumph as closely as I could.

To my surprise and delight, my rough sketch turned into a pond nearly as realistic as Manie's.

"Well done, darrling," she said, giving me an unexpected shot of pleasure and confidence that first inspired me to become an artist.

In the days ahead, I returned to my spontaneous sketches of camellias and imaginary cars with renewed gusto.

I lived for the times that Manie picked me up for an overnight visit, relishing having her all to myself. The house she rented at the top of Seattle's Queen Anne Hill had a breathtaking view of Elliott Bay and the majestic Olympic Mountains beyond. Gazing out the window, I watched the ferry boats drifting to and from Bainbridge Island, their elongated shapes perfectly echoing the landforms of Puget Sound's bluffs and beaches. At night, the beacon of the Alki Point lighthouse pulsed and strobed across the dark, choppy waters. By day, we enjoyed looking down at Pier 91, the navy pier, where the great, gunnery-gray battleships lined up, disgorging hordes of white-uniformed sailors. Behind the pier, the facing slope of Magnolia Bluff rose to confront us. Halfway up its grassy hillside, the dignified white Commodore's house commanded the view back in our direction.

Manie presided over this marine scenery like a muse atop Mount Olympus. Early in the morning, she fixed herself a large bowl of hot, steaming tea, blended English-style with milk. She always drank it in a distinguished ivory-colored bowl with telescoping sides, never in a mug. When she lit her first Camel of the day, the tea's fragrance mingled satisfyingly with the equally fragrant tobacco while she handed me a glass of milk and a jelly donut fresh from the oven. Then it was time to watch TV. I lived for the television because we didn't have one at home. Dad felt it was a needless luxury. Radio had been just fine for him growing up; why shouldn't it suffice for us?

The Lone Ranger and *Gunsmoke* were Manie's favorite TV shows, which was not surprising because, growing up in Paris, she had gone to see Buffalo Bill's Wild West Show. From the moment she saw "Buufalo Beel" onstage, she dreamed of traveling to the American West. Her dream finally came true when she moved to Montana after she met and married Floyd, an American army doctor who was serving in France during World War I.

While Manie longed to live among the cowboys and Indians, I developed a reverse passion for all things French, begging her to tell me stories of her childhood. One day, I asked, "Manie, where did you live in Paris?"

"Oh, darrling, we lived in an aparrtment dirrectly acrross the strreet from Madame Sarrah!"

"Who is Madame Sarah?"

"Madame Sarrah? Oh, mon petit, she was Sarrah Berrnhardt, once the most famous actrress in the worrld! I used to love nothing morre than to step out on the balcony and watch herr carriage drraw up outside."

"Wow, what happened then?"

"Well, Madame Sarrah alighted onto the curb, and you should have seen the beautiful gowns she worre! But do you want to know the best part?"

"What?" I asked.

"Sometimes a gentleman got out with herr, drressed in a top hat and tails. He would kiss herr gloved fingerrtips and prresent herr with a bouquet of a dozen rred roses. When that happened, I got all quiet and hid behind a potted plant."

"Why?"

"Well, because of courrse I had to see whether orr not she would allow him to accompany herr inside. Sometimes she let him in and sometimes she didn't. Sometimes she just gave a little bow, turrned arround and went inside all by herrself."

Listening to Manie's exotic image branded my heart, and from that day forward I longed to experience a moment as exquisitely romantic as Madame Sarah's sidewalk flirtations.

Recognizing my growing preoccupation with my French family roots, Mom urged Manie to teach me French. The result was that one day when I was about ten years old, she sat me down on the sofa and began trying to instruct me.

"*Je t'aime*," she said.

"What?"

"'Je t'aime.' It means 'I love you.' Now rrepeat it to me."

"Je t'aime," I said.

"*Aussi.*"

"What?"

"'Je t'aime aussi.' It means 'also.' You arre supposed to say, 'I love you too.'"

"Oh, je t'aime aussi," I said.

"Merci. Now let's starrt with you saying '*Je suis.*' It means 'I am.'"

"Je suis," I said, but then she snorted and sniffed, wrinkling her upper lip, which was her constant nervous tic. That was the undisputed sign that I was boring her, and in Manie's world, nothing was worse than when someone was "borring." In her impatience, she rose from her seat and never reattempted to instruct me. Instead, I later learned French from an extraordinary high school teacher, Madame Sarah Vyborny.

The diminutive Mme. Vyborny compensated for her lack of height by sporting high heels and a magnificent, shellacked beehive hairstyle that reached for the ceiling like a balloon. Her Polish accent was atrocious but she was a fantastic teacher, and her pedagogical mission drove her to reveal to us a deeper dimension to life than would otherwise occur to our little group of entitled and well-fed white high-school students. Life was tragic, as she had personally witnessed during World War II, when she had lost her entire family in the Holocaust. In time, we, too, would inevitably suffer from love and loss.

Reading Camus's *The Stranger* for Madame Vyborny's French class at home in my room, I glanced over at the wall. Leaning against it below a bank of windows was a large Plan de Paris, a map of Paris mounted on a heavy matte board, which Manie had given me. Not any ordinary map, it was an actual drawing of central Paris in which every building had been rendered in excruciating detail with teeny-tiny etchings. The artist of this remarkable drawing somehow managed to present a bird's-eye view of the city in which one saw not only the rooftops but also the front facades of all the buildings, from the majestic palaces and cathedrals to the ordinary apartment buildings. Extending from the Arc de Triomphe on the left to the Place de la Bastille on the right, the Seine ran like a wide ribbon through the center.

This map figured prominently in my imagination, especially when I read French books in translation, such as *The Count of Monte Cristo*. Alexandre Dumas, the author of *The Count*, assigned his characters apartments in particular Paris streets as if they were social calling cards, instantly revealing each character's individual socioeconomic status. Reading the name of a street, I would pore over my map, trying to locate it. In this way, I learned the difference between the Left Bank, with its students and bohemians, and the Right Bank, with the Louvre, the Opéra, and the grand boulevards. Every French novel I read provided more real estate clues for my virtual Parisian Monopoly board.

In 1970, Seattle was little more than a one-company town with an all-too-recent pioneer past, and it felt as if every resident were descended from Norwegian or Swedish families, offering little cultural diversity. Shortly before I graduated from high school, Boeing lost a big federal contract, and Seattle fell into a deep recession. A famous billboard went up near the airport, reading, "Will the last person leaving Seattle—turn out the lights." I loved my home, with its beautiful mountains, lakes, and Puget Sound, but it was beginning to feel too small and parochial to contain my growing curiosity and ambition.

Daydreaming about places with more sophistication and longer, richer histories, I spent more and more time fantasizing about my Paris map until I lived there in my imagination. I longed to see the real Paris, which eventually inspired me to apply to the American College there. The college had no dorms, but finding a place to live was not a problem. Mom helped me write a letter to Manie's mysterious and erudite older sister in Paris, my great-aunt Muguette, who had held the enviable position of conservator of antique prints and drawings at the Bibliothèque Nationale, the French national library.

A couple of weeks later I was overjoyed to receive an aerogram from Aunt Muguette agreeing to let me board with her in her small Paris apartment. Now all I had to do was book a flight to London so that I could visit Aunt Muguette's daughter and her family in the English Midlands before class started in Paris.

When I got off the train in Burton-upon-Trent, Marie-Cécile Setford smiled and waved as she maneuvered her VW bus into a parking space next to the station. Rays of sunshine shone brightly through a thick layer of clouds while she opened the van's sliding door to accept my luggage.

"Welcome, Brooks!" she said, enveloping me in a big hug.

"Thank you, it's so great to meet you at last!" I marveled at how much she resembled my mother, her first cousin. In that first instant, I already felt maternal love emanating from her, and although she was technically my second cousin, I knew I had gained a dear aunt.

In a flash we were at Arnwood, the Setfords' house, which topped a little knoll above the green floodplain of the River Trent. An impromptu metal table and chairs occupied the lawn, and the Setford children, who were roughly my age, horsed around before we sat down for English tea.

The setting sun painted long shadows on the golden grass under the limbs of a giant oak tree when Marie-Cécile's husband, David, emerged from his little painting shed to greet me, paintbrush in hand. Admiring his unfinished canvases of Oxford's spires, I looked forward to joining him and the others on sketching excursions. The joyous family noise calmed my jet-lagged nerves. How different it was from our serious dinners in Seattle, where Dad lectured about architecture, and Mom, Bliss, and I listened!

Over the coming days, we toured the bucolic English countryside, visiting Chatsworth and Blenheim Palace. Later, we went to Kedleston Hall, an eighteenth-century country house designed in part by the celebrated interior architect Robert Adam. The mansion sat in a pastoral dell, surrounded by hills, and when we arrived at its graveled forecourt, I was transfixed by the loveliness of the clumps of trees hugging the slopes. Their canopies stretched upward above the horizon line, as if to touch a host of fluffy, fast-moving clouds backlit by the sun.

"Look, Brooks," Marie-Cécile said, pointing toward the hills. "This landscape has been deliberately designed all the way up to the ridgelines, in a 360-degree panorama."

Following her gaze, I saw that from where we stood all the views added up to a delightful, organic pattern of grass and trees, light and shadow. The landscape appeared entirely natural, as if no human hand had ever touched it. The linear hedgerows I normally saw in the English countryside had been banished, and all the groves had a random, artless quality.

"It's all in the English Landscape Park style of Capability Brown," Marie-Cécile explained. "He was the most famous landscape designer of the eighteenth century."

"This is amazing!" I said, surprised and intrigued.

It had never occurred to me that it was possible to design an entire landscape of hills, valleys, and lakes. I had never given much thought to individual trees or shrubs, but now I saw that they could be deployed to create a giant canvas, as though they were so many colors in an artist's palette. Even better, Kedleston was three-dimensional—it was as much a living sculpture as a painting, and you could deliberately move through it, as if through a cathedral or a movie set, experiencing it sequentially.

This was such a big idea, so far from the claustrophobic draw-ings of bathrooms and hallways that I had seen in Dad's studio. From that day forward, each time Marie-Cécile took me to visit a country house I made a beeline for the windows, where I gazed out lovingly at the tree-clad pastoral meadows in the distance. Although I still daydreamed about becoming an artist, seeing Kedleston planted a seed of enthusiasm for landscape design in my heart. Could I do something like that? Move from drawing lily ponds on small scraps of paper to creating art outdoors with real grass and trees?

6   AMERICAN COLLEGE IN PARIS

WHEN I LANDED at Orly airport in Paris, my eyes swept the ranks in the arrivals terminal until they focused on a small, dignified elderly lady carrying a sign labeled "Kolb." Dressed in an elegant black suit, a mink stole, and a black pillbox hat with a little veil, Aunt Muguette welcomed me with open arms.

"Bonjour, Brooks. Bienvenue à Paris. May I call you Brooksies?"

She reminded me a little of Manie, but I could already tell how much more dignified and serious she was. This was not a complete surprise, as Mom had long ago told me that Manie was the rebellious younger sister.

In the motorcoach on the way into Paris, Aunt Muguette pointed out the sights and scenes with precision and a quick wit. Disembarking at the Gare d'Austerlitz, we stopped briefly at a traffic light. Immediately, all the sights and sounds of Paris surrounded me—the noisy cacophony of traffic on the elegant, tree-lined boulevards. Having never before been in such a big city, I inhaled the vibrant urban scene with a mix of joy and bewilderment. It was as if I had stepped directly into a performance of George Gershwin's *An American in Paris.*

"Would you like to take my arm?" I asked in French.

"Non," said Aunt Muguette, who was already launching into the intersection, in spite of all the cars rushing by at top speed, headlights flashing rapidly on and off.

So this is how you cross a street in Paris, I thought. *You simply point a toe into the boulevard, as if to test the waters, whether or not the light is green.* Like a duckling lining up behind its mother, I quickly plunged after her, as car after car screeched to a halt. Now she was leading me down the steps to the Métro, where we boarded a train to Porte d'Italie, her stop.

Over the next few days, Aunt Muguette conducted me around all the famous sights of Paris, and they did not disappoint. Apart from the Eiffel Tower and Notre Dame, my favorite was Monet's lily pond murals in the Orangerie Museum. Each painting curved outward toward the viewer, Cinerama-style, in the two oval-shaped rooms. The hypnotic masterworks made me smile, reminding me of how Manie had taught me to draw lily ponds with pastels. Glancing back and forth from the painterly surfaces of Monet's canvases to the tall windows, where brilliant sunlight shimmered off the River Seine, I determined once again to become an artist.

With its mansard roof crowning several stories of windows that diminished in height as they ascended, the American College's main building at 31 Avenue Bosquet in Paris's Seventh Arrondissement blended in with every other stone building on the street, as if it were wearing camouflage. Inside lay a large, bare-bones student lounge. Ranks of ashtrays covered an array of low tables, each tray as large as a box of kitty litter. Long-haired students in dark, baggy sweaters slumped forlornly about, smoking and flicking ash into the litter boxes. All of them bore a studied air of Parisian ennui that might have inspired applause from Jean-Paul Sartre.

Quickly climbing a stairway past the lounge, I arrived on the second floor. There, I was relieved to discover an airy hallway with a lovely wood parquet floor that opened into several white-plastered, gold-trimmed salons with tall mirrors and elaborate crown moldings. Each elegant room looked out into the leafy canopy of London plane trees along the boulevard. Soon their leaves would turn yellow, then drop. Later, the thorny globes of their seedballs would hang from their bare branches like dejected Christmas tree ornaments.

The nearest ornate doorway led into the office of the college president, a woman of indeterminate age, with dark honey-colored hair done up in a severe French twist. Every now and then, she would smile and wave her arms briskly as she paced the room, sometimes tapping a colleague on the shoulder before returning to the task at hand. Although American, her efficient movements and stylish business couture revealed that she was neglecting no detail in her campaign to be mistaken for Parisian. Apart from her American accent, she very nearly succeeded, making me wonder if, by enrolling in the college, I was doing the same silly thing.

I quickly signed up for an art class that met two or three days a week in an authentic Parisian art studio near the Luxembourg Gardens, the Académie de Port-Royal. Toward the back of the long, narrow, dark, and easel-filled space, thick plum-colored velvet drapes theatrically framed a partition that served as the backdrop for a collection of rotting apples and oranges. Arranged just so in a large bowl on a small table, it served as a still-life tableau for all the young Cézannes among us.

The hours I spent in the Académie amounted to nothing more than free time to paint. At first, I attacked my paintings with gusto, the wider the brush the better. I prided myself in my assertiveness with a brush, a confidence born of a lifetime of spontaneous drawing at home. *"I am a bohemian and I am an artiste!"* I shouted to myself, as I flicked thick globs of oil paint this way and that.

In the studio, we were often joined by a group of well-bred bourgeois ladies who must have been taking a course at some other institute. Dressed in cashmere sweaters, they eschewed smocks while devoting themselves to daubing delicately at their Pointillist studies. If a little part of me realized that it was unfair to hurl my brushes so close to their linens and silks, I did not admit it. As they chatted daintily among themselves in their well-mannered way, I chalked it up to the elevated role of the artist in French society that they appeared not to be alarmed by my proximity. That said, it would have been a miracle if none of my wet, red-and-blue globules ever landed on an elbow or a bosom.

At the Académie, there was no official instruction, but the regular painters who inhabited the studio made up for this by joking and criticizing my work. Jean-Pierre was a slender young Frenchman with an unruly mop of thick, black hair, who wielded his long paintbrush like one of the fencers in *The Three Musketeers*.

"En garde!" he said. "En garde!" At this, he leaped gymnastically about the place, lunging and parrying while discharging rapid-fire jokes in French. This was a transparent attempt to amuse his girlfriend, a big-boned receptionist who sat stoically by the door, refusing entry to any nonpaying customers.

Meanwhile, a large-framed man who resembled Gérard Dépardieu loved to make satirical running commentaries on the student work. One day, when I was attempting a landscape inspired by the view from the Setfords' house in Burton-upon-Trent, he jumped to within a foot or two of my easel, proclaiming in loud English, "Loook, loook, eet eez so grreeen, so grreeen! Is grreen perrhaps zee only tube of paint in yourr palette?"

I chuckled uncomfortably, having no retort. But when I took a sharp look at my painting, I had to admit the truth of what he was saying. It was indisputably green, with nary a hint of red or any other color to spice it up. Laughing nervously, I continued to work, but I lost heart and abandoned my easel.

While I loved to paint, I worried that my talent had limits. If I were to pursue painting seriously, I desperately needed guidance from a great teacher, but all I got was a discouraging "crit" from a sardonic French painter. In fact, there was more to it than that: painting for its own sake, as an end in itself, was beginning to lose its appeal. Having discovered a keen interest in European history, I found that trying to create fine art failed to satisfy my intellectual curiosity.

The history of art also appealed to my thirst for knowledge. Happily, the Louvre dispatched one of its staffers to the American College to instruct us young ignoramuses in the history of Western art. Buxom Madame Dane began with prehistoric fertility symbols and pressed on past the classical period of the Vénus de Milo, until she eventually arrived at the nineteenth-century French salon painters. This she accomplished in a series of well-orchestrated, vividly scripted slide lectures, except that there was something slightly off about her presentations, a certain *je ne sais quoi* that I couldn't quite explain.

One of my classmates knew exactly what it was.

"Madame Dane?" The girl's hand shot into the air as she attempted to get our professor's attention.

"Yes?"

"Madame Dane, you've got the slides in backward," said the student.

Madame had been surveying the tradition in European painting of a female figure reclining upon a divan, a genre that began in Venice with Giorgione's *Sleeping Venus*, continued in France with Ingres's *Venus*, and terminated with Manet's groundbreaking *Olympia*. At that moment on the screen, I beheld Madame Récamier, the famous subject of Jacques-Louis David's canvas, and sure enough, Madame Récamier's feet were pointing to the left, not to the right.

"But," objected Mme. Dane, rolling her *r*'s with a flourish worthy of my French grandmother, Manie, "what différrence could it posseebly make?"

Never had I encountered a more perfect example of French logic, and there was certainly no point in disputing it. Seeing Madame Récamier reclining in the wrong direction made us all vaguely uncomfortable, but it was impossible to claim that reversing her direction made the painting any less of a masterpiece.

After Christmas break, I attended a party with several classmates on the Right Bank, near the Hôtel de Ville. One particularly nice young American woman took an affectionate interest in me—perhaps she had a crush on me. When it was time to leave the party, she took my hand and we walked back toward the college along the fabled Quais de la Seine, the cobblestone walkway halfway down the riverbank. She was pretty and this was Paris. Night had fallen, and the lights of the *bâteaux-mouches* bounced lyrically off the undulating waves of the Seine, so the moment should have been romantic, but it was torture for me. In my uptight young take on life, holding hands with a girl for more than a few minutes meant that you were admitting to some sort of commitment, and I was afraid of being cornered.

It reminded me of one lunch break in high school when a pretty classmate named Donna had spotted me from afar as I entered a grassy playfield. Jumping off a swing set, she came running to me, arms outstretched, a big smile on her face. I knew she wanted to hug me, but I froze. In my anxiety and fearfulness, I somehow thought that hugging her would signify that I desired her, that I wanted her to be my girlfriend. Reading the reluctance on my face, poor Donna's smile faded and her arms drooped as she slowed to a crawl.

Why hadn't I hugged her? Why was I so distant and cold? Donna was an intelligent, sweet girl, and there was no reason not to have hugged her except for my inexplicable inner torment. Now, as with Donna, I only wanted to escape from the girl in Paris, and I finally managed to part with her at a Métro stop. It didn't occur to me that my discomfort might be due to my sexual orientation.

Toward the end of winter, I saw a poster stapled to a kiosk on the boulevard. Written in French, it invited students on a tour of Italy during *la Sainte Semaine,* or Holy Week. This seemed like a perfect opportunity because I longed to see the Renaissance frescoes we were learning about in my art history class, and especially

Michelangelo's *David*. Thus, during spring break, I found myself at the Gare de Lyon, ready to board a train to Florence. Gathered on the platform, the other participants included about twenty French Catholic students, mostly girls, with a handful of boys.

Among the boys, a friendly young Canadian named Kevin smiled at me when we shook hands. He and I quickly fell into effortless conversation, free of the barriers I was used to from boys. When we shared a cappuccino at a little cafe in the shadow of the grand old Duomo, as I learned the cathedral of Florence is called, our easy rapport reminded me of my friends at home. Gazing into his kind eyes, an undercurrent of attraction buzzed between us, but I discounted it, telling myself I was misjudging the situation. I wasn't bold enough to risk rejection by caressing his cheek or trying to kiss him. What if he got angry and took offense?

After a couple of delectable days touring the Florentine masterpieces, it was time to head to Assisi by motorcoach, where we were expected to express as much piety as we could muster over Good Friday. Then it was on to Rome.

On Easter morning, we joined the crowds filling Bernini's magnificent, enormous oval piazza in front of St. Peter's, where we secured prime places reserved for us for the Papal Mass. A crystalline sky backed Michelangelo's dome as the pope emerged on the porch of the basilica, bestowing blessings on all of us in Latin. Amid the ancient pomp and circumstance, I did not have to be Catholic to feel an unaccustomed spiritual energy—the sheer hope and joy of the Resurrection—surge through me and the entire crowd.

After the Mass, it was time to tour the Vatican Museum, to which we were led down a long, open-air hallway overlooking the lovely Vatican gardens, with their tall palms and fragrant citrus. My buddy Kevin accompanied me as we bumped along through the crowd, and when I paused to gaze over the parapet at a fountain, an enormous wave of horniness suddenly shot through me like an electric shock. Far from targeting Kevin as the object of my lust, I forgot he was even there. My body and brain were so far out of alignment that my mind blocked the perception that he was attractive and might also be available. Instead, I wanted to plough anything that moved, even the wall below the open arches. Hell, I wanted to plough the Sistine Fucking Ceiling, which was our destination.

Although I was no stranger to masturbation, I had not managed to indulge recently, due to the close proximity of my traveling companions. When I did jerk off, I was so dissociated from my desires that I scarcely fantasized about the boys I was attracted to. I certainly didn't fantasize about girls.

Powerful demons were raging inside me as I lifted my eyes heavenward to behold Michelangelo's masterpiece for the first time. Even though I was not Catholic, let alone religious in any way, it felt wrong—sinful—to be filled to the brim with horniness in God's most holy of houses. Especially to be horny for boys. At that moment, the crowd pushing me from behind deposited me directly below the world-famous central panel. As I gazed upward at God bestowing the spark of life on Adam, no matter how self-censoring my thoughts were, they did not prevent His painted finger from looking exactly like a you-know-what.

That night, tucked into my cot in the male dormitory of a monastery, I lay stiffly in the dark, waiting until I was fairly sure that all the others were asleep. Finally deciding that it was safe, I let one hand creep gingerly under the covers so that, at long last,

I could relieve the monstrous burden of my lust. At that exact moment, Kevin's voice reverberated from clear across the ranks of beds.

"Brooks, are you okay?" he asked, in a stage whisper.

"I'm f . . . fine," I croaked, struggling to stifle the enormous moan of my relief.

Kevin was undeniably sexy, and part of me hoped that he would pursue me more aggressively the next day. Another part was terrified that he might actually do so. In the morning, though, he simply smiled at me over our caffe lattes.

"Buongiorno," he said, without irony or innuendo.

I nodded to him over my coffee cup. The situation was so ambiguous that the fog of it exceeded the habitual haze of confusion that accompanied me everywhere. Once again, I deliberately put my sexuality out of my mind.

7

HIGH-RISE SOUTH

SINCE THE American College in Paris offered only an associate degree, I decided to transfer to the University of Pennsylvania. When I returned to Penn after fall semester in Low-Rise North, I was not surprised to be reassigned to High-Rise South. Opening the door to my new room on the twenty-third floor, the skyline of Center City appeared in the window, reflecting a constantly shifting play of light and shadow against the crowd of tall buildings. I was lucky to get a room facing east, toward downtown: the south-facing apartments looked out on dramatic orange and blue flames dancing high into the night sky from the giant oil refineries lining the Schuylkill River below.

I quickly signed up for a class in eighteenth-century English literature taught by Dr. Paul J. Korshin. With his jet-black hair and long sideburns, our youthful and vigorous professor had thick lips and swarthy, olive-colored skin. Dandyishly dressed in wide-lapel, tailored Savile Row suits accessorized with a velvet bowtie at least three inches tall, he lectured like a prosecuting attorney making his final argument to the jury.

Addressing the class as if he were Samuel Johnson and we were the denizens of a London club, he enjoyed employing the Socratic method.

"You, sir, are clearly a gentleman and a scholar," he said to one of the students. "What is your opinion of landscape imagery in the poetry of Alexander Pope?"

"Umm . . . landscape imagery?" my classmate said, clearly flustered.

This did not deter Dr. Korshin, who was soon quoting from Pope's poem, "Epistle IV to Richard Boyle, Earl of Burlington," often called "The Genius of the Place."

In the poem, Pope contrasts the French landscape design of André Le Nôtre, which he abhors, with the new English Landscape Garden, which he very much admires. First, he assesses Le Nôtre's slavish devotion to symmetry:

"Grove nods at grove, each alley has a brother,
And half the platform just reflects the other."

Next, he offers his own design manifesto, expressing his admiration for Lord Burlington, an early patron of the English Landscape Garden style:

"Consult the genius of the place in all;
That tells the waters or to rise, or fall . . ."

My ears perked up, remembering my almost visceral emotional response to the lovely, seemingly random, tree-studded hills surrounding Kedleston Hall. How supremely they contrasted with the regimented boulevards and parks I had observed the year before in Paris.

Now, to my immense surprise, Dr. Korshin was teaching us the intellectual underpinnings of the English revolution in landscape design, which threw out symmetry and geometric planes in favor of undulating hills and valleys, serpentine lakes, and picturesque bridges. How ironic and unexpected it was that an English professor should be the one to spark my growing passion for landscape design!

That semester, Dr. Korshin took an unusual interest in me, singling me out for special attention. When, after class, he first called me up to the lectern to inquire about my background and educational goals, I basked in the glow of his regard, as if he were a substitute father. Soon my feelings for him became nearly as complicated as the conflicting emotions Dad inspired in me. Dr. Korshin's eloquence overshadowed Dad's, but while Dad always pushed me toward architecture, it was not clear what sort of future Dr. Korshin had in mind for me. I felt sure that he had some sort of plan, but what was it? Much as he encouraged my literary insights, I knew he didn't intend for me to become an English professor because he kept reminding me and my classmates how narrow the odds were that we could land a faculty job if we were foolish enough to pursue a PhD in English.

The next fall Dr. Korshin offered me a work-study job assisting him in his new role as head of the American Society of Eighteenth Century Studies (ASECS). While I sat and labeled newsletters bound for the ASECS members, Dr. Korshin—whom I now called Paul—held forth on a variety of topics between phone calls. His sentences were as persuasive and articulate, as devoid of hesitations, as written paragraphs.

When the phone rang, he sat back in his swivel chair, placing his polished black Italian shoes on top of the desk. Framed in the window overlooking Walnut Street, with its academic buildings, trees, and parade of students, he cradled the phone in one hand

and reached up with the other to smooth his perfectly parted black hair.

"What do you mean you can't deliver the conference programs by Monday?" he shouted into the phone with a rising note of impatience, working himself up into the fuming and furious but tightly controlled demeanor of a British prime minister standing for Questions in Parliament.

Paul's self-assurance magnetized me. Reveling in how he treated me more like a colleague than a mere student, I wanted so much to emulate him—to be as suave, polished, and in command of my role as he was. At a time when I longed for a mentor, there he was, but I wasn't sure where his mentorship was leading me or if I even wanted to go there. Here was a man I admired as much as Dad, who apparently had my best interests at heart, but who also rode roughshod over other people's feelings, like the lowly printer he had just shouted at. To be successful in your career, did you really have to be so arrogant? I hoped not.

In junior year, I was still a nerdy A-student. One exciting new class was nineteenth-century French literature, taught by Mme. Vivienne Rappeleux, an erudite woman with a fine Parisian pedigree. With her bright brown eyes, short brown hair, and a smile that varied between enigmatic and vaguely enthusiastic, she conducted her class entirely in French, and we worked our way dutifully through Flaubert, Balzac, Stendhal, and Zola. Still fresh from my year in Paris, my French was good enough that one day La Rappe, as my new roommate, Rich, liked to call her, asked to see me after class.

"I've written a paper in French, and now I have to present it in English at a conference," she explained. "Would you be willing to translate it? Let me be clear that I want it in *colloquial* English, *bien sûr*," she added. "I want it to sound the way people actually *speak*, not like academic, written English." Although I knew I was a good student, I was stunned by the honor she was bestowing on me. Naturally, I agreed, and over the next few days I began translating. Then, one afternoon while I worked at my desk, Linda Dunn, my friend from Low-Rise North, came up for a visit.

"What are you doing?" she asked.

"Oh, I'm translating a paper into English for my French teacher. She has to read it out loud at a conference." At that, Linda approached and stood right behind me, her long hair grazing my shoulder. Placing her finger on the text in front of me, she chuckled.

"You know what would be really funny, Brooks?"

"What?" I asked.

"If you wrote, 'I bet you're not even listening to this' and stuck it somewhere in the middle of the translation," she said, laughing musically.

"Oh my God, really?" I said, wondering if I had the balls to do it. I wasn't one to break rules or pull pranks. Basically, I was a goody-two-shoes, but I was also highly impressionable. As much as I wanted to please Dr. Rappeleux, I also wanted to please Linda, but I couldn't please both of them at once. It was a conundrum, but Linda was persistent.

"Yes," she insisted, "yes," and she laughed again.

I stifled a laugh thinking about it. I could just imagine Mme. Rappeleux at a lectern in a giant ballroom, her bright brown eyes flashing across the dignified audience. Like the Mona Lisa, her enigmatic smile would be pasted on her lips as she listened modestly to her pompous introduction by the provost of This-or-That

University. Next, she would begin reading, and then, ten or fifteen minutes in, she would intone, "I bet you're not even listening to this," as if reciting robotically from a teleprompter. At that, the audience would gasp in horror at her effrontery, or her galling display of French ennui, and *voilà* (!) the talk would be over.

Laughing at Linda's devilry, I took my pen, shuffled the pages as if they were a pack of playing cards, and inserted the deadly phrase randomly into the text. Linda never moved from her supervisory position above my shoulder until she saw the ink go down on the page with her own eyes.

A few days later, I nonchalantly handed my completed translation to Madame, and a few days after that, the phone rang in my dorm room. Mme. Rappeleux was hysterical.

"Brooks, I demand to see you right now," she said angrily.

"Where?" I asked, my voice cracking.

"Meet me on Spruce Street in front of High-Rise South. I'll be in my car." She slammed down the receiver.

Trembling, I approached the elevator bank. While the elevator paused multiple times on the way down, I had plenty of time to berate myself for having been so foolish as to agree to Linda's prank. By the time it finally thudded to a stop in the lobby and the heavy stainless-steel door inched open, I had convinced myself that my academic reputation lay in ruins.

As promised, Madame was parked on Spruce Street in her Volvo station wagon.

"Get in," she said, so I opened the back door and got in. Next to me, a young boy sat playing with blocks and behind the back seat, a large dog panted and paced.

"This is my son," said the professor matter-of-factly, as she took off at top speed. It had never occurred to me that Madame had a family, but meeting her son didn't make me feel any better. We circled the campus three or four times as waves of angry French poured over me. I had no idea where Madame intended to take me. It appeared that she was merely running laps.

After Mme. Rappeleux made it perfectly clear how much I had disrespected her, and how unthinkable—truly unthinkable—it was that I had stuck that sordid phrase into her paper, which, by the way, was entirely too *colloquial* a translation, she returned me to High-Rise South as abruptly as we had left.

"Needless to say, I will never ask you to translate something for me again!" she yelled. "Now get out!"

At that, she disgorged me onto the sidewalk and sped off again, if it can ever be accurate to describe a Volvo as speeding. Returning shamefacedly to the twenty-third floor, I wondered why I had been willing so quickly to accede to Linda's demand. At first, I couldn't answer my own question, but later I realized that it revealed I had a long-repressed rebellious streak. Yes, indisputably, there was a tiny, suppressed part of me that wanted to overturn the authority of Dad, Dr. Korshin, and now, Madame Rappeleux. My gratuitous attempt to have fun had backfired, and the lesson I drew from it, once again, was that I should remain true to my straight-laced ways. It was the first time I consciously thought of myself as being divided between two conflicting identities—an ambitious conformist struggling with an adventurous spirit. I had no idea how to reconcile them, but if I couldn't tap into that subversive part of myself in a more positive way, how could I possibly know what I wanted out of life?

8

TEN ARTHUR'S ROUND TABLE

WITH A cartoonish *beep, beep*, Paul Korshin's orange VW Beetle screeched to a halt in front of the Wynnewood, Pennsylvania, commuter rail station. After surprising me by inviting me to dinner, he had come to "collect me" at the station. Not sure what I had done to deserve this honor, it made me nervous. Yes, I was a good student, but so were most of my classmates. Over the years, I have repeatedly asked myself what it was that Paul saw in me, without ever clinching it. Maybe he recognized that I was genuinely interested in what he was teaching, as opposed to taking his class merely because I needed the credit. Regardless of the reason, I had enthusiastically accepted Paul's invitation.

When I hopped in the car, Paul took off at a rapid clip, regaling me with amusing stories over the loud buzz of the engine.

"Rocco and those other bozos at the printing company are about as bright as Nixon's dirty tricksters," Paul said. "Thank God they're not in the English PhD program!"

"You cracked me up when you were talking to him," I said. "How did you ever get him to make the printing deadline?"

"He just needed to listen to reason! Nothing like a little intelligent analysis to persuade people to do what they already assured me they could accomplish. You don't have to be a nuclear physicist to run the offset printing machine on time," Paul explained, completely unaware of how imperious he sounded.

After darting to the left and then to the right, we pulled up at a little cul-de-sac. We had arrived at Ten Arthur's Round Table, one of a matching set of Tudor houses with half-timbered gables and steep slate-tiled roofs. *What a perfect address for an English professor*, I reflected—the very name was steeped in Arthurian legend.

Paul led me to the lilac-colored front door, which was decorated with a wrought iron peep window and massive ornamental hinges. Just as I was observing how the door managed to look at once inviting and imposing, it swung open, revealing the hospitable figure of Paul's wife, Kate, whom I had not yet met. With her chestnut-colored hair swept into a ponytail, she wore wire-framed glasses and a large white apron over a simple housedress.

"So you're Brooks," she said with a warm smile. "Come on in."

"Thanks. So nice to meet you," I said.

In the comfortable living room, sofas and armchairs huddled around a coffee table on a Persian carpet, under a high-coved plaster ceiling. The effect was elegant yet casual, which meant that it was as charming as a renovated cottage in the Cotswolds. Sitting on the sofa was a well-dressed academic couple that Paul introduced to me as his colleagues in the comparative literature department.

Gazing around, I noticed that all the rooms were painted in warm pastel shades of tangerine, salmon, and watermelon. Beyond the living room, a wide archway led into the dining room, which was furnished with a long oak table and eight or ten dining chairs. At the far end of the room, a nondescript swinging door led into the kitchen.

While Kate served glasses of wine, the doorbell rang, and within a few minutes three other guests arrived. Paul had prepared me for one of them in advance, explaining that Dan Tennant was an announcer on one of Philadelphia's two classical music radio stations. This was the station that annoyingly repeated cloying ads for "The More Than One Hundred Extraordinary Shops of Chestnut Hill" with mind-numbing frequency throughout the day.

After serving canapes, Kate excused herself to finish the dinner preparations. As the kitchen door swung behind her, the cocktail phase of the evening slipped into high gear. Paul was chatting intently with another guest in one corner of the living room, and soon I found myself face-to-face with Dan Tennant, with absolutely nothing to say.

Tongue-tied, I finally blurted out, "So . . . I hear you're a DJ." At this, Mr. Tennant leaned backward slightly, then drew his chin up as high as he could manage.

"I am *not* a DJ, I am an *announcer*," he said, clearly taking umbrage.

"Um, well I know that you're in charge of programming at W . . ." I responded, trying desperately to remember the station's call letters.

Later on, I managed to steal a private moment with Paul, who was highly amused.

"Nothing wrong with what you said, Brooks, he's had that coming for quite a while."

Surprised that Paul was actually proud of me for pushing Dan off his pedestal, I began to wish that I had done so deliberately. In those moments of confidence, Paul's approval felt like warm sunshine, just as it did when we were working in the office and I managed to say something witty enough to make him laugh.

Then again, Paul's pleasure at my inadvertent put-down of the radio announcer only reinforced the intimidation technique I had witnessed him use on the phone. Once more, I found myself conflicted between basking in his approval and cringing at his elitism. There was something so well-bred about it, something that no doubt helped him achieve his goals, but where did that leave me? I didn't want to go through life being a bitch to everybody. Still, I felt sure that he had my best interests at heart. He was not going to steer me wrong.

Suddenly, we heard the loud trill of a kitchen timer. After a short pause, it buzzed again, and Kate emerged from the kitchen, wiping her hands on her apron. "Dinner is served," she announced, and we filed into the dining room with heady anticipation.

I don't remember the name of a single dish served at that theatrical dinner, but each one was an ingenious and delectable mélange of exotic ingredients.

Later, while we savored our chocolate mousse, Paul continued to hold forth, as he liked to call it, on current events and scholarly topics with equal panache. After we licked our spoons, he glanced at his watch and announced that it was time to run me up to the station. It was precisely 10:30 p.m., and with a little luck I'd make the 10:40 train. I jumped up from the table, thanked Kate, and got into Paul's Beetle for the return run. Zipping to the station, he energetically shook my hand and bade me good night. For a fleeting moment I wondered if he was sexually attracted to me. An energy flowed between us that sometimes verged on an electric current, but he never touched me, and the whole situation was wrapped in ambiguity.

The train took a long time making its way back to the city, allowing me to reflect that, despite having been in the midst of a fabulous set of A-listers only moments before, now I felt lonely and bereft. Unsure why Paul had singled me out for the privilege of dining at his home, and even less sure of what he expected from me, I was a bit shaken. Although grateful for his attention, I felt unworthy, as if I were an imposter. Now, like Cinderella at the stroke of midnight, I was reduced once more to the bohemian milieu of student life. Clearly, I didn't belong among the rarefied professors, but where exactly *did* I belong? I had no idea. I badly needed guidance from an older male mentor—either Dad or Paul or both. But I needed a mentor who "got" me as a whole person, not someone who wanted to mold me into an architect or a worldly intellectual.

Many similar dinner parties ensued, each one ending when Paul checked his watch and ran me up to the station, where I'd rush to catch the train just as it was pulling into the station.

The next year, he generously hosted my twenty-first birthday party, inviting two of my classmates to accompany me. At the party, Paul presented me with two gifts: a copy of Alastair Cooke's *America*, which was currently a PBS television sensation, and what he called a lifetime supply of tabasco sauce. A lifetime supply turned out to be a box of ten small bottles.

Just as he was getting ready to spirit me off to the station, he said, "Brooks, I have something to show you."

He and Kate led me to one of the dining room windows. Lifting the blind, Paul pointed to a tiny cactus on the windowsill. A porcupine pin cushion, the diminutive blue-green object stood erect in its pot, rising above two small needle-covered spheres, one on each side.

"You see that cactus?" Paul asked.

"We decided to name it Brooks," he said.

Blushing, I didn't know what to say. So was it true that he was attracted to me? And was his wife too? Did they honestly want a threesome with a lowly college student who was still, to his shame, a virgin? The situation was so enigmatic that it only added to my confusion.

Three little windshield wipers rattled back and forth as my roommate's white MGB barreled down the freeway with the top up. We had just finished our junior year, and our butts felt the shock of every pothole all the way from Philadelphia to Seattle, where Rich had kindly offered to drop me off on his way home to Los Angeles. His background was fascinating—he had grown up in London, where his father had produced the two Beatles movies, *A Hard Day's Night* and *Help!*. He actually knew the Beatles personally, but he was too unassuming to brag about it, so naturally I made it my business to boast about it for him, as loudly as I could, wherever I went on campus.

"Yes, my roommate knows the Beatles," I would assure everyone, regardless of whether or not they had posed the question . . . and why would they?

One night, Rich and I pulled into a roadside motel in Spearfish, South Dakota, and asked for a room. When we approached the desk, the aging proprietors, a married couple, clenched their eyebrows and frowned with agitation. After much sighing and stalling, they produced a key and pointed us toward a cottage next to a narrow driveway. Entering the room, we saw that it had only one double bed, so we returned to the counter.

"Hey, mate, could we get a room with two beds?" Rich asked, whereupon the proprietors sighed with relief, managed to make tight little smiles, and handed us a key to a double room. Their unreasoning fear of gay men was so palpable that I wondered what it was about us that marked us as queer. Then I got it. Having been raised in London, Rich was exceedingly polite, and neither one of us came across as macho. Rich liked to talk in his mid-Atlantic accent about girls, but he rarely dated. Meanwhile, I gestured awkwardly and must have looked femme enough to be a bully's target. That was all the evidence they needed to frame us as gay.

The instant we entered the town's diner for breakfast the next morning, the loud buzz of conversation slammed to a halt. Clinking their coffee mugs on the counter, a line of beefy truckers swiveled on their red vinyl stools to stare at us. Nobody smiled or nodded. It was the only place in town, so we stayed to order coffee and pancakes, but their malice unnerved us.

"They don't seem to like us here," Rich observed when he was sure nobody was eavesdropping.

"I know what you mean," I whispered. "Obviously, they think we're gay. Let's get the hell out of here."

"I don't know, mate, I'm not gay. It must be you."

I frowned but nodded. Despite continuing to deny I was gay, I clearly didn't fit in with the straight crowd. At the same time, I was too scared to jump into the mysterious gay one, which in any case was entirely hidden from me.

Gazing at the endless telephone poles passing by us on the monotonous miles through eastern Montana, I had plenty of time to reflect about our hostile reception. It was my first *visible* dragon, the first concrete evidence that I had reason to be afraid of coming out. Granted, Spearfish was in the middle of South Dakota, a part of the country so culturally behind the East and West coasts that it might as well have been Dorothy's Kansas.

Still, that didn't make the coasts particularly hospitable. Whether in Seattle or at Penn, I hadn't met a single person, male or female, who admitted that they were gay, and I hadn't even heard of the Stonewall riots that had taken place in New York only five years before. Thousands of young gay men were flocking from rural places like South Dakota to the safe haven of San Francisco, but I didn't know that either.

After the tension of our long drive, it was a relief when Rich and I pulled into Seattle, where Mom and Dad celebrated by treating us to dinner at the Space Needle. As our table slowly revolved, high above the city, I excitedly pointed out the sights to Rich. Mom grinned while Dad peppered Rich with questions about his studies and interests. He couldn't converse without lecturing, but he was good at asking questions.

"So how do you like Penn?" he asked Rich.

"It's okay," said Rich. "But I miss London. It's so much more cosmopolitan. Then again, I like LA too. I'm thinking about transferring to UCLA."

"Good," said Dad. "But why don't you stick it out and finish at Penn?"

Of course, Dad would look at it from the academic angle. I enjoyed sitting back while he focused like a laser beam on Rich, glad that for once someone else was in the hot seat. Paul Korshin's approval had made me more confident, but I still squirmed at Dad's architectural harangues. Tuning him out, as I so often did, I found myself daydreaming. What if I confessed to him that I might be gay? I shuddered at the thought, unable to imagine telling him something I was still actively denying.

When my senior year arrived, I often found myself on the ground floor of Van Pelt Library, attending to one of my endless reading assignments. Glancing up from the card catalog one day, I noticed a narrow white door that appeared to lead nowhere. On it, a small, discreet sign proclaimed 'Gay Student Union.' Despite my curiosity, I wasn't about to traipse past the ranks of card files to try opening the door. *What if someone sees me?* The irony that the gay student union appeared to be housed in a broom closet completely eluded me, but now that I had seen the message on that door, it became my mission to clock any person entering it.

In my few remaining months at Penn, I never once saw a single person go in or out. Did the student union really exist? Either way, it appeared to have no members. Even though the sexual revolution was in full swing off campus at rock concerts and nightclubs, and even though David Bowie and Elton John delighted in celebrating androgyny on their album covers, the sexual norm on campus was strictly hetero. My classmates' sexual liaisons appeared to occur during or after the rowdy frat parties that rollicked up and down Locust Walk, the central spine of campus. Sometime during their beer-drinking binges and their retching, the grinding and making out began, soon to be forgotten as quickly as the next morning's hangovers. No matter how much I wanted to think of myself as straight, I was revolted by that scene and stayed away. It felt like the opposite of romance to me.

ONE AFTERNOON before I was due to graduate, Paul cornered me on the sidewalk in front of Bennett Hall, otherwise known as the English Department.

"Brooks, have you thought about what you're going to do for a career? Are you planning to apply to law school?" he inquired.

In those days, long before software engineering became the quickest route to riches, law was one leg on the three-legged stool of career preparation at Penn, the other two being medicine and business.

"No," I said. "I don't want to go to law school. I just need to take a few months off and think about my next move, maybe travel a bit." I felt I was on solid ground. It was not unusual for kids my age to take a break between college and graduate school, maybe sail around the world. Lots of my high school friends were pursuing those types of experiences. Hell, one of them was even building a boat on a beach in Bellingham, Washington, *before* sailing around the world. However, such a beach-bum approach to personal growth was not sufficiently serious-minded for Paul.

"So what do you expect to do, become a **Stevedore**?" he retorted in a loud voice, all his scorn fully deployed. I could tell that **Stevedore** was capitalized in bold italics, as if he had lifted it from a line in a satirical poem by Alexander Pope.

"No, Paul, I don't plan on becoming a stevedore any more than I see myself becoming a lawyer. I just need to take a few months off and figure it out."

But Paul trained one of his scornful glances on me, dismissing my boyish logic. Instead, he unexpectedly proposed that I should apply for a prestigious scholarship called the Thouron (pronounced "Touron") Fellowship for British-American Student Exchange. Having already studied in Paris, it had not occurred to me to seek another year of study abroad, but since Paul was recommending it, it deserved my consideration.

"Do you really think I have a chance to get in?" I asked, knowing that the fellowship was intensely competitive.

"Yes, I do," Paul said. "You should go for it. Now all you have to do is find an MPhil. course, the British equivalent of a master's degree, and apply for both the Thouron and the MPhil." Without further ceremony, he consulted his watch and scurried back into Bennett Hall.

I stood on the sidewalk, stunned. It impressed me deeply that he cared enough to nudge me to apply. Paul had my back—he wasn't about to let me become one of those West Coast college bums who drift from one bartender job to another year after year, supposedly trying to find themselves. As long as I could find a British degree program that would engage my artistic talents and lead to a paying career, I couldn't really see a downside.

The next day, I met Paul in Bennett Hall. "Okay, I've decided to go for it—I mean to apply for the Thouron. Thanks for suggesting it!"

"Good man, you won't regret it."

After an intensive application process, I was delighted to receive a letter naming me as a Thouron semifinalist and inviting me to a weekend at a swank New Jersey country club. There, fifteen or sixteen of us were observed from dawn to dusk by a panel of Penn faculty from both sides of the pond, as if we were contestants in a sort of proto *Big Brother* reality show. Apart from several rounds of stimulating one-on-one interviews and panel discussions, the trickiest part involved proving that our table manners were equal to the test of picking up the salad fork at the appropriate moment during the formal dinner parties. The bar of British protocol was set so high that a couple of Black male applicants hastened to assure the regal English lady who led one of the panels that, if selected, they would not fail to speak the Queen's English in lieu of the African American vernacular that American academia had recently enshrined as "ebonics."

A few weeks later, I was at home in Seattle when a dignified envelope bearing the logo of the Thouron Fellowship arrived in the mail. I took a deep breath and quickly tore it open.

"Mom! Dad! Guess what? I got in! I got picked for the Thouron!" I said, practically leaping over the sofa in my excitement. I was one of only eight designees, four women and four men, including the two Black men.

"Oh, that's wonderful, darling," Mom said.

"I'm so proud of you," Dad added. "So, city planning, then?"

"Yes," I said, knowing that Dad was skeptical. As far as he was concerned, architecture was superior to urban planning or any other design profession.

Ignoring Dad's biases, I discovered that University College, London had a graduate program in what the Brits called "town and country planning." I blithely assumed that this meant the design of outdoor spaces, the boulevards and parks that give any city its form. Those design elements were the closest modern equivalent I could think of to the ingenious landscape design that had so moved me at Kedleston Hall. Landscape intrigued me not only for its giant scale but because it was a *living* canvas, lit by the sun, shaded by clouds, and buffeted by the wind. Landscape was alive and kinetic—a vast, natural stage on which people moved about, enjoying the view. Drawing plans for towns and cities sounded like the most engaging and satisfying career I could imagine, one that would marshal my artistic talents to create something for public use and enjoyment.

The next fall, class started in London's Bloomsbury District with an orientation session around a giant conference table. Our new professor began by asking each of us fifteen incoming planning students where we were living. Having just barely managed to secure my place in a college dorm after roaming futilely around the great city, chasing down apartment rentals listed on the bulletin boards of coin "laundrettes," I was glad for this opportunity to become acquainted with my new classmates.

"I found a place at Max Rayne House," I said proudly, when my turn came.

"I live in bloody council housing," the next student said, spitting dramatically into a nearby dustbin. He turned out to be a firebrand from Glasgow who had nothing but contempt for public housing.

"All private property in the UK should be banned!" he added, slamming his fist on the conference table. "The British government should appropriate private property and redistribute it to the masses!"

A heated debate ensued, but it was fairly clear that a sizable majority of the students agreed with him. Being a good American capitalist, I was shocked. Never had it occurred to me that a bunch of London planning students would be Marxists, if not flat-out communists. Just as I was processing this unexpected information, however, a female student raised her hand. A well-coiffed lady with wavy, chestnut-colored hair, quite a few years older than the rest of us and dressed in a respectable business suit with a string of pearls, she explained in a plummy accent that she was returning to university after a stint in the business world.

"Oh, . . . and I live in the Village of Radley, in Oxfordshire," she added, almost as an afterthought.

Although she was too polite to express her opinion, it was abundantly clear that she was a Tory who did in fact believe that people should be allowed to own property. Imagining her leaving her darling Anne Hathaway–style thatched roof cottage for the drive into central London in her Mercedes sedan, I felt a wave of relief, although the ratio of Marxists to capitalists was still about thirteen to two. But I was confused. Why were we talking about economics when I thought we were going to learn how to design parks, plazas, and boulevards? A little sliver of anxiety crept into my excitement about the program.

Filling out my class schedule, I discovered that real estate economics was a required course. Taught by a young statistician, the curriculum promoted the theory that an economic formula of descending and ascending property values dictates where any urban business locates. According to the rule, the closer to the center of any city a business chooses to locate in, the more profit-able it is likely to become.

Something about this disturbed me. Why was nothing mentioned about how the unique geography of a specific city, its rivers and railroads, its steep hills or floodplains, might affect how and where a business locates? Recoiling against the teacher's axiom of economic determinism, I despaired. How foolish I had been to assume that town and country planning meant the design of urban outdoor spaces, when apparently it was actually all about sociology and economics for people who wanted to work for—or maybe against—the British government.

After a few days of anxiety, I learned that I could transfer into the architecture department, where I signed up for introductory environmental design classes. Freed from the rigors of real estate economics, I had plenty of time to explore London after class. At the Tate Gallery, I tried to work up enthusiasm for the Turners. Wrestling with the atmospheric drama of England's mists, fog and rain, his almost abstract brushstrokes triumphed.

In spite of Turner's genius, I was drawn more toward the prosaic Constables. In the Constable landscapes, the sun shone brightly, and hard outlines of buildings, meadows, and trees could be seen in sharp relief against the sky. Constable's paintings recognized that earth is an equal building block in the construction of a scene, along with water and sky. It dawned on me that you could design real landscapes that would end up looking like Constables, whereas any scene, designed or not, might end up looking like a Turner, given the right vagaries of light, cloud, or mist.

Having read Reyner Banham's book on the architecture of Los Angeles, which was rebooted as a PBS television special called *Reyner Banham Loves Los Angeles*, I was delighted to discover that the celebrity professor taught in the architecture department. When I signed up for his intriguing spring course on the neo-Palladian movement in British architecture, I learned that the great Italian Renaissance architect, Andrea Palladio, had directly influenced the architects of the eighteenth-century English estates.

These same country houses, surrounded by Capability Brown's landscapes, were in turn painted by Constable. Like Kedleston Hall, they were the estates described in Pope's poem. While stately, symmetrical mansions anchored the properties, the gigantic, asymmetrical landscapes that enveloped them were paramount in the vision of their creators. The Palladian movement, Banham explained, eventually crossed the Atlantic, inspiring the designs of Monticello and the White House, along with their grounds.

With his bushy gray beard and giant aviator glasses, Banham cut a dashing figure. One afternoon, while the other students and I awaited his arrival at the National Gallery, the mad London traffic parted, revealing the rapid approach of a bicycle with heavy leather saddlebags. It was Banham, of course, dressed in a tweed suit and matching wool cap. What could be more stereotypically English than a cyclist in tweeds? I chuckled at the thought that he could have been a character in an Agatha Christie murder mystery.

Leading us inside the museum, Banham introduced us to the neoclassical paintings of Nicolas Poussin and Claude Lorrain, both of whom painted Greek temples or Roman bridges set in bucolic, naturalistic landscapes. In each of the paintings, trees framed a perspective divided into foreground and middle ground, with a background of hazy hills and clouds. Figures clothed in classical robes, often shepherds with their sheep, were dotted about, adding an element of depth and scale. By contrast, a third painter named Salvator Rosa painted dramatic Alps and moody storms. The first two artists represented neo-classicism; the latter, a nascent Romanticism.

Both "isms" played an important role in the design of the neo-Palladian landscapes, and I was fascinated to learn that these landscape paintings directly inspired Capability Brown and the other English park designers. I reveled in the idea that a two-dimensional piece of art could be translated into a three-dimensional reality that people could move through and enjoy. But there was even more to the story. Banham explained how late-Renaissance theatrical designers working for the Commedia dell'Arte in Florence had used the newly rediscovered art and science of perspective to design their bucolic stage sets.

Nowhere were the precepts of theater design inspiring classicist landscape paintings, and of paintings in turn influencing real landscapes, more evident than in Henry Hoare's masterpiece, Stourhead, where the house no longer served as the focal point of the site. Instead, it was built off to one side of a lake, playing a secondary role to the giant park surrounding it.

When we set out to visit Stourhead in mid-May, sunshine had finally come to Britain, along with unseasonably warm temperatures. Banham chartered a bus and we barreled down the motorway to Wiltshire, singing songs. After a picnic on the lawns of Longleat House, a National Trust property reminiscent of *Downton Abbey*, we continued on to Stourhead. Just as in Pope's poem, its beautifully sculpted valleys became hills, hills became valleys, lakes were dug, bridges were built to span across the new lakes, and hedgerows were converted into artistic groves dotting the horizon. Many temples nestled into the graceful hillsides surrounding the central, serpentine lake. These pavilions or follies were stone fantasies inspired not only by Greek and Roman myths but also by a Romantic, pastoral view of life. Why else would they have been inhabited by shepherds and nymphs, actual actors that Banham explained were paid to dwell in them by the upper-class twits who originally owned the place?

Until I saw Stourhead under Banham's guiding eye, I had always assumed that nature was simply nature, and design was design, yet here was concrete evidence of how brilliant people could actually design *with* nature. I was so moved that I decided I wanted to be a landscape architect.

Ironically, I soon learned that most British landscape architecture students went to, of all places, Penn, due to the fact that Ian McHarg chaired Penn's landscape architecture department. McHarg was a dashing Scotsman whose seminal book, *Design with Nature*, had become an influential manifesto for enlightened ecological planning, and I rushed out to buy a copy. Devouring it, I quickly concluded that if I wanted to become a landscape architect, I couldn't do better than to return to Penn.

When I called Dad about it, he said I should talk to Bob Hanna, a former student of his who taught landscape architecture at Penn. Bob was on sabbatical that year, having won the prestigious Rome Prize at the American Academy, so I decided to pay him a visit in Rome over spring break. At the venerable Villa Aurelia, the sixteenth-century palazzo that houses the American Academy, I was escorted down wide hallways to a lofty, frescoed room where Bob received me.

"I hear you might want to come back to Penn," Bob said.

Of medium height, with rugged features, gray-green eyes, neck-length brown hair, and a thick beard, his manner was so deadpan that I felt as if Bob Newhart were receiving me in the Hall of Mirrors at Versailles.

"Yes. What do I need to do to apply?"

"Well, we'll need to see your portfolio."

Bob's tone was self-assured and soothing, and I gleaned that I had a reasonable chance to be accepted into Penn's master's program. Now I was on a mission to create a portfolio that would make me stand out from the other applicants, and I hurried back to London to accomplish it.

BACK HOME in Seattle to take a few prerequisite classes before returning to Penn, I found a summer job in, of all places, the University of Washington Dental School. There, I was surprised to discover an attractive young woman sitting at the desk opposite mine, next to the window. She had a mane of thick, honey-colored hair; a long, slender neck; graceful fingers, and jade-green eyes. But the most wonderful thing about Jayla, apart from her amazingly good looks, was the way she would sigh, then smile and roll her eyes, before finally emitting a musical laugh as she mused over the foibles of our coworkers and grumbled about the injustices committed by our boss. Her eyes twinkled with an appealing mixture of amused irony and sad resignation at the world's absurdity that reminded me of Linda Dunn, my friend from Low-Rise North.

"Jayla, I have to say, you look so much like Farrah Fawcett!" I told her one day. I was thinking of the ubiquitous poster that every straight college man had on his wall in the mid-seventies, the one where a beaming Farrah is seated on the floor, her head propped up on her left elbow while her right arm angles back, supporting her. A giant corolla of wavy blonde hair flows across her forehead and curls over her shoulders, making her look like a sexy lioness.

"Oh, please—give me a break. Don't even go there!" she replied. She was a real woman, not a pinup girl, and she was not about to be compared to the star of *Charlie's Angels*.

At first, I was astonished at her reaction because I had thought that comparing her to Farrah was a huge compliment, but my surprise quickly turned into embarrassment. Still, despite my gaffe, I took a deep breath and opened my mouth again.

"Would you like to go out to a movie?" I asked, biting my lip in case she said no.

"Yes, sure," she said, to my surprise and pleasure.

The problem was that I had to pick her up in Dad's new car, a giant, white Oldsmobile Delta 88 sedan, and I knew in advance that she would smirk and mock me for it. The Oldsmobile was a haven of quiet luxury, but it could not have been more unhip. The front wheels felt as if they were miles from the steering wheel, and you had to be the captain of *The Love Boat* to maneuver it through a turn.

Sure enough, Jayla tittered when she beheld the arrival of my cruise ship, grinning broadly and saying, "*This* is your car?"

I quickly explained that it was my dad's, which in itself was vaguely embarrassing, and we were off to the movies.

After a few dates picking Jayla up in the Olds, I was invited up to her large, tidy apartment in a venerable brick building in Seattle's University District. Before I knew what was happening, she was lying on her back on a faded oval rug and pulling me down on top of her. We began kissing, but something was wrong. I don't know what demon possessed me, but all at once I sat up on my knees and exclaimed, "I'm starving. Let's go out to eat!"

While my sudden but unwelcome hunger was real, no doubt the real culprit was a tiny, uninvited voice at the back of my brain that whispered, "Give it up, Brooks. You're a homosexual."

"You're hungry and you want to . . . *eat*?" she asked, with one of her ironic laughs.

"Yes," I said meekly, and off we went to some nearby, completely forgettable student eatery. No doubt that was the moment when Jayla concluded I was not boyfriend material, and I couldn't say she was wrong. She was the sexiest, most attractive young woman I had ever met, and I wanted very much for my body to agree with me, but it was on strike.

After dinner, we returned to her apartment, where she invited me to share her bed, although not her body, and I spent an eternal chaste night lying next to her.

When morning finally came, I peeked sideways through the window blind, gazing abstractedly at the giant, pale terracotta heads of Indian chiefs in feathered headdresses that supported the faux cornices above every window on her floor. I felt so incredibly foolish and ashamed, such a failure when it came to hetero dating. But while I mused forlornly, Jayla yawned, stretched, and opened her lovely green eyes. Fortunately, she was smiling as pleasantly as ever, flashing brilliant white teeth that were every bit as perfect as Farrah's.

There was an inviting kindness, a lightness, and a delicacy about her, but when I left her apartment that morning, I stood on the sidewalk and looked back up at her window. *The next time I make out with someone*, I thought, *I bet it will be with a man.* That was the most honest I had ever been with myself, but I was still not ready to act on it. Where the thought even came from, I wasn't sure. Apart from furtively admiring the men I saw everywhere, I had still not formed a crush on anyone, not at Penn and not in London.

A few days later, Mom found me on the sofa in the living room, listening to Hall and Oates's hit song, "She's Gone," which I was playing and replaying on the record player. I must have looked like I was brooding because she asked me, "What's wrong, dear one?"

"I'm thinking about having an affair," I answered unguardedly, referring to my still-unformed plans to try once more with Jayla. I just had to figure out how to ask her out again without making a fool of myself.

"Don't," Mom said, and that pretty much put an end to the matter because I was still so young and naive that my first impulse was always to obey Mom. Honestly, I was not being truthful with myself. Hall and Oates were singing about a woman who had left, but I should have known that I was lamenting not the loss of a woman but the persistence of an illusion—the illusion that I was straight. It must have been cracking, though, because a couple of weeks later, riding home with Mom from the supermarket, I said, "Mom, there's something I need to tell you. I'm—I'm attracted to men. I don't know what it means, but it's very powerful."

Mom pulled up in the driveway and sat quietly for a moment without unbuckling her seatbelt.

"Well, there it is, dear one," she said at last. After a pause, she carefully added, "It's a hard life, you know. I hope you realize that." Although she had nothing more to add, I knew from her calm tone and loving attitude that she would support me if I ever summoned the courage to act on my feelings.

I didn't know what to say, so I said nothing, but I was gratified by her accepting and loving tone. I was so grateful for this assurance that when I came out, or *if* I came out, she would not disown me. Hopefully, Mom would not tell Dad about our conversation, but if she did, I prayed that he would go along with her, as he did in most things, adopting her tolerant attitude. Whatever the case, I put it out of mind, because I was due back at Penn in just a week to begin my master's program in landscape architecture.

DRESSED IN an Izod shirt and jeans, Professor Jake Borgum paced the auditorium stage, ready to lead the incoming landscape architecture graduate students in a chorus of the famous Beatles song "Yesterday."

After we dutifully parroted the first verse, he lifted both arms toward the audience. "Now, hear this, all of you. Your yesterdays are over and your troubles are about to begin. If you're wondering how, let me explain. Are any of you married? Raise your hands if you are." A smattering of hands rose timidly from the audience.

"Well, in that case, good luck making it to the end of the year! You will soon be divorced," he warned. "And as for you singles out there, you might as well forget about starting a relationship."

While I found his attempt at intimidation distasteful and bombastic, it made me nervous. Relieved for once that I was single, and therefore not on the verge of divorce, I recoiled at the idea that I would once again have to put my personal life on hold after all my years of undergraduate studies, during which I had remained resolutely in the closet.

After Jake's warning, the long, hard slog of my three-year master's program began. Having spent my undergraduate years studying for the sake of knowledge itself, it felt great to be learning something that would lead directly to a paying career. Best of all, I was at last embarking on a path that *I* had chosen, rather than merely following in the footsteps of my distinguished architect father.

Although Bob Hanna had encouraged me to apply, Ian McHarg was the big international draw for Penn's landscape architecture program. Everybody who was interested in environmentalism or concerned about pollution had a copy of his *Design with Nature*, along with Rachel Carson's *Silent Spring*. The era of computer mapping had not yet begun, so when you entered the large, messy landscape architecture studio on the third floor of the Graduate School of Fine Arts, you smelled the heady chemical fumes of hundreds of felt-tip markers deployed to create layer-cake models revealing the intricate way that certain plant communities crowned specific soil types, which in turn overlaid specific geologies, all on a particular rural site.

Every now and then, the heroically tall figure of McHarg strolled through the studio, smiling authoritatively from behind his impressive handlebar moustache. Dressed in a tweed jacket with suede elbow patches, he brandished one of the brown More cigarettes that were so popular with all the professors. Bubbling over with excitement at such poetic topics as fluvial morrphology, he stopped to criticize one student's work as "insalubrrious" and another's as "arrbitrrarry and cappricious." I felt sure that he selected those particular phrases because they contained the largest possible number of the rolling Scottish *r*'s he so loved to impress us with.

I smiled to myself, rejoicing that McHarg's maps represented an approach to regional planning that relied entirely on physical geography, rather than on the abstract real estate economics I had been taught in London. Moreover, unlike the tedious architectural drawings in Dad's studio, these were colorful graphic representations of living, breathing landscapes.

During the same week that Jake Borgum made us sing "Yesterday," I met my future housemate, Birgyte. Of course, once again I had to find a place to live, so it was serendipitous when I spied a "Roommate Wanted" notice tacked to a telephone pole, jostling for attention against a collage of competing messages. Four blocks off the Penn campus in West Philly, the place turned out to be in a dilapidated four-story brick apartment building behind a scruffy lawn.

After climbing a steep staircase to the fourth floor, I knocked on a once-elegant black door.

"Come in," said a voice from within.

Opening the door, I found myself in a dark hallway with a scuffed wood floor. Beyond the hall, the living room was bathed in afternoon sunlight. There, an extraordinary young woman lounged upon a heavy, crippled sofa, her bottle-blonde head propped up on one elbow. Clad only in a pink bikini, her languid pose was pure *Madame Récamier*, as I recalled from Madame Dane's art history class in Paris.

"I'm Birgyte," the intriguing young woman now said, breaking my reverie with her radiant smile, blue eyes dancing above pink lips. Even her eyebrows and lashes were blonde, and although her pose had solid precedent in French painting, the effect was entirely American. More specifically, it recalled Marilyn Monroe. As I registered all of this, a beautiful black cat with white boots circled the sofa and jumped up, settling at Birgyte's feet. Boz Scaggs's new hit song, "Lowdown," played softly in the background.

"This is Katyte," Birgyte said. "That's Lithuanian for 'little cat.'" Then, abruptly changing the subject, she said, "So, about the rent. It's $74 a month, utilities included, and there's a shared phone. Your room is down the hall to the left." At that, she waved me off to look about the place.

Down the hall, the lofty, north-facing room was all white except for a glossy sky-blue window frame, and I imagined how warm it would feel with my new yellow-and-green-striped Madras bedspread. But what would it be like to share a home with Birgyte? I was already magnetized by her, but what exactly did that mean? It didn't feel like an overt sexual attraction—not the kind that makes you want to jump into bed right away. Instead, my reaction was more subtle. I had the subliminal feeling that she might help loosen me up, free me from my by-the-book, good-student ways.

When I returned to the rundown living room, she beamed. "So would you like to be my roomie?"

"Yes, please, I'd love that!" I said, and in consenting so quickly, it suddenly occurred to me how unlikely it was that anybody had ever said no to her.

"Oh, and by the way, are you a Penn student?" I asked.

"No, I'm in the PEP Department at Temple University." Whatever that meant, it seemed fitting because, despite her languid manner, I could tell that she was quite a peppy young lady. Before I could ask, she volunteered, "Psycho-Educational Processes. PEP."

"What are psycho-educational processes?" I asked.

"It's all about organizational development. We're taught to infiltrate large companies and upend their sclerotic organizations, making them better at team building. Kind of like Outward

Bound for corporations." That clicked with me. So many of my high school classmates had enrolled in Outward Bound, the summer program where you ventured deep into a forest with a bunch of new buddies, pitched a tent, gazed at the stars, and then, the next morning, learned to trust your pals by falling backward into their arms while blindfolded.

Apparently, Birgyte was very much into that sort of thing. "The *best* exercise," she was explaining, "is the one where everybody ties a bunch of sheets together to make a rope. Then you grab the rope and follow one another deep into a cave without a flashlight. As long as you don't lose your grip on the sheets, you'll be fine."

When the movie *My Dinner with Andre* premiered, the descriptions that André Gregory shares with Wallace Shawn about his intense experiences, including briefly being buried alive on Halloween night, were right out of the PEP department playbook. When Shawn's character says that living as intensely as André is not possible for most people, he could have been talking about me. Birgyte was André, and I was Wallace Shawn, preferring less risky pleasures like drinking a glass of wine.

But what is not possible for most people was an everyday part of Birgyte's life. As she explained it, she worshipped a goddess called Passion.

"Brooks," she said one day. "Who could possibly be more romantic than Elizabeth Taylor and Richard Burton? Everyone knows they're tempestuous, but so what if they argue and fight all night long? They never get bored with each other! Anger is passion, and passion is the highest form of love!"

"So Burton and Taylor . . . you think what they have is true love?" I asked. I was skeptical. Their relationship sounded exhausting to me.

"Well, let me put it to you this way. True love is when a man and a woman are gazing intently into one another's eyes while hanging side by side from a cliff, clawing a few tufts of grass to save them from crashing onto the jagged rocks below." At this she sighed, confessing that she had not yet met her Richard Burton.

Privately, I reflected that this was because she reminded everybody of Marilyn Monroe and absolutely nobody of Liz. But I wondered what my own feelings were about passion. How important was it in a relationship? Contemplating this every now and then, I eventually concluded that passion is indispensable for propelling an intense love relationship, but that Burton and Taylor's brand of passion is destructive. Couldn't there be another form of love, a love grounded in a sunnier, lighter, happier version of passion? I sincerely hoped so.

Birgyte and I became running buddies, over time growing close enough to call each other 'Ducky.' My classmates all assumed that I was in love with her, but more accurately, I was in thrall to her. It was hard not to be. After all, this was a woman who attracted men like fireflies to a flame. We could not go anywhere, not even down two flights of steps to pay a call on our building's dope dealer, without a swarm of eager young men surrounding her.

Somehow, I had managed to get all the way through high school, college, and my year in London without once taking a toke on a joint. The acrid smell of the stuff put me off, and I prided myself in not giving in to peer pressure, but my opinion was about to change. One evening, we sat down in Birgyte's room—I on a beanbag, she on her ornately carved red throne. She lit a joint and passed it to me while placing an LP on her record player.

Why not? I thought. At that moment, toking didn't seem to be about trying to be cool. Birgyte's example showed me that it was actually about feeling good and having fun. It was even about getting creative.

"I don't think I'm high yet," I said, after one or two tokes.

Birgyte just smiled, laughed, and we both took another hit. At that moment, I heard the opening strains of "The Fever," a rollicking bluesy number by Southside Johnny and the Asbury Jukes. Southside Johnny was a New Jersey band that regularly opened for Bruce Springsteen, and they were wildly popular in Philly. In an instant, I became their newest fan. The minute I heard Johnny sing the first line over a soulful background texture of saxophone riffs, Birgyte didn't have to tell me that I was high.

She and I developed a pattern. Every evening, I worked diligently on my drawings in the landscape architecture studio until after 9:00 p.m., then walked home from campus, longing for fun and emotional release. Rounding the corner of 44th and Locust, where the pathetic Acme supermarket stood, I zeroed in on Birgyte's window from a block away. If it was lit up, there was a good chance we might laugh and get high, but if it was not, I would have to content myself with solitude. When her light was on, my heart leapt with anticipation.

Granted, this sounds like a major crush, but even though she oozed sex appeal, I was curiously immune to her on a physical basis. Although I could not have put it in words, she appealed to me by offering access to my rebellious and fun-loving side—that other, repressed side of my personality that I normally kept strictly in check. Forever having hunches, which she valued above logical reasoning, Birgyte taught me to worship at the altar of intuition. Until I met her, nobody had ever encouraged my id at the expense of my superego. It was a new, refreshing experience to explore this looser, more open side of my personality, without censure, under her guidance.

During those wonderful high times together, when the clock stopped, Birgyte confessed her latest loves, confiding in me enough to grab my attention while holding back her innermost secrets. Those she reserved exclusively for her romantic partners. Eschewing the droves of college men inside and outside our building who followed her around nonstop, she even discounted her handsome and faithful boyfriend. This despite the fact that Jerry was a dapper Le Creuset salesman who drove a burgundy Oldsmobile Cutlass Supreme coupe, one of the hippest cars of the mid-seventies.

"I've met someone," she said conspiratorially, one night after we were good and high. For extra effect, she brandished her long, black cigarette holder, waving it around like a magic wand. Birgyte was the only person I had ever met who sported a cigarette holder.

"You have?" I asked. "What about Jerry?"

"Oh, Jerry's nice," she said. "But he's not Richard Burton." At this she gestured dramatically with her cigarette holder and took a puff.

"Okay, so who *is* this Richard Burton?"

"Don't tell anyone, but it's my professor in the psychology department—Raoul. He's getting a divorce."

"He's married? Are you sure that's a good idea?" I asked, concentrating as usual on the practical, earthbound aspect of the situation.

"Raoul sweeps me off my feet," she said simply.

I knew that settled the matter because Birgyte had always explicitly stated that the quality she most sought in a man, apart from nail-biting passion, was the mystical, romantic, and no doubt drug-fueled ability to make her feel as if she were the only woman in the world.

Meanwhile, I was terrified of revealing how vulnerable I was. My chief form of armor in those days was to deflect attention from myself, turning it back on whoever was talking to me. If I could keep the attention on Birgyte, I could hold on to my deepest secrets, such as the loneliness and secret shame I felt when I overheard her making love with Jerry. This was extraordinarily easy because she so enjoyed talking about her own desires and romantic visions.

Still, she was a sympathetic listener, so one night I surprised myself by throwing off all my armor. "You know, Birgyte. I . . . I think I might be gay," I said.

"I always assumed you were, Ducky," she replied, with a conspiratorial wink. Her completely nonjudgmental reply meant that, happily, at long last I had an ally. It didn't mean, however, that I was ready to share my secret with anybody else. Just as when I had told Mom, my confession amounted to no more than an unusual instance of my id crawling out like a crab from underneath the rock of my superego, and while that felt safe to do in Birgyte's company, I wasn't ready to own it yet. I was still determined, as if through sheer will, to find the drive to pursue women with as much zest as all the boys pursued Birgyte. The last thing I wanted was to be a freak on the sidelines.

12 LORENZO THE MAGNIFICENT AND BORING BOB

AFTER TWO introductory semesters taught by McHarg, we turned from regional planning to designing actual landscapes on smaller sites. Bob Hanna, the unassuming professor I had met in Rome, became my lead teacher, along with his more colorful colleague, Laurie Olin. A tall, slim, and affable man with horn-rimmed glasses, the unusually named Laurie was as articulate as Bob was taciturn. Since both were former students of Dad's at the University of Washington, I had a special connection with each of them, and I quickly came to think of them as mentors. Unlike Dad, they were prepared to mentor me on the path I had chosen for myself and in the subject that most interested me—landscape architecture.

Bob and Laurie traded off assigning us an exciting and diverse array of design projects, each at a different scale. We converted abandoned quarries to parks, plotted hundreds of housing units on steeply sloping suburban sites, and designed a linear park along an abandoned industrial canal in a small Pennsylvania town. But the project that most intrigued me was my design for a pocket park in the dense core of Center City, Philadelphia. It was the smallest site we had investigated, which meant I could zero in and study it in detail. I placed a large waterfall against a wall in the small plaza, which became the focal point of my new gathering space.

Despite their close affiliation, Bob's and Laurie's teaching styles could not have been more different. Where Bob's desk "crits" were meticulous, Laurie spoke grandiloquently and gestured theatrically while sketching brilliant doodles illustrating grand design concepts. These he invariably referred to as "my notions." Laurie's sketches were the most beautiful landscape design drawings I had ever seen, and they inspired me to try to become as skilled at landscape drawing as he was.

One day in the landscape design studio, when we were supposed to provide emergency vehicle access to a row of multiuse buildings, one of my classmates called out to Laurie.

"How wide should I make the fire lane?" he asked.

At this, Laurie grabbed the student's roll of yellow tracing paper, which, along with our pencils and erasers, was the most important tool we had, and pulled out a generous length. Given that we were poor students living on peanut butter and jelly, all of us were keenly aware of the high cost of yellow trace, but that didn't stop Laurie from teaching us never to hoard the stuff. The more we doodled, the looser and more imaginative we got, or so was the theory. In this case, once he had pulled out a five-day supply, Laurie began sketching with his Eagle Prismacolor #947 pencil. The warm, burnt-umber tone of the 947 looked especially vibrant against the flimsy yellow paper.

Drawing rapidly, Laurie began a long discourse for every student within earshot.

"You can see how long and tall a fire truck is," he explained, and as we looked on, a gigantic hook and ladder truck emerged, cab, wheels, hoses, and everything in between. When he got to the ladders on top, he extended them upward at a slight angle, revealing how the upper section overlapped and slid above the lower section.

"There you have it, chief," he said at last. "An American LaFrance fire engine."

For some inexplicable reason, Laurie had the habit of calling all of us "chief," even though we all thought of ourselves as lowly grunts. The drawing was perfect in every detail, and I marveled that he could even identify the truck's brand name. Then, as he sauntered jauntily away to consult with the next student, I noticed that he had left a three-foot-wide swath of blank tracing paper between the fire truck and the rolled end, which the student wasted no time recapturing for later use.

"Okay, but how wide should I make the fire lane?" my classmate shouted toward Laurie's back.

Reflecting on this incident, I saw how it revealed the depth of Laurie's knowledge as well as his artistic genius, but it seemed odd that he had never actually answered the student's straightforward question. Was his performance an elaborate kind of stalling, a cover-up for his inability to inform us about an important dimension, enshrined in the fire-fighting codes, because he didn't actually know it? It was hard to say. However, I couldn't help but admire Laurie for his talent and his serene, seemingly bottomless command of landscape history and theory. Wanting to emulate him like nobody I had ever met, I returned to my design assignments with gusto and a reinvigorated sense of purpose: to produce a design or at least a drawing worthy of Laurie's praise.

It worked. One day, he looked over my shoulder as he passed from student to student, reviewing our drawings.

"Good work, chief," he said. "Keep it up."

I soon formed a strong friendship with a talented classmate named Beverly Briggs. Hailing from Winston-Salem, North Carolina, for which the two leading brands of cigarettes were named, poor Beverly had no choice but to become a nonstop smoker. Curvaceous, with a perpetually upward-turned gaze, she wore a white T-shirt emblazoned with a little palm tree and the words *Beverly Hills* printed over her chest.

"I checked with Bob Hanna," she said. "He said we should make the fire lane twenty feet wide. I think we're supposed to make it go all the way across the site so the truck can reach every damn building. I wonder how steeply it can slope?"

"I don't think it can be much more steep than a train track," I said, staring down at the closely spaced contour lines on her plan.

"Hmm, I don't think this is gonna work," Beverly said, raising her cigarette, inhaling and exhaling dramatically at the natural pauses in her narrative. Several years older than I, she was returning to school after a divorce, and she approached her design problems doggedly, relying on her cigarettes to keep the stress at bay. Being myopic, she wore contact lenses pretty much all the time, and her eyes would get red and puffy during our late-night studio charrettes.

Unlike Beverly, I dealt with the tension of our constant deadlines by promenading around the studio, taking numerous trips to the bathroom or the coffeepot. Having sketched all my life, I drew rapidly and often finished my assignments ahead of Beverly. Convinced that I was trying to act superior, she accused me of being "facile," implying that if I finished a design quickly, it must be mediocre. I didn't know if I was facile or not, but her verdict gave me something new to worry about.

Two male classmates also made a big impression on me. Both were British exchange students—Richard Weston was an Englishman who later went on to an improbably successful career in British fashion, and Alistair McIntosh, a Scotsman. Perfectly aligned when it came to the witty sarcasm they deployed to lampoon our professors, they referred to Bob and Laurie as 'The Masters.' Due to Laurie's love of all things Italian and his mastery of drawing, Richard dubbed him 'Lorenzo the Magnificent' after the wealthy Medici prince and patron of all the great Florentine Renaissance painters. Meanwhile, poor Bob Hanna was nick-named 'Boring Bob.' Rumpled and hunched over like the TV detective Columbo, it was a wonder that Bob didn't smoke Mores, since brown was his favorite color. When giving desk crits, he would gaze down at our sketches of a town plaza and inquire, "Did you include a place where one can get a drink and a sandwich?" By a drink, we soon learned that he meant a beer, if the sandwich was served at lunch, or a dry martini if served at dinner.

No matter the design problem, part of the requirement was to draw an eye-level perspective view, and we were supposed to insert human figures, both to convey a proper sense of scale and to enliven the sketch. After my classmates and I had pinned up our drawings a few times for faculty juries, I had a fascinating insight: each of us subconsciously sketched our own body image. One female student's figures were as tall and svelte as she was, whereas Beverly's were rounded and shapely. Possibly hoping to have a baby, her drawings inevitably included a small child leading her mother around by one hand while carrying a bouquet of three brightly colored balloons in the other.

Noting this, logic dictated that my figures must also resemble my own body. If so, what did they look like? I saw that they were all men, usually seen from the back or the side, mostly because it was harder for me to draw a person from the front. While they were tall and muscular, no doubt their awkward shoulders and stiff knees represented my insecurities about my body. Unsure whether or not I was a hunk, staring at my figures made me worried that I was not sexy.

But something more than just my body image troubled me: I felt increasingly embarrassed and humiliated that I was still a virgin. The late seventies were the high-water mark of the sexual revolution, and in spite of Jake Borgum's warnings, quite a few of my classmates were partnered up. I was missing out on all the fun, but I hadn't the slightest idea where to find it. The girls in the program were either unavailable or unappealing, and while several of the boys were handsome, none of them showed more than a cursory interest in me. There didn't seem to be a gay boy among them, not that I was even on the lookout for one. I had convinced myself that if I just waited a bit longer, surely my hetero drive would kick in, despite all the evidence to the contrary.

Since we lived near one another, Beverly and I often arranged to walk into class together. She was rapidly becoming my closest friend in the program, and she was always full of the latest gossip, so we took the opportunity to dissect all our professors and classmates, as well as our latest projects.

One morning on our way into the studio, Beverly opened up to me about something completely unexpected. After a rambling preamble, she finally came out with it.

"Brooks, I'm dating Bob," she said. "We're getting really close."

"Bob," I said. "You don't mean—"

"Yes, Bob Hanna," Beverly said.

I thought for a minute, and then everything fell into place. Of *course* she was dating Bob, who was divorced from his wife, a well-known photographer. She was dating Bob because dating our professors was a "thing"—both Laurie Olin and Ian McHarg were also dating students. It then occurred to me that Beverly and Bob were undeniably well suited to each other. Each was extremely meticulous and methodical, both oozed integrity, and both were chain-smokers.

Good for them, I mused, although it seemed unfair that my dear friend was now no longer quite my equal, being newly elevated to some sort of vague social status halfway between student-hood and professor-dom. Soon afterward, her witty Beverly Hills T-shirt went back in the drawer, never to be seen again. Gradually growing her hair out, she took to wearing oat-colored Harris Tweed jackets with cotton turtlenecks in matching earth tones, paired with khaki slacks. She was dressing the professional role that our program was preparing us for, and she and Bob started looking more and more alike, in the semi-androgynous, his-and-hers sort of way that so epitomized the late 1970s.

When my second year wound down, it came time to look for a summer job. Several of the graduating students had found permanent positions at The Radio Station, which was what everybody called McHarg's firm, Wallace, McHarg, Roberts and Todd, because its call letters were WMRT. Still, the only place I wanted to work was a small, gutsy landscape studio called Hanna/Olin. The lively colored-pencil drawings that Bob and Laurie created on yellow trace were its most recognizable hallmark—their beauty was "incandescent," as McHarg would have said. Admiring those drawings as much or more than anyone else did, I approached Bob one day and asked him for a summer job.

"Come down to the office," Bob said, "and we'll talk."

The office was a bohemian affair on the second floor of a small, white, two-story building at the corner of 19th and Market. Next to the front door, an elderly African American man shined shoes all day long at his outdoor stand, smiling and shooting the breeze with passersby. The ground floor was occupied by a dive bar. No matter how bright a day it was, the bar stools inside lurked in a permanent gloom. For some inexplicable reason, the establishment specialized in pickled onions, and as they pickled away, the sour, stale stench wafted up the walls into Hanna/Olin's office, where it blended with the acrid smell of Bob's interminable cigarettes.

Opening the street door, I climbed a flight of stairs to find Bob sitting at a corkboard table, hard at work on a drawing. Behind him, dozens of yellow-trace drawings hung pinned floor to ceiling on a long, white wall, lending an artsy, dynamic, and urgent air to the proceedings. As usual, Bob exuded integrity, despite our relentless lampooning of him as Boring Bob. As I approached, he looked up from under a protruding sheet of translucent visqueen, explaining that the painters had not yet finished their work.

"Hi, Bob, I'd really like the opportunity to work at Hanna/Olin this summer. I can't think of any firm I'd rather work for," I said.

"Hmmm, oh really?" he said at last, tapping his unlit cigarette on the desk. That was his constant refrain, the phrase he invariably used to respond to any new piece of information. "Well, I'd like that, but we don't have enough drafting stations. I wish we had more, but the ones we have are all taken . . ." His voice trailed off while he gazed across the long, narrow room, as if scanning for an empty desk.

Before Bob lit his next cigarette, I had a sinking feeling. Would I have to knock on the door of Collins and DuTot, a highly competent but uninspiring firm? But he was speaking again.

"Actually, Brooks, what we could really use just now is a secretary. Do you type?"

"Yes," I immediately answered, deciding on the spot that I'd rather be a secretary at Hanna/Olin than a junior draftsman at Collins and DuTot.

Thus it was that I spent my summer days typing, retyping, and again retyping constant revisions of the letters that Bob and Laurie drafted to their clients and overlords, prestigious New York architecture firms like I. M. Pei and Partners, which was then at the zenith of its international influence. Every day as I typed away, the office activity swirled happily around me, and I arguably learned more about the business of landscape architecture than I would have had I been producing yellow-trace drawings at a drafting table.

Still, when August loomed and it was time to start my third and final year of grad school, who was going to type Bob and Laurie's letters? After five or six duds answered the want ad I placed in the Philadelphia *Inquirer*, a young woman came in who had presence, personality, and fire power. Nora Hyamite was short and full-bodied, with curly black hair and mirthful, violet eyes. When I finally managed to convince Bob and Laurie to hire her, we quickly became friends.

Mom and Dad flew in from Seattle for my graduation, and I proudly escorted them around the studio, showing them my best work. Naturally, I had assumed that this occasion would be my moment in the sun, but when I excitedly began explaining my latest designs to Mom and Dad, Bob and Laurie quickly approached.

"How nice to see you, Keith," Laurie said. "How goes teaching at the University of Washington?"

"Well, the latest crop of students doesn't amount to a hill of beans. It really hasn't been the same since the late sixties, when all my students boycotted class to protest the Vietnam War. How were they ever going to become fine architects? I had to flunk a lot of them."

"Hmmm, . . . oh really?" Bob said.

"My notion is that you have to inspire them with the best design examples," Laurie said. "If they were all standing in the Piazza San Marco in Venice, sketch pads in hand, perhaps they could be motivated. If that doesn't work, I don't know what will," he added, chuckling.

"Tell me, what projects are you designing these days?" Bob asked.

"Oh, well I did a Bio-Science Building at Washington State University in Pullman, and now I'm working on the Puget Sound Blood Center," Dad said, clearly relishing the beginning of one his long lectures. At that moment, the new dean, Lee Copeland, sauntered up.

Oh Lord, I said to myself, *now I'm done for*. Lee was yet another of Dad's former students. I glazed over, disappointed that nobody seemed anxious to praise me and my accomplishment graduating from what had been a rigorous and challenging program. Why couldn't Bob say, "Brooks did a great job! He got the faculty medal in design!"?

While I was proud of Dad and pleased to see what a strong influence he had been on my professors, this was my big moment, and I felt like he was snatching it away from me. When they continued to fawn over him, my disappointment turned to resentment. It seemed that no matter how hard I worked, no matter how much I tried my best to emulate Bob and Laurie, I still wasn't good enough to please Dad or for him to notice how far I had come. Was I always condemned to live in his shadow, or could I at least get Bob and Laurie to recognize my own promise?

As soon as I moved into my new grown-up apartment on Kater Street in Center City, I resolved to try even harder, starting with my first real job.

13 APPRENTICE TO THE MASTERS

WHEN I returned to Hanna/Olin in the fall to start my first official job as a landscape designer, Nora Hyamite welcomed me with a rush of excitement.

"I mean, Brooks, you're not going to believe this, but Bob just asked me to buy toilet paper for the office, and I mean, he asked me to buy *brown* toilet paper. I mean, can you believe it?"

"You've got to be kidding!" I didn't know whether I was laughing because Nora couldn't begin or end a sentence without saying, "I mean, you know what mean?" or because of the lengths to which Bob went to express his preference for the color brown. Either way, I rejoiced to be moving from the typing desk to a proper drafting table. Now in good company among the burgeoning staff of fifteen designers, I was delighted to find that I enjoyed being a full-fledged member of a working team even more than producing the beautiful landscape drawings we were assigned.

The nicknames we gave one another underscored the lighter side of life at the office. Dennis McGlade, a tall senior staffer with an aristocratic nose and prematurely white hair, dubbed Nora 'The High and The Mighty,' and insisted on calling me 'Young Kolb,' but most of the staff were known as 'Doctor' in mock recognition of the PhDs none of us had.

Whenever Dr. Barry Gazso had to leave a message on the phone, he declaimed in a loud, energetic voice, "My name is Gazso—G, A, Z as in zebra, S as in Sam, oh."

"Moderation in all things . . . including moderation," Barry said, getting off the phone. This was a direct quote from his favorite comedian, Rodney Dangerfield, and one of his everyday axioms.

"Come on, we've got to maintain an even strain," he added, repeating the mantra that best summed up his philosophy. What it meant for us grunts in drawing production was that no matter how stressful a deadline, we should always keep up a productive, but not frantic, pace of work.

My erstwhile classmate Alistair McIntosh liked to move from table to table, pretending to be a design professor delivering crits. On more than one occasion, he crept up behind me and noiselessly placed a hand on my shoulder, which made me jump. Then he stared at my drawing, his right hand hovering over it like a helicopter. Suddenly, his thumb dove to within a quarter inch above the drawing surface, where it came to an abrupt stop.

"Fault!" Alistair cried, pointing at the spot. I nearly jumped again.

Not to be outdone, Dennis strode nervously through the office, pausing now and then to gaze critically at one workstation or another.

"Hmmm, what tangled webs we weave, Young Kolb," he said, alighting at my desk. "You obviously need discipline."

Dennis loved to talk about tangled webs and how we all needed discipline, which never failed to make me laugh. The best thing about being part of this quirky but cohesive team was the crazy inside jokes we all shared, especially the absurdity of producing elaborate drawings for meetings at the New York offices of I. M. Pei and Partners, fancy affairs that we weren't invited to attend.

My first days at Hanna/Olin were a bit of a shock because, while Bob and Laurie had both been outstanding and encouraging teachers, they were much more exacting as bosses. Early one morning, Laurie instructed me to do a pencil drawing of a new design for the Pitney Bowes corporate headquarters.

"We need a bosque of trees right here, chief," he said. "Draw them on a grid at fifteen-foot spacing."

"Okay," I said, getting to work while Laurie left to catch a train. Finishing the sketch by early afternoon, I moved on to another of the myriad drawings we were assigned. Later that afternoon, as I was getting ready to leave for the day, Laurie returned from New York and approached my desk.

"Where's that sketch for Pitney Bowes, chief?" he asked. I pointed to the drawing, proud of the grid of trees I had drawn, each with its own trunk and shadow line rendered in dark pencil.

"Oh, but this is all wrong!" he exclaimed.

"I thought you wanted the trees on a fifteen-foot grid."

"No, no, no—that's not what I asked for! What's needed, chief, is a subtle pattern, with variations on the grid—some of the trees might be twelve feet apart, others seventeen. How could you not understand that?"

Now he was really piqued.

"You see? That's a much better effect!"

He was already overlaying my drawing with a new layer of yellow trace, sketching trees that were far lovelier and more distinctive than mine. I watched with shame as he covered my efforts with a perfect drawing in a manner of minutes when it had taken me hours to produce my overworked impasto of colored pencil marks. At that, he snatched my roll of trace and took it to his desk, where he finished the drawing on his own. I felt like a complete failure, wondering if I could ever reach the professional zenith that I aspired to, the level that Dad, Bob, and Laurie had already achieved so many years ago.

The labor-intensive aspect of our work reached its apogee one afternoon when Laurie announced that he needed help producing an after-dark site lighting plan for the Pitney Bowes project. Bordering Long Island Sound in Stamford, Connecticut, the site included a peninsula park with a shoreline loop road. Measuring about four feet by five feet, the giant drawing first had to be rendered in dark blues and grays with Prismacolor pencils. Working alongside Laurie and three or four colleagues, I colored the background gradually darker and darker. Just as Laurie had promised, the yellow pools of light dazzled in contrast, but when I left that night at 2:00 a.m., I wondered if the Pitney Bowes executives really needed to see those yellow pools of light against a blue-gray background to be sold on the lighting concept. I would never know, as I wasn't invited to client meetings.

One evening, as we dashed down the steps to grab a quick bite before returning for the night shift, Laurie must have seen the troubled look on my face.

"Don't be crestfallen, chief. Be of good cheer."

I couldn't remember ever hearing the word "crestfallen" spoken on American soil—it seemed to belong exclusively to English children's books like *Mary Poppins*. More to the point, whenever Laurie said "Be of good cheer," it was ominous because it meant that we would most likely be working all night, which I loathed. I loved my work and prided myself in my dedication to it, but at some point, toward the end of every day, I needed to rest and recharge.

Somewhere along my lengthy and intensive educational path, I had gambled with my emotional health—putting my personal life on indefinite hold while I jumped on the fast-track to academic and professional achievement. Like a hamster, I had been running on a treadmill for years, and every day I felt obliged to run faster. Now I couldn't help but see the endgame. We were not going to finish this one tight deadline, then sit back on our laurels and chill for a few weeks. No, we were going to continue working at the same breakneck pace for at least the next half century.

On one of the occasions when I accompanied Laurie to New York to assist in the drafting pool at I.M. Pei's office while Laurie attended meetings, I nearly reached a breaking point. Inevitably, our trip began with a sprint down Market Street to the 30th Street Station.

"Hurry, chief," cried Laurie, who was already several paces ahead.

"I'm coming!" I shouted, rushing to catch up.

Pulling the glass doors open and running down the stairs to the platform, we barely managed to hop aboard the north-bound train before it pulled out. As usual, I arrived at my seat stressed and panting, the sweat pouring off me until the air conditioning could work its welcome magic. Meanwhile, Laurie sat down cool as a cucumber, pulled out his *New York Times*, and began to read out loud to me. We didn't exactly work on the train, this being before laptop computers were invented, but the trips were still stressful, as I had to remain alert to respond intelligibly to Laurie's running commentary.

On arriving in New York, we took a cab to Pei's Midtown office for an intensive charrette that was due to last all day. I didn't like working in other offices, even ones as grand as I. M. Pei's, because I never had a clue where to find the drafting equipment, which equipment I was allowed to use, or even what was expected of me. The employees were usually too busy to assist me while Laurie abandoned me to go to lunch with his soulmate, founding partner Harry Cobb. Over lunch, Laurie and Harry enjoyed showing each other the paintings they did in their spare time, exchanging gifts of fine watercolor paper and Montblanc fountain pens. Laurie left his pen behind so often that it was not unusual for the odd Montblanc to show up in Hanna/Olin's morning mail in envelopes bearing the return addresses of some of Midtown Manhattan's finest restaurants.

Despite my reservations, there were distinct perks to be found at I. M. Pei. At midmorning coffee breaks and again at lunch, a fashionable young woman in a French maid's outfit, starched white apron over black skirt, complete with dark nylons and high heels, propelled herself through the giant studio, balancing a tray hanging from her shoulders on black velvet ribbons.

"Cookies?" she asked politely, pointing to the fresh, home-baked domes that were laid out in a perfect architectural grid on her tray.

"Yes, please!" I said, delighted by the unexpected treat.

After a couple of hours scribbling with his Montblanc pen and discussing his design "notions" with Harry Cobb in a nearby conference room, Laurie came back into the design studio.

"I've got to leave for another meeting downtown," he announced, addressing Pei's project architect, to whom I'd been assigned. "Don't worry, though. Brooks here is at your disposal—he can stay as long as you need him, including overnight."

The architect nodded while I cringed, no doubt looking more than crestfallen.

I should have been pleased that I had finally made the cut—I had become accomplished enough that Laurie was prepared to lend me out to someone as august as Harry Cobb. Instead, I resented being a pawn that Laurie could march hither and thither, ordering me around without prior warning, as if I were a private in his army. I had always idolized him, passionately hoping to become as brilliant and skilled as he was, but now I was beginning to think that it came at too high a price. I worried that it meant permanently sacrificing my personal freedom, strangling the loose, fun-loving side of my personality that had recently and unexpectedly shown up to claim its turf. Like an embryo, it was kicking me from inside, struggling to break out of the womb of discipline and structure that I had thus far so relentlessly pursued.

14 ROLLING ROCKS AND DANCE STEPS

DUBBED DR. Dalbeau, Kip Dalbert was the most important "doctor" in our midst because when the clock finally said 5:00 p.m. on Friday afternoons, it was his job to make a beer run for our weekly happy hour. After Laurie stood up and started joking around, calling everybody "chief," Dr. Dalbeau sprang into action, dashing out the door. As soon as he returned with burlap bags of peanuts and six-packs of Rolling Rock, we created a mellow ambiance by switching off the fluorescent lights and aiming our drafting lamps upward. Then we popped a cassette tape of Stan Getz's bossa nova album into a player that lived next to Laurie's desk. With "The Girl from Ipanema" playing and the lamps bathing the ceiling in warm light, the office began to feel welcoming and relaxing. Soon the floor became as thickly littered with discarded peanut shells as the layers of needles on the sandy ground in the New Jersey Pine Barrens, whose delicate ecology we were constantly studying.

Once in a while, Beverly joined us for happy hour. Drifting slowly through the room to speak sequentially with one person and then another, she invariably had an agenda—something distinct and different to convey to each individual. She liked to take her time, preferring the intimacy of one-on-one chats to the group huddles of a cocktail party. Having an agenda of my own, which was to tell Beverly some bit of gossip I had been dying to share with her all week, I once made the mistake of breaking in on one of her intimate tête-à-têtes. When I attempted to wedge myself into her conversation, she turned toward me, blinked rapidly five or six times, lifted her fluttering eyelids to some obscure and invisible point on the ceiling, and inhaled deeply on her cigarette. Then, she exhaled audibly, at last returning to her conversation partner, without a single word to me. I learned quickly and resigned myself to waiting my turn for a proper audience.

As the months flipped by like cards in a rolodex, I became more and more discouraged about not having a personal life apart from the weekly happy hours. Unless I had to work late, my evenings were empty, and much as I disliked working weekends, at least that offered companionship. To make matters worse, my virginity had become an increasingly heavy chain to drag around. How could I possibly be twenty-six years old and still a virgin?

Determined to change the situation, I decided to make one more valiant effort to meet women. Thus, it was auspicious that, when walking to work, I noticed a small sign high on the corner of a building on Walnut Street. In black linework on a white background, it depicted four or five steps rising from left to right. On the steps stood the silhouetted figures of a dancing couple, the woman's shoulders arching backward as the man leaned over her from the step above, his arm encircling her waist. Below the dancing couple, tall narrow letters spelled out "The Next Step Dance Studio." The sign promised the romance and joy of real ballroom dancing. What better way could there be to meet women?

When I showed up for my first evening class, I discovered that there were two instructors, a man and a woman. The woman was a strikingly tall, thin "creature," as Henry James might have called her, with high cheekbones and a mane of curly, flame-red hair. Layers of blue eye shadow accentuated her latte-colored skin, and she wore high heels with what appeared to be a gold lamé one-piece swimsuit. With her Creole looks and clipped Bermuda accent, Anastasia was as much like a drag queen as a real woman could possibly be, unless of course she was transgendered, which was such an esoteric category that I had never heard of it.

By contrast, the man was a short Puerto Rican in cargo pants and black patent leather dancing shoes. Slim and athletic, Carlos was extremely versatile on the dance floor, just as proficient at dancing the woman's part as the man's. When I gave myself to the lesson, trying to learn the complex, rousing Latin rhumbas and cha-chas that played on a small phonograph on the floor, I found myself relaxing in the embrace of his strong arms as he deftly maneuvered me around the room. He was leading me by following, and I had absolutely no idea how he made me execute the moves. Dancing with the tall Dominatrix was fearsome; with him it was pure joy.

After one lesson led to another, I found myself looking forward to the pressure of my hand on Carlos's waist, his hand clasped firmly in mine, as the ballroom spun around us.

Closing my eyes while dancing, I flashed back to a childhood memory of my swimming lessons at the Olympic Swimming School in Seattle's Lake City neighborhood. One sunny day, the instructor decided it was time to help me overcome my fear of deep water. I was splashing around in the pool with another ten or so excited little kids when, suddenly, he reached over and scooped me up, drawing me toward him. As he began paddling on his back into the sparkling water, holding me on his chest, I felt as if I were a baby otter out swimming with my papa. He was strong, well-muscled and deeply tanned, and the nest of brown hairs on his chest had a pleasant, soapy-sweaty smell, as if it were the scent of summer itself. He must have been no more than twenty-five, but to me he was youthful and mature at the same time, an ageless god in my embrace. Never had I felt so physically attached to anyone besides my mother, but my euphoria was fleeting because he quickly returned me to the shallows and reached for the next kid.

When I opened my eyes, the memory didn't stop me from fooling myself because I still felt it was incumbent upon me to ask Anastasia out. After all, I had joined the class with the intention of meeting women, and she was the only woman in the room, apart from a couple of highly forgettable wallflowers with acne and badly cut hair.

It took me two or three weeks to rally my courage, but one evening as class was letting out, I casually said, "May I take you out to dinner next week?"

Lowering her formidable lids, so that the entire cloud of blue eye shadow faced me above her perfect lashes, she brusquely replied, "No thank you," in her clipped accent, before pivoting on the toes of her high-heeled pumps. That was the end of the matter. Truthfully, I felt more relieved than humiliated, but there were more dance lessons to come, and I would have to face her again at the next one.

After a couple of classes, I couldn't resist sharing the news of my new extracurricular activity with my coworkers.

"Guess what?" I whispered to Barry Gazso, during one of our happy hours. "I'm taking a ballroom dance class."

"Do you hear that, guys?" Barry asked, raising his voice. "Young Kolb is taking dance lessons. Don't forget to maintain an even strain on the dance floor, Brooks!"

"That sounds like fun!" chorused a slew of my coworkers.

Much to my astonishment, one, two, then three, four, and even five of my colleagues said they'd like to join in. Within twenty minutes, I had signed up eight more students for the Next Step Dance Studio's evening class in Latin ballroom dancing. Dr. McGlade came to class, and so did one of the newer employees, Diana Shue. Even Bob and Beverly came to one or two sessions before Bob had to beg off, no doubt because the lure of sipping martinis at the office after dinner, while working on his drawings, was too strong to resist.

Rats, I thought, *there goes my plan to meet women,* for how could I possibly start chatting up a young lady while surrounded by six or eight of my crazy coworkers, each of them observing my every word and gesture?

One night, three or four weeks later, Carlos and Anastasia were attempting to teach us an especially tricky dance move. From across the room, I noticed that short and stocky Diana Shue had stretched her arms upward as far as she could reach, where they were wrapped in a tight knot around Dennis McGlade's neck. Bent forward over Diana, his tall, slim body appeared as contorted as Michelangelo's *Laocoön,* so I wasn't about to waste a golden opportunity to hit him with the very line he loved to drop on us.

Approaching, I burbled, "What tangled webs we weave, Dennis. What tangled webs we weave!"

While walking to and from work in those dance class days, I became intrigued by a nondescript door in an equally nondescript building that I kept passing on 12th Street. Above the mysterious door, a small sign bore a single word: *Equus*. In the morning the door was always locked, but in the evening, it opened regularly, as if on cue, to disgorge one or two men who ducked out quickly, scurrying down the street. I pictured myself walking up and turning the doorknob, but I didn't dare. If it was a club, wouldn't they just kick me out because I wasn't a member? The more curious I got, the more impossible it seemed to approach the door, so I clenched my hands in my coat pockets and hurried past.

15 EQUUS

ONE SUNNY Saturday afternoon that spring I was gazing out my third-floor apartment window at the balmy clouds floating by. Opening the window to sniff the sweetly acrid scent of cherry blossoms on the breeze, a flood of hitherto suppressed longings welled up from somewhere deep inside me, like a lake in a cave. Although they were familiar to me, I had never acknowledged them before. But now it was as if a mysterious neural switch that had forever been jammed in the "off" position suddenly and unexpectedly turned on, making me ready and eager to go to bed with a man for the first time. Standing at the window, I finally admitted to myself that all the long years of denial and self-suppression had never worked. Ergo, I might as well try acceptance. My anticipation just had to turn into action. But how would it happen and who would it be with?

Just at that moment, three figures came marching toward me down the middle of narrow Kater Street. Riveted, I noticed that they were holding hands and practically *skipping*. All three young men were undeniably handsome, and out of nowhere, I couldn't help fantasizing that they were the tin man, the cowardly lion, and the scarecrow from *The Wizard of Oz*. But then where was Dorothy? Excuse me, maybe *I* was Dorothy?!

The man on the left had black hair and five o'clock shadow; the one on the right was fair and clean-shaven, with blazing blue eyes and red hair combed straight back from his high, shiny forehead. Holding down the center was a tall, beautiful man with butterscotch skin, gray eyes, and an oh-so-sexy, frizzy, brown goatee. Could it be, I wondered? Yes, it could. The man in the center was none other than my next-door neighbor. He must have moved in recently because I had encountered him only once or twice passing in the hall, leaving me without enough time to register how handsome he was.

I heard a key turn in the street door, and all three men came bounding up the rickety stairs and into the apartment across the hall, joyous laughter following their loud footsteps. How I wanted to join them, I mused, but what would be my pretext? I couldn't just knock on the door. What would I say? *Hi, I'm your neighbor?*

No, it was just too awkward. I decided it was best to bide my time now that something so vastly significant had been revealed: my neighbor was unmistakably and deliciously gay.

But there was something else about the way he looked, something I couldn't quite put my finger on. Then it hit me. His full lips had opened into a delightful, unguarded smile. It had to be the smile of someone who was nonjudgmental, someone in whom it would be safe to confide my desires. And yet there was even more to it. The way he related so easily and happily with his two friends reminded me of Alonzo all those years ago in Low-Rise North, giving me my first glimpse of how accepting gay friendships could be. Something melted inside me at that moment.

For years I had been keeping my guard up, trying to pass myself off as straight, and here was a man who, simply by his breezy example, demonstrated that I could cast that heavy burden aside and be myself. *Fuck it,* I thought. *All that pretending is such a waste of time!* Suddenly, I was ready. I couldn't wait to dissolve all my barriers and leap into a new current—a gay river. It was the queer equivalent of the conversion of St. Paul—there was a God and He had a Plan. I just had to find an excuse to talk to the man.

An evening or two later, I found myself facing my neighbor's door on the narrow, shag-carpeted landing. My hand was shaking as I made a fist, working up the nerve to knock. When I heard my discreet tap, I held my breath, waiting to see if he would answer. I knew he was home because I could hear Donna Summer singing on the record player inside. Before I could exhale, the door opened, and the muscular form of my gorgeous neighbor appeared, lips widening into that sexy smile again. The next thing I knew, he introduced himself as Ken and invited me in. Could it be that romance was waiting just across the narrow little hall? Afraid of losing my opportunity, I sat down in an armchair and quickly got to the point, without subtlety or preamble.

"Ken, um, I have to tell you something," I said. After a quick pause, I blurted out the rest. "Um, I want to go to bed with a man. I've never done it before. But . . . I want to go to bed with you. I very much want to go to bed with you." I abruptly stopped and fixed him with my best puppy-dog eyes. I thought of following up with "Would you be my guinea pig?" but deemed that unwise.

Meeting my gaze, Ken smiled again—the second of two green lights in a row. "That can be arranged," he said at last, after a flirty pause, and then he smiled again, looking deep into my infatuated eyes.

Did we go to bed at that moment? No. Instead, he coyly suggested that we take it slow and made an appointment to see me later. When I returned to my apartment, I kicked the door closed, took in a big gulp of air, and exclaimed "Yes!" to the universe at the top of my voice. In my mind, I was already at the altar, in a gauzy veil, with my finger out ready to receive Ken's ring.

Fortunately, he didn't keep me waiting long. A few nights later, there was a knock at *my* door. I opened it, and in he came, looking sexy as all get-out. I gestured toward my couch, where after sitting down, he promptly wrapped an arm around my shoulder, smiled again, and gazed into my eyes. His were an exotic gray green. He began murmuring in a soothing voice, gently stroking my cheek, then the back of my neck. He clearly had a knack for soulful love chat, as if he were a tenor-voiced Barry White, and I was eating it up.

The delicious caressing and fondling continued for a few minutes or perhaps an eternity, with soft whisperings between us. Then, before I knew it, I found myself lying on top of Ken on the lawn of my green shag carpet. We began to kiss, my first male kiss, and I could feel my hard-on swell against his, inside our tight jeans. As our tongues explored the inside of each other's lips, I knew beyond a shadow of a doubt that I was a homo. I was not a convert; I was merely a person who had awakened from a long sleep.

In the days that followed, Ken initiated me into the shadowy mysteries of gay sex, exactly as I had hoped. As far as I was concerned, he and I were going to get married and live happily ever after. After all my years of self-denial, it seemed so simple, so joyful. Unfortunately, though, he had other plans. Being no fool, he proceeded to explain, in a friendly tone, that it might, no in fact it most certainly *would*, cramp his style to have a boyfriend living directly across the hall. Never in the history of the world would sexual ambrosia turn so rapidly into nasty jealous drama.

For these well-considered reasons, Ken let me down gently, explaining that although he had been quite happy to initiate me, we weren't a "thing." As a consolation prize, though, he promised to introduce me to his friends and be my guide in navigating Philly's gay scene.

Of course, I was crushed, but some tiny part of me recognized the wisdom of his pronouncement. Then a new thought occurred to me: perhaps I had been just as conditioned to expect that life would bring me a hetero vision of monogamous marriage as to assume that my partner would be a woman. Having crawled for so many years across the desert of my repressed sexuality, I was not about to perpetuate my suffering by succumbing to my newfound pain. This was no time to mire in self-pity. No, now was the time to relish the new horns I felt sprouting from my forehead, rejoice in playing the field, and claim my true identity. I had already come out to Ken; now I was finally ready to come out to the world.

Soon, I confided to Beverly about what had happened with Ken. When she heard the news, she inhaled quickly on her cigarette and then let out a long breath.

"Brooks," she said, "I love you, but I have to tell you something. You know how everybody has synaptic gaps between their neurons that the messages leap across? Well, your synaptic gaps are wider than most people's. It takes a long time for those messages to get across—too long. I already figured you were gay, of course. But Ken? You have this weird tendency to want a quick fix. How on earth did you think you could simply come out and find the love of your life all in one day?"

I felt sheepish about it, but I had to admit she was right.

Resigned to just being friends, I began to visit Ken often. One Saturday morning, as the strains of "Funkytown" pulsed through the crack below my door like a spring breeze across the turf of my green shag, I knocked on his door. He smiled and let me in, whereupon to my surprise I discovered that he was entertaining a female guest: a chic and beautifully coiffed young African American woman, whose skin tone was only slightly darker than Ken's. She smiled at me from his couch when he introduced her as his girlfriend, explaining sotto voce, without embarrassment or irony, that he was bisexual. Even though I knew we were not dating, I was devastated. It hurt so much to learn that he had a girlfriend when he could have had me.

Still, I was intrigued by the word "bisexual." I hadn't even considered the existence of this sexual territory, assuming that the world divided itself neatly between straights (the vast majority) and homosexuals (a tiny minority). That there could be a category bridging both groups fascinated and disturbed me—it seemed too wishy-washy. After denying my sexuality and hiding it for nearly two decades, I felt an urgent need to label myself as gay. Ken's bisexuality seemed like an exotic but annoying diversion, since it meant he didn't have all his time available for men, by which I meant me.

As he had promised, Ken showed me around, instructing me about where to go to see and be seen. One of these conversations eventually prompted him to escort me to Equus on a Friday night. First, he had to get dressed, and that meant trying on and rejecting about thirty tight T-shirts and seven pairs of ripped jeans before settling on just the right combination.

"I need to look fierce," he explained.

Although this was the first time I had heard that term, still popular with the RuPaul crowd for showcasing the aggressive side of the feminine side of the man, I instantly knew what Ken meant. For a man to look hot, it was important to create the illusion that you were a gorgeous, fire-breathing wild animal with a head full of sharp teeth.

When Ken finally looked fierce enough, we set off on foot for the club, the heels of our Frye boots clicking rhythmically against the hard pavement. Before I knew it, we arrived at 12th Street, and that mysterious door opened to me at long last. Once inside, I beheld a darkened room, filled to the rafters with men. Under a spotlight, beautiful young men crowded three or four rows deep around a central island bar.

The sight of so many men crammed into the small space, laughing and joking while raising their cocktails to their lips, hit me like a revelation. I suppose I had imagined there would be only a handful of guys, reflecting what I had always assumed was the tiny percentage of gay men in the general population. How could I not have known there were actually so many of us? So many *handsome* men, some of them still wearing suits, indicating that they had come directly from their jobs as lawyers or businessmen. The fragrance of their cologne mingled with their salty sweat into a heady aroma of lust. When Ken handed me a bourbon and seven, the sweetness of the 7-Up balanced the whiskey's kick, perfectly blending with the aphrodisiac scent in the air.

I was content to spend the entire evening standing at the bar, drinking in the heady atmosphere, and trying to catch a glance from one of the many attractive men, but Ken wasn't having it. Before we could order a second round, he grabbed my sleeve, leading me to the back of the room and around the corner to a broad staircase. I followed him up to the mezzanine, where men draped themselves over the railing, but he rounded another corner and on we went up to the third floor. When we reached the top of the stairs, a wall of sound enveloped us. Adjusting my eyes to the gloom, I glimpsed moving spotlights aimed at a mirrored wall behind a dazzling white dance floor, lit from below. A reflecting ball revolved on the ceiling above a multitude of young men jerking and swaying to ecstatic disco rhythms. Men clustered at a long bar buying drinks while others hung on a railing, gazing down at the sunken dance floor, which resembled an ice rink. Oh, the Observers and the Observed—to see and be seen! Then, huge puffs of dry ice fog suddenly pulsed across the floor, concealing everybody's feet and accentuating the dancers' frenzied movements.

Ken led me down two steps to the dance floor, and as we began to dance, everything clicked into place: the attractive men, the disco music, and the brightly lit floor, which was an exact copy of John Travolta's club in *Saturday Night Fever*. All at once, I felt free to be myself for the first time in my life. It was such a relief to no longer pretend I was not attracted to men. The constant burden of being on guard against the crushing conformity I felt around straight people fell off my shoulders and disappeared forever into that beautiful, dry-ice fog.

Concentrating on the music, I reveled to Abba's hit "Lay All Your Love on Me." Then, the next song cued up, and for the first time, I heard Diana Ross belt out her new single, "I'm Coming Out." What could possibly be more serendipitous than the timely convergence of Diana's huge hit with the transformation taking place inside me?

In the following nights, I went to Equus as often as I wished, which was to say very often indeed. Each time, I walked up to that strangely unmarked door, took a deep breath, and opened it all by myself, at first cautiously, then later with scarcely a look over my shoulder. Inside, I had more fun than I had ever had before; more, in fact, than I had ever imagined I could have. Although I still pined after Ken, part of me realized that I had been silly to pin all my hopes on him. I began to think of Hanna/Olin in a new way as well. Instead of being the entire focus of my life, it now began to assume its proper role as just one part of my identity, though admittedly a central one. But a whole new world had rushed in to fill the vacuum in my personal life, and it was both deliciously pleasurable and deliciously secret.

Ken was also kind enough to invite me to a few social events. One Sunday afternoon, after brunch, I was walking down the hallway of a large apartment building on my way to a party. Toward the end of the hall, a tall drag queen towered over the carpet, a latte-colored figure in a wavy, shoulder-length chestnut wig, full mascara, and heavy eye shadow.

"Hi," I said, "my name's Brooks."

"Hello, I'm Amber," she purred, extending her immaculately manicured hand to mine, enameled nails pointed demurely downward. After this cursory introduction, she attempted to open the door, but her shockingly long, tapered nails prevented her from turning the knob.

"Here, please allow me," I said, reaching for the door, and we entered the party together. Who was there, what music was played, and what jokes were told, I have long forgotten, but Amber was a big hit. The episode delighted me because while I was obsessed with looking butch enough to attract the manly men I wanted, meeting Amber taught me that gay self-expression didn't need to stop at coming out. It could expand and expand until it embraced whole new costumes and identities that thumbed their noses at the straight establishment. There was no need to show the world only one persona.

With her wig and mascara, Amber seemed to be telling me, "Honey-chile, you can be whoever you want to be!"

One afternoon after the party, in my heavenly, new state of coming out, I was walking home from the A&P on 3rd Street, which seemed to be the only supermarket in all of Center City. Clutching a bag of groceries to my chest as I sashayed down South Street, I heard somebody call my name. Turning, I recognized the smiling blond head of Gary, a new junior colleague at Hanna/Olin, who never failed to make me laugh. We fell in together and walked a few blocks toward our respective apartments.

"I just *knew* you were gay! I knew it the minute I saw those two phallic baguettes sticking out the top of your bag as you minced down the street!" Gary exclaimed.

"Um, okay," I said, tongue-tied. There was nothing else to add. I was busted, and the baguettes were to blame, but I was overjoyed to find out that I had a gay workmate. The next thing I knew, he and I were going to Equus every Friday and Saturday night, and often to Sunday tea dance as well. Gary lived an absurdly sophisticated life with his lover in an apartment on the twenty-first floor of Hopkinson House, which had an actual porte cochere and a doorman, just like in Manhattan. He enjoyed inviting friends over for steaks, which he broiled after stuffing them with garlic chips.

One evening, Gary invited a bunch of friends over for a big party. After the preliminaries, several of us sat outside on the balcony overlooking Washington Square, enjoying the balmy summer night. Gary was holding forth, amusing us with his banter.

"What an astounding group of young homosexuals!" he suddenly exclaimed, gesturing emphatically toward all of us with raised eyebrows, his face a model of faux sincerity.

I laughed at the unexpected quip, reveling in the thought that I had never been so definitively and gloriously *labeled*.

WHEN KEN had first initiated me, he popped a cork deep inside my body, and now a champagne of lust coursed through my veins. I thought of it as a toast to my newfound male fantasies with a glass of Veuve Clicquot. Now that I had finally stopped suppressing them, they were becoming increasingly graphic and vivid, tied to beautiful faces and hot bodies in magazines and attached to furtive glimpses of mustaches, beards, pecs, biceps, torsos, and of course "baskets" in the locker room at the YMCA.

Forced to turn my back on my big crush, I had no choice but to start cruising, but I informed myself that my cruising was not just for its own sake. On the contrary, it was a means to an end. Its explicit goal was to find another man as much like Ken as possible. No matter how long it took, I wasn't going to stop until I found Ken's clone. Then, when I finally found him, he would wrap me in his arms and I would never hit the bars again. As foolish as it sounds, that was my overriding fantasy and I was sticking to it.

The problem was that, as late as I was entering the game, I had only the vaguest idea how to play it. The one thing I knew how to do was to ask guys to dance, hoping a dance might lead to a date. From this tried-and-true method, I scored several encounters, some of them erotic and others merely amusing.

One night after gyrating amid the clouds of dry ice with a very young Black guy, I asked him for his number. After a couple of dates, Jed casually said, "My mom is going to meet us at Equus next Saturday night."

"What?" I asked, genuinely stunned. I had never seen a woman at Equus, any woman, but going with a date to a gay dance club, to meet his *mother*? That was a curveball in a whole new game.

"Don't worry; you'll like her."

"Okay," I said.

A few nights later, just as we were walking up to the club, a motorcycle roared to a halt at the curb, and its two leather-clad riders slowly dismounted, removing their helmets. When they shook out their hair, I realized that the two figures were women, the first dykes on bikes I had ever seen.

Brightening, Jed waved toward the motorcycle, exclaiming, "That's my mother and her girlfriend!"

I turned to get a closer look, surprised to learn that not only was his mother joining us at Equus, but she was a lesbian. Not just any lesbian—she was even a motorcyclist!

"Hi, I'm Marina," Jed's mother said, warmly extending her hand.

"And I'm Sabrina," the girlfriend added, smiling and shaking my hand in turn.

"You didn't tell me their names rhymed!" I whispered to Jed, pinching his shoulder. *Now I have seen everything*, I mused, as we entered the club, where apparently all four of us were going to dance together. Clearly, there was much I still needed to learn about all the nuances of the gay and lesbian community.

When we left the club, Marina mounted her motorcycle and Sabrina climbed on back. "Why don't you come over to dinner next week, Brooks?" she asked.

"I'd love to," I said, glancing at Jed, who nodded shyly. Thinking this was yet another first, I duly presented myself at their apartment in the Art Museum neighborhood on the appointed date. Sitting down to dinner, I found myself engaged in fluent conversation about Philadelphia politics and the arts with Marina and Sabrina, who turned out to be edgy professionals. Jed barely said anything, and only a few minutes into the salad course, I noticed that he was sulking in his chair at the corner of the table.

What's wrong with him? I wondered. After dinner, he clumsily ushered me out the door, muttering something unintelligible, without explanation. After that, he stopped returning my calls. Disappointed at having been rejected twice in a matter of weeks, I concluded that he must have been threatened by my easy rapport with his two mothers, who were only a few years older than me, since I was quite a few years older than Jed.

Days later, I ran into Marina on the street.

"I'm so sorry that Jed dumped you," she said.

"That's okay," I replied awkwardly. "I liked him and I really enjoyed meeting you and Sabrina too."

But, as we waved goodbye, it occurred to me that Marina had been pushy to invite me over without first consulting Jed. No doubt he must not have been ready to welcome me into his family circle. And when your mother approves of your romance, there's got to be something wrong with the romance, doesn't there? At least that's how I explained it to myself.

Meanwhile, I could no longer deny it—I was hopelessly attracted to Black men. While I also found Italians and Mediterranean types attractive, African American men were *it* for me. Part of my attraction had to do with the fact that the group of Black men who hung out at Equus seemed honest and "real," not prissy and stuck on themselves like so many of the white guys. But I wondered why all the Black guys hung out in a pack at the back end of the dance floor, farthest from the stairway. Why didn't they mix more?

One busy night a few weeks later, lining up to get into the club, I got my answer. Up ahead, I watched as the bouncer folded his arms over his chest to prevent a Black guy from entering. Squinting and standing on tiptoes to see over the heads in front of me, I witnessed the bouncer lift his arm and point toward the street, as if to say, *Get lost*. At that, the man turned on his heels and loped down the line toward me, eyes averted. Scowling, he tugged his jacket over his right shoulder and shoved off into the night without a glance back at the club. There was only one possible reason for his expulsion: the bouncer had done a head count and decided the club had reached its quota of Black men for the evening.

This came as a shock. It reminded me of how Alonzo had been so dismissive toward me. Then, I had just been confused, disappointed, and a little humiliated, but now I saw that he must have had good reason to be guarded. How was he to know that I wouldn't one day become an obstacle in his path? Maybe I would rise to a position of power, where, like the bouncer at Equus, I would refuse him admission to a club or a restaurant or even to a job opening or an entire career. It seemed that every day in Philadelphia I was learning a little more about racism, even though as a white person I was fundamentally sheltered from it.

As strong as my attraction to Black and brown men was, I did also notice hot white men. One was a guy I passed on Spruce Street every morning on my way to work. Although we both strode in tandem toward City Hall, I always spotted him on the opposite side of the street. Walking fast, I usually overtook him, but each time I saw him, I found him increasingly attractive, reassuring me that I didn't have just one "type."

One day, after I nodded and waved, he smiled and waved back. Feeling my confidence building, I asked myself, *Are we actually flirting?* I couldn't say for sure, but after this little ritual repeated itself over several days, I said to myself, *Fuck it, I'm going to meet him.* Throwing caution to the wind, I crossed the street mid-block and went right up to him, saying, "My name's Brooks. I see you every morning, so I just wanted to say 'hi.' And . . . um . . . would you like to go for a drink one night after work?" I cautiously suggested a straight bar in the neighborhood, just in case.

"Sure, that sounds good," he replied without hesitation, and we arranged to meet a few nights later.

When I showed up at the appointed hour, I spotted him already seated at a bistro table. We ordered Rolling Rocks, and after a requisite dose of small talk, I took a deep breath, and said, "I suppose you're wondering why I asked you to go out for a drink."

"No," he said, shaking his head as if to indicate that it was totally normal for a guy to ask a bro out for a brewski—even one he had never met before.

Taking this as an encouraging sign, I doggedly pressed on, driven by a lusty assertiveness that conquered my customary shyness and fear. With my usual complete lack of subtlety or guile, I managed to spit it out.

"I find you very attractive and I'd like to go to bed with you," I said.

At that, he calmly glanced up from his pilsner, looked me in the eye, and said, "Um, I'm not gay . . . but I'm flattered that you're attracted to me."

While heartily relieved by his kindness and tolerance—he could just as likely have taken offense and yelled out "Faggot!" at the top of his lungs while pounding his fist on the table—I was filled with shame and embarrassment. I had to pinch myself to maintain my side of the awkward conversation without freaking out, but of course there was nothing more to say. We nonchalantly extricated ourselves from our beers and scrammed. I never saw him on Spruce Street again; he probably switched one block over to Pine Street to avoid me.

The humiliating lesson could not have been more clear: in the future, I would have to improve my "gaydar," the art of scanning a guy's body language and fashion cues to identify him as a queer brother. But mastering the art of cruising was only one part of a broader education—I also needed to learn how to navigate the world as a gay man.

For that, I relied on two gay friends who represented opposite viewpoints. Gary, my workmate friend who had caught me hoisting a sack of baguettes, excelled at campy innuendo. Wearing his queerness like a pride flag, he didn't care who knew about his latest trysts or antics, with or without his boyfriend. In the other corner stood my new friend, Jeff, a young landscape designer that Beverly had introduced to me. Jeff was fundamentally conservative, a sort of gay family man who attended church regularly and longed for a world in which he could legally get married to a man.

While I admired both men's points of view, I wasn't sure where I fit in with their contrasting approaches to the art of being gay. Sometimes feeling iconoclastic and adventurous, I yearned to be out and proud like Gary. At other times I preferred to avoid the limelight, dreaming like Jeff of finding a stable, monogamous relationship. Happily, after many months of feeling whiplash between their divergent outlooks, I finally realized that I didn't have to choose between them. Nobody said I couldn't chart a middle course, if I wanted, and in any case, there was no pressure to choose one man's viewpoint over the other's.

One day at an impromptu picnic in Rittenhouse Square, near the office, Jeff said, "Brooks, I've met somebody, and I think I'm falling in love."

"You have?" I asked, surprised.

"I like him so much that I asked him if he wants to move in together, and he said yes. We've been apartment hunting, and we found a great trinity." Jeff smiled at me, pleased to be moving forward toward urban nesting and eventual nuptials. We all called Philly's narrow row houses trinities because they almost always had three stories. They were also known as Father, Son, and Holy Ghosts. But how had Jeff already found somebody to move in with?

"Congratulations, that's wonderful," I said. But I was envious—Jeff had come out even more furtively than I had, at least a month or two later, and now he was already leapfrogging ahead of me in the dating scene.

Meanwhile, I had an important hurdle to cross: I had to come out to Mom and Dad. After putting it off week after week, I decided I couldn't wait to tell them in person because I wasn't planning to visit Seattle any time soon. I would have to phone them.

One evening after work, I took a deep breath, lifted the receiver, then stopped and held it in the air. Pausing before dialing, I thought back to the time, several years before, when I had more or less already come out to Mom. Shaking myself out of my reverie, I put the receiver to my ear and punched the keys with a trembling finger. Mom answered and Dad got on the upstairs extension. I took another deep breath—this was it. Would they reject me or would they tell me they still loved me anyway? I had made up my mind that either way, there was no turning back. If they rejected me, I informed myself that I would just have to go forward without them.

As usual, I simply blurted it out. "I want you to know that I'm attracted to men and I'm, basically, a homosexual."

"But women are so attractive," Dad said. "How can you not see that?"

He sounded genuinely perplexed, but he didn't appear angry or recriminatory. I sighed with relief, laughing inwardly at Dad's combination of innocence and ignorance. Even though he didn't understand my sexual orientation, he was still Dad, and it seemed that I was still his son. Mom murmured a couple of soothing phrases, and I felt optimistic that she would explain it all to Dad after we got off the phone.

"Don't you want to tell Bliss?" she asked. "He's here visiting," she added, handing him the phone.

"Hi, Bliss, I have something to tell you . . . I'm gay." I paused, waiting for his reply. I hadn't talked to Bliss in a long time, and we rarely saw each other, since I lived clear across the country from him.

"Oh, so that explains it," he said. "I always noticed you were kind of femme, so I just kind of assumed you were gay all along." Bliss's matter-of-fact tone spoke volumes—he appeared to be no more shocked than Mom had been.

When we said goodbye, I took another deep breath, grateful to be assured of continuing love and support from all three other members of our little family. However, a tiny drama queen hidden inside me was a tad disappointed that our phone encounter had been such an anticlimax. Ready to put up her dukes and slap somebody, my inner queen wasn't quite ready to remove her makeup at the first sign of a white flag of surrender. *What a ridiculous reaction*, I thought to myself, and went to bed smiling.

New Year's Eve was approaching, and I had plenty to celebrate, but the celebration I craved was a romantic date, not a night of drunken revelry, so I invited the latest lad I had met on the dance floor to spend the evening at my apartment. To my delight, he accepted, and I bought a bottle of champagne, but when the last day of the year slipped resolutely into night, he was a no-show, and I spent an agonizingly lonely New Year's Eve. I have no idea why I didn't simply strike out to the clubs, but in those prehistoric days before cellphones or even answering machines, it was not an unusual thing to stay in, hanging by the phone, no matter how unadvisable that was.

The incident shone a spotlight on the heady, chaotic, and ultimately lonely world of cruising. When someone took the bait and followed me home, it could be so exciting to spend a night of passionate lovemaking with an all-but-anonymous partner. But when the guy got up in the morning, the first thing he did was to reach down for his rumpled underwear and the wrinkled shirt and pants that lay huddled together on the dusty floor. Then he disappeared into the morning, never to be seen again. When the door closed behind him, I felt as if a curtain of emptiness had been pulled across me, separating me from the world outside.

At those moments, cruising felt like no more than a meaningless game. It rarely triggered my sense of guilt or shame, but it left me feeling depleted. I had expended so much energy and *time* to hunt the lads down, and for what reward besides the temporary high of our intertwined bodies, the exhilarating exertion of our mutual climax? Now, I would have to begin all over again in my quest to find an emotional connection that could outlast one short night.

On the other hand, as disheartening as cruising was, I had to admit that I was becoming addicted to its highs—to those exciting moments when I could boast of bagging the latest man. If I had taken the time to think about it more clearly, I might have realized that the universe rarely if ever grants you the opportunity to enjoy the highs of any situation without suffering its lows— they are two sides of the same coin.

On the morning after my New Year's Eve no-show, Gary and our mutual friend Ron spirited me off to that most uniquely Philadelphian of New Year's celebrations, the fabulous Mummers' Parade, where they refused to heed my lamentations. The Mummers' elaborate and colorful costumes shimmered in the bright sun as we stood in our thick winter coats on Broad Street watching them march by.

"Oh, sweetie, don't fret," Gary said. "We'll go dancing again!"

There was a long weekend ahead, and the three of us made up for my depressing New Year's Eve by partying with renewed vigor. I was so grateful to Ron and Gary for restoring my spirits. Better yet, although I could not have known it, fortune was about to smile on me.

17 A PART-TIME PRIVATE EYE

ONE EVENING at Equus, an acquaintance tapped me on the shoulder.

"Brooks," he said, "a friend of mine wants to meet you."

Lifting my eyes from the swirling fog of dry ice, I surveyed the crowd hanging on the railing above the dance floor. There on the top step, leaning elegantly against a post, stood a young African American man with mocha-chocolate skin. His well-muscled legs tapered from his toned hips to his pointy-toed, high-heeled gray ankle boots, and his shimmering black hair dazzled. Most memorable were his huge, smiling eyes—there was so much mirth in them! Catching my glance, he batted his luxuriant eyelashes several times, raising his eyebrows in a faux-demure expression, as if he were at once flirting with me and parodying his own flirtatiousness. Right away I was intrigued. Then, his alluring expression gave way to a full-stop grin, followed by a hearty laugh.

"Come here, you foo—" he said, enveloping me in a hug while he bent his knee and kicked his heel up behind him, just like Mary Tyler Moore in *The Dick Van Dyke Show*. Now I was smitten. He had picked me out from all the other men in the bar, which of course made me feel special, and from the start, I liked him back. After I brought him a bourbon and coke, we clinked glasses and had a little introductory chat.

"What do you do?" I inquired. That was the standard question we white college graduates asked one another, now that we were all working and beginning to claw our way to the top.

"I'm Clarissa Grant, full-time secretary and part-time private eye," he gushed. "Clarissa is my drag name, that's the private-eye part."

"So what type of mystery does Clarissa solve?" I asked.

"I'll give you an example," he replied. "Say my friend Gabe knows his lover is cheating on him, but he doesn't know who the other guy is, he will enlist Clarissa to find out, and when she does, she will present Gabe with the indisputable evidence."

He then set the scene with more detail. Gazing at the clock in the secretarial pool while donning her pumps and her fashionable clutch, Clarissa would rush out the door on the strike of five, so that, sniffing the air like a good bloodhound, she could quickly gather evidence. She always had her ear to the ground for the good tea, dish, or gossip, and since the tea usually pointed to a mysterious puzzle if not a downright betrayal, it was Clarissa's job to get to the bottom of it, like Poirot cracking his toughest case.

"But who's the full-time secretary?" I asked.

"Chad is my daytime name—that's the secretary part. I'm taking classes to be a court reporter. In court, I'll be typing shorthand on a portable keyboard they give you. It's really light-weight—it has a slender post that makes it easy to carry around," he explained, adding that the little keyboard would also come in handy to type up the fruits of Clarissa's research.

"Are you from Philly?" I asked.

"No, Downingtown, PA. It's a small town beyond the outer suburbs."

These revelations were all so unexpected and bizarrely endearing that our evening ended in bed. Our tryst turned out to be the beginning of my first relationship with a real boyfriend, as we started dating regularly and then exclusively. Soon he began to call me "bo-fre," short for boyfriend, and I eagerly responded in kind. He loved to grab my sleeve, bat his luscious lashes, and ask, "Is you is, or is you ain't ma baby?"

"Oh honey, ah IS!" I responded, heartily amused. Many years passed before I discovered that this line was a quote from a Louis Jordan song, which in no way diminished its appeal.

And I *was* his baby. I had never had a relationship in my whole life, not in high school, not in college, and certainly not in graduate school. After all my long, painful years of love drought and self-denial, I was all the more ecstatic to have at last found a boyfriend, especially one as charming, energetic, and cute as Chad. When we held hands and when we made love, a strong current of affection passed between us. We were having so much fun that I never stopped to question how deep our love was or whether it could last.

Limber and photogenic, Chad was always in motion, often jumping in the air at the moment I clicked my camera's shutter. Shifting into Clarissa mode, he would describe a scene in which one queen upbraided another, pronouncing, "She read him up one side and down the other." Then, pointing to a queen wearing pancake makeup, he loved to say, "Her face is *beat*!" Just as I had learned the meaning of "fierce" from Ken, these were delightful terms for my shiny new queer lexicon.

In the heady days and nights to come, Chad conducted me about town, introducing me to all sorts of clubs. One evening he unexpectedly said, "Wanna go to a wrinkle room?"

"What's a wrinkle room?" I asked.

"Come, I'll show you," he said, chuckling at my ignorance. Taking my hand in his, he promptly led me across town to an anonymous building near the Reading Terminal Market. Upon arrival, I noted that the club had an ordinary sign hanging over the street that most definitely did not say "Wrinkle Room," but the mystery revealed itself soon enough. When I passed a clutch of men huddled inside the front door, a grand piano materialized out of the smoky gloom near the back wall. A gaggle of much older men in suits and ties crowded around the piano, forming an impromptu glee club. A gray-haired old queen in a maroon blazer sat at the piano, banging out melodies, while the chorus sipped martinis and sang harmony.

"He takes requests," whispered Chad, as we pushed and prodded our way to the piano.

When we got close enough to see the black and white keys, the elderly pianist glanced in my direction, and raised an eyebrow. I didn't want to miss my opportunity.

"Um, do you do 'New York, New York?'" I asked, whereupon he nodded and quickly dove into the tune. As soon as the glee club voiced its thrilling opening line about their small-town blues fading away, I knew that I would never forget what a wrinkle room was.

On other occasions, Chad escorted me to a couple of gay clubs called Odyssey and Odyssey II. One night, he took me to the original Odyssey to catch a live performance of a Black disco diva. A standing-room-only crowd filled the darkened space as Loleatta Holloway approached the makeshift stage. The music cued up, karaoke-style, the crowd hushed, and sturdy Miss Holloway grabbed the microphone. As she rolled her head back and opened her jaws, revealing a full set of brilliant-white teeth, she belted out the first of many loud and impressively sustained high notes. Chad grabbed me and put his lips to my ear.

"Look, it's Lethal Holler!" he said, with a grin.

We went dancing a lot, mostly at Equus, and sometimes at Odyssey. The only club we didn't go to was the DCA. I had heard a lot about the DCA from the guys I met, so I knew that it was reputed to contain a full-size, semi-truck cab. The cab was said to have working headlights that pulsed in strobe-like beams across the loud dance floor, where men boogied their way to ecstasy. Into this Detroit icon of redneck masculinity, butch guys in flannel shirts crept in discreet pairs to grab a quick orgasm, groping one another against the steering wheel and across the inconveniently located gearshift. I never went to the DCA, not only because you had to pay an annual membership fee, but also because it didn't open before midnight, and despite being a newly minted "dazzling urbanite," the moniker that *Philadelphia* magazine had recently bestowed on the young nightclubbing set, I was never a night owl.

Chad was a fashion-forward person, always sporting the latest styles and forever ironing his shirts. When he left for work, he often paired a dark T-shirt with a sports jacket, a style I came to admire. Quick to find bargains, he often took me shopping at the Salvation Army store, which he dubbed "Sally Ann's." He knew how to look his best, it showed, and this endeared him to me, especially because I had such little fashion sense myself.

One of his "girlfriends," as he called them, was a slim, dark guy with a pencil moustache who lived near Temple University in

North Philly. When we visited Rondel, trash overflowed the bins in front of the stone stoops of the dilapidated brick row houses, and drug deals ricocheted back and forth like speeding bullets. Chad and I felt like winners if we walked a block or two without being shot, and we were careful not to be seen holding hands.

Rondel had a serious disposition tempered by a sneaky sense of humor. He was always looking for a boyfriend. Whenever he found one, no matter how briefly, he would point to the guy, saying, "That's my *hus*-band!" I loved the way that he and another of Chad's friends, Binky, accepted me unquestioningly, without ever trying to peg me by my background. It was so refreshingly unlike the way white people always wanted immediately to place me, to put me in a box, the box that informed them of my parents' social status, the type of neighborhood I came from, and how prestigious my college was. All that mattered to Binky and Rondel was whether or not I was good company.

18 I LEFT MY HEART IN . . . PHILADELPHIA?

THE WORLD Chad and I occupied as a couple was limited to our free time. It never occurred to me to invite him to the office or that I could offer to meet him at his secretarial job. Now that I had finally found it, the gay scene was a delicious secret that I couldn't get enough of, a dazzling underworld completely hidden from normal, workaday life. Reveling in my new clandestine identity, I didn't stop to reflect that the secrecy of the gay world might impede our rights, or that its very invisibility had for so long trapped me in my lonely self-homophobia.

At first, it felt glamorous to have two separate identities. It was exciting, even intoxicating, to pass through that unmarked door at Equus, as if I were crossing into another dimension. Although I was "out" to more and more people, including at work, all it really meant was that I had confided in them about my attraction to men. The actual life I was leading was my exclusive business, completely invisible to them, and I liked it that way.

Over time, though, my separate identities began to weigh on me. Sometimes I felt as if I were split in two, fully belonging neither to my official straight professional milieu nor to my underground gay one. And I began to tire of what at first I scarcely realized was the effort it took to keep my two identities separate.

For example, when colleagues invited me to parties at their apartments, I automatically made the choice not to bring Chad.

Gradually, I began to recognize that by hiding him from my work friends, I was unwittingly devaluing him. By definition, didn't that mean I was also devaluing myself? Moreover, would I have introduced Chad around if he had been white? I hoped I didn't have a double standard, but I couldn't say for sure. As unconscious as my behavior was, I now wondered if perhaps it cloaked a sneaky, underhanded form of unintentional racism, a demon that could not help but infect our relationship.

Sometimes my two worlds collided unexpectedly, and then I was forced to out myself in a way I had not prepared for. One day Chad and I were standing on a street corner, waiting for the light to change, when a Latino friend from my undergraduate days suddenly appeared facing us across the street. He could not avoid seeing that we were holding hands, so I had no choice but to say, "Hi, Andrés. This is my boyfriend, Chad." I tried to sound proud, but Andrés blanched, frowned, shook his head, and quickly departed, without saying a word.

It was even more painful and alienating when Beverly confided in me about Bob.

"Brooks, I told Bob you're gay," she said one day, flicking ashes into a small tray.

"What did he say? How did he take it?" I asked anxiously.

"You know how he always pauses, and then says, 'Hmmm, oh really?'"

"Yes."

"Well, after the 'hmmm,' he said you probably just haven't found the right girl yet."

I knew Bob meant well, but that disturbed me. It seemed to suggest that my long and difficult struggle to attain self-acceptance was no more than a foolish illusion. It further implied that I should simply walk right back into the closet, snap the door shut, and resume the useless script I had performed for years, always trying desperately and unsuccessfully to find the "right" girl, without ever really wanting her.

A few months into our affair, Chad decided to move to an apartment on North Broad Street, where the rent was lower. Well beyond Center City's northern boundary, he liked to joke that it was the summer palace, referring to his old southerly apartment as the winter palace. The summer palace was in a rough part of town—we couldn't board a North Broad Street subway car without being accosted by a German shepherd police dog on a tight leash, held back by a uniformed cop. The first time I spent the night there, the bedroom lit up every few minutes all night long, blazing like lightning from the sparks the Broad Street streetcar threw up when its metal wheels screeched against the track as it lurched past below. Chad slept like a lamb, but the grating noises and blinding lights so unnerved and exhausted me that, after a couple of weeks of sleepless nights, I came down with mononucleosis.

However long in coming, my illness was almost inevitable: I was burning the candle at both ends, working long hours at the office and going out disco dancing several nights a week. My body was stretched tight as a drum, the switch to my overstimulated brain stuck in the "on" position.

One morning, I dragged myself to the office, feeling heavy as lead. I went through the motions of trying to work, but it was no use, so I walked unsteadily home, where I put myself to bed. There I remained for several days, aided by powerful antibiotics. Chad hopped in to visit me a couple of times during my sickness, brightening the room with his lively step and quick humor. During one visit, I propped myself up in bed and he crept in next to me. Drawing the blankets up to our chins, we laughed at the latest antics of Jane Curtin and Dan Aykroyd on *Saturday Night Live.*

Two or three days into my bedrest, I received a home visit from The High and The Mighty, Hanna/Olin's executive secretary.

Bounding into the room, Nora said, "I mean, Laurie is asking everybody are you really sick, you know what I mean? I mean, he's saying maybe you're playing hooky or something, you know?"

"You mean he sent you as his personal emissary?" I asked.

Nodding and rolling her eyes, she took a hard look at me, verifying that I was in fact ill. We chuckled about it, her violet eyes dancing to the music of her husky laugh. What an unpleasant surprise it was to discover that Laurie, like Chad, was also a bit of a part-time private eye. It hurt to learn that after my all-nighters and years of loyalty, he still doubted my integrity. I had tried so hard to prove myself, to show Bob and Laurie that I was worthy of the same regard that they held for my father, but his latest move seemed to imply that I could never earn it.

One Saturday night after I recovered from my illness, Chad and I were sitting facing the aisle on the Chestnut Street bus, heading to the clubs. As the bus passed 19th Street, I gazed one long block up to the corner of Market. There, a small yellow square of light beckoned to me from a second-floor window. Framed in the window, I could just make out Bob Hanna's silhouetted head as he hunched over his table, intent on one of his drawings. A sharp wave of guilt washed over me—guilt for not being in the office helping him—but as the bus continued past the intersection, the feeling passed, replaced by a visceral sense of relief that I was instead on my way to a fabulous gay nightclub.

Even after my recovery from mononucleosis, my long nights at work continued to take a toll. One afternoon, I trailed after Bob and Laurie as we crossed Chestnut Street on our way back to the office after lunch. Catching up with them, I managed to butt into their conversation. "Um, I love my work," I said, "but how much longer are we going to be working evenings? I'd love it if I could go home earlier."

"Don't worry, chief," Laurie said. "Be of good cheer. We know you deserve to have a life, and we're planning to hire some new people soon."

"Oh, good," I responded skeptically. My doubts were well-placed because as the days lengthened into weeks, no new employees materialized, and our days and nights remained as strenuous as ever.

Laurie's disbelief that I had been sick, paired with Bob's comment that I should wait to find the right girl, increased my sense of alienation. An added stress arose from the incestuous nature of the Philadelphia landscape architecture community, so much of which revolved around Penn, Bob, and Laurie. Well informed by all her intimate little one-on-one chats, Beverly kept me up to speed on the minutest personal details about our classmates, professors, and colleagues in other offices: who was sleeping with whom; who had just got what new job; and who had quit or been fired. She knew it all.

Listening to her intel without ever requesting it felt increasingly claustrophobic and suffocating. Eventually, I realized I didn't even want to know it all—it felt like an invasion of other people's privacy. Besides, what was she saying to others about *me*? Was there anybody out there who didn't know my business? I longed to live in a place where I could have more privacy, where my colleagues did not need to know everything about me.

My conflict came into sharp focus one weekend afternoon while Chad and I sat on a westbound bus. When the bus stopped, who should get on but Lee Copeland, dean of the Graduate School of Fine Arts, former dean of Architecture and Planning at the University of Washington, and colleague of my father's. Recognizing me as he walked down the aisle, Lee offered his usual mild, noncommittal smile, with a quick side-glance at Chad. Chad bounded off the bus, blew me a kiss, and skipped down the street, waving back.

Oh well, I thought, *Lee might as well be the latest person to know I'm out of the closet.* Still, his influential position as dean, which came with what I assumed to be his power to augment or hinder people's careers, brought back all the fears of coming out that I thought I had vanquished, fears that had also kept me from presenting Chad as my partner at professional events.

Mulling this over as I stepped off the bus, I remembered a large poster I had recently seen on the wall of a travel agent's office. In the dramatic San Francisco scene, a perfect shot of the Bay Bridge gleamed from a narrow slot of blue sky, bookended by a hilly canyon of skyscrapers where the iconic cable cars climbed and descended. I had loved San Francisco from the time I had first visited it with my parents at the age of thirteen, and now I began to fantasize about moving there. By then I knew that thousands of young gay men from all across America were moving in droves to San Francisco because it promised gay freedom unequaled in any other city in the world, not to mention escape from their judgmental or abusive parents. At the same time, San Francisco had a multitude of landscape architecture firms, maybe more than in any other city, so my chance of finding a desirable job there seemed promising.

Dad had given me a piece of advice after I graduated.

"Get lots of experience working in different firms, Brooks," he had said. "There's really no need to stay at any one office longer than around two years, unless you really like it."

I had already been at Hanna/Olin for a little over two years, and maybe now was the right time for me to move on. But if I was really going to do it, obviously I needed to talk it over with Chad.

One day, when we were hanging out in my apartment, I put it to him.

"Honey—I've been thinking a lot lately, and . . . I've pretty much decided I want to move to San Francisco. I'm sick of how I always feel like I'm living in a fishbowl here, with Bob and Laurie and all the other landscape architects looking over my shoulder and no doubt gossiping about me." I waited for Chad's response.

"Frisco, huh? That's cool, I guess . . ." Chad turned his head toward the window and gazed out noncommittally.

"Oh! Don't get me wrong," I hastened to add. "I don't want to break up with you. I want you to move out there with me. What do you think? Would you like to move to San Francisco? I hope so! It's such an amazing city. You'll love it there, and it's a magnet for gay men. No, it's *the* magnet! What do you say?"

"Aaaaaghh!" yelled Chad, covering his ears.

That was the dismissive scream he always employed when he didn't want to hear something he would otherwise have to argue about.

"Oh, come on," I said, pressing him.

"I'll think about it," he replied, after a long pause.

In the days to come, though, I couldn't get him to open up about it. I couldn't tell if he was deeply hurt that I appeared to be moving on or if it was just some sort of minor inconvenience for him. We had never discussed our future. Although we had tacitly agreed to be monogamous, at least for the time being, it was not clear how serious we were about each other or how long-lasting our relationship might be. Now, like an actor with uncontrollable stage fright on opening night, that glaring omission appeared for the first time in the beam of a powerful spotlight.

Later that night, I thought about it. I didn't want to leave Chad, but if the choice came down to staying with him or moving to San Francisco without him, I was ready to move. For such a long time, I had so badly wanted a relationship, and now I had one, so I hated just to walk away from it, but I had to admit that I wanted it both ways. With the tendency that Beverly had pointed out to me—my tendency to want a quick fix—I felt sure that, with time, I could convince Chad to move to San Francisco . . . if not right away, then later.

But for now, San Francisco was too alluring to turn down.

Next to coming out of the closet, giving notice at Hanna/Olin was the hardest thing I ever had to do in my young life. Leaving meant walking away from a brilliant future at one of America's most promising landscape architecture firms. But there was more to it than that. By now, despite the tensions between us, I viewed Bob and Laurie almost as surrogate fathers. After all, I had been guided to them by my actual father. Dad, Bob, and Laurie were a mutual admiration society, and due in no small part to their admiration for Dad, they had invited me into their rarefied society. For those reasons, quitting felt more like breaking up from a long-term relationship than leaving a job. However, I felt compelled to move on.

Every morning in early October, I told myself that today was the day I was going to give notice, but every day I chickened out. Finally, one sunny morning, I couldn't stand it any longer. *The time for action is now*, I decided, willing myself to act. The office clock ticked loudly, and I heard everybody's parallel bars and triangles clicking against the soft murmur of background conversation. My hearing became almost supernaturally acute as adrenalin pumped through my veins, but each time I got up the nerve to approach them, either Bob or Laurie picked up the phone for yet another of their incessant calls to New York. The minutes dragged by agonizingly—9:00 became 10:00, then slipped another half hour. I broke into a sweat, my heart beating loudly. *At long last,* I said to myself, *this is it. It's now or never.*

Trembling as I approached their desk, I forced the words out.

"There's something I, um . . . I wa-want to tell you," I said, my voice faltering and cracking. "I've decided to move on to new things and go back to the West Coast. I'm leaving and . . . and I'm giving two months' notice."

"Hmmm, oh really?" Bob said in his trademark deadpan phrase.

"I'm sorry to hear that, chief," Laurie said in a more authoritative tone. "Are you sure that's what you want?"

He sounded unusually concerned above the preternatural hush that had taken over the drafting stations behind us, everyone else in the room shushing each other to listen in on our awkward conversation.

"Yes," I mumbled, and having nothing more to say, I returned to my desk.

After expending so much emotion, I longed to fade into the wall of white particleboard where all our lovely yellow-trace drawings were pinned, hanging layer upon layer like so many moths in a museum vitrine. I wanted to go back to working normally, as if nothing had happened, but when I picked up my Eagle #947 burnt-umber pencil exactly where I had left it, my wrist was shaking so hard that I couldn't draw a straight line.

Laurie and Bob jumped up from the table where they always sat facing each other like Bliss and I had as children, donned their tweed jackets, and exited rapidly down the stairs, most likely to go off and confer about their future staffing needs. The instant they left, my compatriots rose in a hearty round of applause, which startled me almost as much as hearing myself voice my resignation out loud only moments before. I found myself looking into the face of Anne James, our newest employee, who was beaming and clapping enthusiastically. I could only conclude that some of my colleagues, in their heart of hearts, wanted to resign as much as I had, and were living vicariously through me. Touched by their support, I knew that they wanted the best for me.

Once my pulse finally returned to normal, I calmed down enough to continue working. It was a tremendous relief to have risen to the challenge, to have stood up for myself by announcing my decision. Now I could get on with an exciting new life of freedom, a life of my own choosing.

In the two months remaining before I left Hanna/Olin, we moved to a new, larger, and more luxurious office on the second floor of 2020 Chestnut Street, which Bob and Laurie were renovating. It had workstations in trendy diagonal patterns, with several modules of four desks arranged in the form of a cross. On move-in day, the remodel was nearly complete, but a few odds and ends still needed finishing.

One morning, as I got down to work, Barry Gazso was engaged in a quiet huddle with Bob and the contractor, but Bob had just stubbed out his cigarette, consulted his watch, and dashed down the stairs with a roll of drawings.

No sooner had Bob departed than we all heard a sudden outburst.

"That man should be given his last cigarette and shot!" the contractor shouted, delivering his final verdict. At that, he picked up his measuring tape and carpenter pencil and headed out, as if in pursuit of Bob. When the tension cleared, we all chuckled, knowing how exacting Bob could be.

Early one morning, just when I was beginning to regret my decision to leave, I discovered a handwritten note on my desk from Bob. The message expressed displeasure that, instead of cleaning up my pencils and drawings at the end of the previous day, I had left them in a messy heap, visible from the entrance. This irritated me, buoying my sense of justification at leaving, especially because I was nearly always fastidious about arranging my drafting materials.

As December approached, Chad still had not given me a definitive answer about moving to San Francisco. I brought it up from time to time, continually stressing how much I wanted him to move West with me, but he always evaded me, and perhaps I was deluding myself. I loved Chad, but somewhere buried in my heart, I knew it was a sort of puppy love that might not be deep enough to stand the test of time. In the end, we settled on a practical approach: I'd move out West and get situated. Then, if he felt like it, he'd come out and join me. That seemed sensible, although I got the sense that he didn't feel any urgency about it.

Before I knew it, only three weeks remained until my departure. I was running around town frantically packing, sending my belongings ahead by Greyhound Package Express. When I called my landlord to give notice, I mentioned that I had found someone who could take over the lease.

"What's his name?" my landlord asked.

"Chad Williams."

"Oh, I would never rent to a Black person," he said.

In my sudden anger, I was about to hang up, but then curiosity got the better of me, and I broke in. "Okay, he *is* Black, but how did you know?"

"His name is Williams," the landlord said, and hung up.

How could my landlord be so sure that everyone named Williams was Black? I wondered. Obviously, there were plenty of white people named Williams. His rejection of Chad came as a shock not only because it was unjust but also because it was so arbitrary. After all, he had had no problem leasing to Ken, who was also Black. Or perhaps Ken was so light-skinned that he "passed," like Sandra Dee in *Imitation of Life*? Either way, the situation was deeply unfair.

I was hurt for Chad, and it hurt me even more to tell him, but it didn't occur to me to try to change my landlord's mind or to appeal his decision to some sort of rental oversight board. While one may have existed, I had never heard of anybody doing such a thing. Sadly, the bottom line was that racism had extended its ugly hand to snatch opportunity from a young man as charming and decent as Chad, and, as far as I was concerned, that gave me yet one more reason to leave Philadelphia. My blinders had been ripped off—I could no longer ignore how pervasive racism was in Philadelphia.

Still, I wasn't prepared for the extreme emotion I felt when, on December 1, I boarded a night-flight home to Seattle, which would be my base camp for my San Francisco job search. My faithful cat, which Birgyte had given me when we graduated and I had renamed Catita, accompanied me in a little crate under the seat.

Exhausted and heartbroken over leaving Chad, I burst into tears the minute the plane taxied up the runway, and I didn't stop until we climbed to thirty thousand feet. Would he ever again say to me, "Is you is, or is you ain't ma baby?" I was afraid he would not, despite our heartfelt promises to phone each other nearly every day. I calmed down a bit as the plane flew relentlessly westward into the night, but I couldn't help thinking, I may be going to San Francisco, but . . . I left my heart in Philadelphia.

Golden Gate Bridge from Buena Vista Park, San Francisco

PART 2

Open Your Golden Gate

Freedom is too enormous to be
slipped under a closet door.

—Harvey Milk

A FLAT ON PAGE STREET

THE GREY Rabbit bus coughed and growled as it lurched onto the freeway, bound from Seattle to San Francisco, where I had landed a job with Omi Lang Associates, a boutique firm known for assisting Lawrence Halprin, an internationally renowned landscape architect. Halprin was already famous for designing Ghirardelli Square in San Francisco, a dramatic waterfall in downtown Portland, Oregon, and Seattle's Freeway Park, built on a lid over the I-5 freeway. The Portland and Seattle projects had received high praise for the way their dramatically corrugated concrete walls conjured an abstract vision of the Sierra Nevada, the rugged mountain range that Halprin so admired. Now he had been hired to design a memorial to Franklin Delano Roosevelt on the Tidal Basin in Washington, DC. Omi Lang was selected as the assisting landscape architecture firm, so my new job promised work on an exciting and nationally significant project.

The Rabbit was just one of two hippie alternatives to Greyhound, the other being the Green Tortoise, so I was not surprised that my fellow passengers were long-haired student types with grungy backpacks. The great thing was that, unlike on Greyhound, the luggage rack above the seats was reserved for beds, so at nightfall I climbed up to my bunk and snuggled into my sleeping bag. When morning light finally came in through the slot windows below the ceiling, a gentle rain was falling sideways against the pale-green, oak-studded hills of the Bay Area. Soon, all the passengers were awake and upright.

"Breakfast is ready," the guy who served as our informal tour director announced, observing several of us climbing down from our roosts. With a little flourish, he lifted the lid of what appeared to be a large plastic garbage can, revealing a giant vat of peanut butter.

"Dig in," he added, handing out plastic spoons. Lining up in the aisle, the hippies took turns dipping their spoons into the communal peanut butter.

"Take me to Starbucks," I might have said, except that, in those days, Starbucks was still confined to a handful of locations in Seattle.

Not more than an hour later, the bus rolled up onto Market Street in San Francisco. As it slowed and sputtered to a halt, I couldn't help noticing a handful of dapper young men scurrying along the sidewalk, each one heading toward what appeared to be an important business destination. They were universally fastidious, cute, and obviously gay. *Thank God*, I thought, *I'm among my own tribe at last!* Thrilled to be once again surrounded by the upbeat urban tempo that never failed to energize me, I rushed off the bus and hustled to get away from the hippies.

My first destination was the Atherton, a small, European-style, gay-friendly hotel in the Tenderloin, where I had booked a few nights. Buying a *San Francisco Chronicle*, I immediately began scanning the apartment ads.

"Arre you going to find yourrself a nice leetle aparrtment in the Marrina?" my French grandmother, Manie, had asked offhandedly, before I left town, and I had rolled my eyes. How could she not know there was no way I could afford the Marina District?

That afternoon, I strolled over to Polk Street, where I bar-hopped. Polk Street had preceded the Castro as San Francisco's preeminent gay quarter, and a few of its bars remained popular, if no longer fashionable. When I strolled into one called Giraffe, a delicious shiver went through me: I was completely free. Nobody knew me. I was just a gay man among other gay men, and we were all equals. I was certain that I could do anything I felt like without fear of censure—there were effectively no barriers or roadblocks in my path.

After a couple of drinks, though, my initial excitement gave way to an undertone of loneliness. It was still too early for the after-work crowd, and the handful of guys at the bar were all ignoring me. Apart from the cute bartender, nobody even bothered to say hello. It was the flip side of what had made me shiver with pleasure only half an hour before: nobody knew me.

In Philadelphia I had enjoyed a strong sense of community, first at Hanna/Olin and then, in its own way, at Equus, but I had felt like I was caught in a claustrophobic bubble and I longed for freedom. Now, suddenly and for the first time in my life, I was experiencing what freedom really felt like. Why wasn't I elated? It had never occurred to me that you couldn't acquire freedom without paying the price of anonymity. The joy of liberty and the loneliness of social invisibility were two sides of the same coin.

Suppressing my dawning realization that big-city freedom had its price, I returned to the hotel, where I fell asleep to the romantic moans of the iconic foghorns, my good mood restored. I was in San Francisco at last, and it did not disappoint.

The next day, I began apartment hunting in earnest, as I was due to begin work at Omi Lang within a few days. It seemed that all the available studio apartments were on Nob Hill, which turned out to mean its rundown south slope, not the fashionable hilltop neighborhood around Grace Cathedral, where all the cable cars converged. Invariably, the apartments were described as cozy, and just as inevitably, cozy meant tiny. Whitewashed and clean, some of them had attractive, old crown moldings, but the kitchenettes were impossibly small and the cabinets didn't close properly. Only the new coats of white paint on the walls and fire escapes made the little rooms look fresh. Dismayed to learn that they were more expensive than in Philadelphia, I resolved not to spend money on a place that wouldn't make me happy.

After a couple of days, I decided that my only option was to find a roommate—the prices demanded it. In *The Bay Area Reporter*, San Francisco's preeminent gay newspaper, I spotted an ad for a roommate exchange on Castro Street and decided to check it out. When I arrived at Castro and Market, what caught my eye was the famous Twin Peaks, the first gay bar in the world ever to boast plate-glass windows, deliberately putting its patrons on display for all to see. It crowded up against the romantic Mission-style Castro Theater, with its Spanish red tile roof.

Descending the long, graceful sweep of Castro, I found "Roommates Unlimited" about halfway down the block. When I climbed the staircase to the second floor, a line of apartment-seekers had already formed, so I grabbed one of the application forms and returned to the sidewalk, where I started to fill it out. Just then, a thin young white man came bounding up. I felt him before I saw him, but suddenly he was in my face.

"Are you looking for a rental?" he asked, beady brown eyes searching mine. Apparently, I was desirable, if not as a bed partner, then at least as a paying tenant.

"Umm, yeah," I said. "My name's Brooks—what's yours?"

"I'm La-Lyle," he stammered, offering a limp hand. "My lover, Stuart, and I live in a flat in the Haight, and our housemate just moved out. We need a new one."

Lyle had a little goatee and brown hair combed back from a tall forehead. His body was as elastic as an unbaked gingerbread man.

"Wanna come take a look?"

"Sure," I said, thinking that while Haight-Ashbury was not the Castro, which was my first choice, at least it wasn't the south slope of Nob Hill.

"Come, follow me," he said, gesturing toward the hill behind us, and he led me back up Castro Street, which turned into Divisadero after you crossed Market.

Passing the fog-laden Monterey cypresses of Buena Vista Park, we soon arrived at Masonic Avenue, in the heart of the Haight. On Masonic, Lyle turned left onto Page Street. Much quieter than the commercial bustle of Haight, it was an attractive, leafy street of tall townhouses. Lyle's was number 1763, and his flat—San Francisco jargon for an apartment with a direct door onto the street—was on the third floor.

Rustling around in a sort of man-bag he was carrying, he produced keys. When the door opened, I beheld a long, steep staircase, reminiscent of ones I had seen years before on a trip to Amsterdam. Once we reached the top landing, I saw that the analogy was apt because Lyle was pointing at a large metal lever on the wall.

"You can open the door with this," he explained, giving it a push, and sure enough, the front door swung slowly open, about a thousand steps below. "Your room is in front," Lyle added, conducting me around the banister and opening a door.

Beyond lay a large, light-filled room with oak floors and two ample bay windows facing the street. Above the rooftops, I could see the lovely umbrella canopies of towering eucalyptus trees undulating in the breeze and announcing the nearby presence of the Panhandle, a boulevard extension of Golden Gate Park. I smiled, thinking that I had really lucked out—it looked like the perfect place to shape my new identity in San Francisco.

"But this is so nice," I said. "How come you and Stuart don't live in this room?"

"We prefer the back," he replied. "I'm a musician, and it's quieter back there." The street didn't sound loud to me, though. The room was bright, airy, and just right.

"How much is it?" I asked. It turned out that the room was less than two hundred bucks a month. "Okay, great," I said. "I'll take it."

"Wonderful," said Lyle. "When do you want to move in?"

"Tomorrow."

The next day I met Stuart. A friendly guy prepping for a career in radio, he spent hours practicing voice-overs in a small room he appropriated as his recording booth. He and Lyle were friendly and supportive, but it was clear from the start that we were not going to be more than housemates. Our different enthusiasms and clashing personal styles were not likely to lead to a closer friendship. For one thing, they were a couple, and as had happened to me so many times before around couples, I felt completely redundant, as if my presence were unnecessary and might as well simply be erased.

One source of friction had to do with music. I liked to place my little cassette radio on the kitchen table, crank up the volume, and play soul music while I cooked. Meanwhile, Lyle was a classical violinist who often hosted other musicians practicing chamber music in the back bedroom. When I got the funk music going, Lyle's door usually slammed shut. One day, dressed in bedroom slippers and a navy-blue robe cinched at the waist, he slouched into the kitchen, where I stood at the stove.

"Can you cut that noise, please? I'm trying to rehearse!" Lyle said. I looked at him. Really, his posture was atrocious—his head hunched forward between raised shoulders like a turtle's, giving him the appearance of an old man in a young man's body.

"Okay, will do," I said with annoyance as I reached for the volume knob. Much as I loved my tunes, I had to admit that he was right and I was wrong. Not only was he the head roommate; he was also a professional musician. It shouldn't have surprised me that the stylings of Parliament/Funkadelic would be too wild for him, interrupting the silence he needed for his rehearsals.

After the radio incident, peace was restored. Mostly I held my own counsel in my large front room, which was lovelier than any place I had lived in Philadelphia. Unrolling the large ink rendering of Philly's Rodin Museum that I had produced in Bob Hanna's drawing class, I pinned it up over the bureau. Catita was especially pleased. She loved to sun herself in the open side window in one of the two bays. On more than one occasion, she jumped nonchalantly out one bay window and over to the next, flying directly over the sidewalk far below.

Unlike at Hanna/Olin, my work at Omi Lang designing a corporate campus for Chevron Oil on a one-hundred-acre suburban site was orderly and methodical, with plenty of people to execute it. It turned out that the firm was strictly hierarchical. Below the managing partners, George Omi and Willy Lang, a senior associate named Ricardo doled out our work assignments.

On my second morning at work, Ricardo said, "Brooks, we need a utility tsar."

"What's a utility tsar?" I asked.

"Well, what we need you to do is diagram all the underground utilities, coordinate them, and make sure they don't collide or surface in awkward locations. Can you imagine how terrible it would look if a manhole came up half in lawn and half in paving? We need to avoid that like the plague."

"Oh, so you want me to plot all the utilities?"

"Yes."

"So, how many of them are there?" I asked.

"Well," Ricardo said. "There's the storm drain lines, the sanitary sewers, the mechanical service, the electrical conduit, the domestic water supply, the fire department connections, the fire hydrants . . ."

The list went on and on, and I was already glazing over. "Okay," I said, knowing I didn't have a choice in the matter. Soon I was on the phone with mechanical engineers, plumbing engineers, electrical engineers, sewer engineers, and civil engineers. Until then, I had never known that there could be so many types of engineers, but with their help I managed to create a complex and colorful map on which all the underground utilities were superimposed, one over the other. I knew the exact depth of each one, as well as its horizontal alignment, making sure that none of them crashed into any of the others.

"This is not a Swiss watch!" Silvio Petrus cried into the phone one day. The venerable Swiss-born mechanical engineer was piqued by my latest inquiry about a series of pressurized pipes.

"Well, we want it to look as much like one as possible," I countered, realizing that the whole point of the exercise was faintly ridiculous. The goal was to limit the number of surface manholes and pinpoint the locations of fire hydrants, enclosing them in tasteful concrete walls. We were busily creating a giant, minimalist campus of matching red-brick buildings connected by identical tree-lined roads and surrounded by acres upon acres of lawns. Not only did the resulting landscape look boring, but it wasted amazing amounts of water in an arid region. All along I had been led to believe that I would be working on sexier projects like the Roosevelt Memorial and a new cultural campus for downtown San Francisco called Yerba Buena Center, but so far, those more desirable projects had not materialized.

Still, my new job had a big advantage: I didn't have to work nights, and due to our shortened work week, free Friday afternoons rolled out in front of me, offering wide horizons for outer and inner exploration in this often sunny, always spectacular city. After all those structured years on the academic and professional treadmill, I could finally take some time to discover myself. Basking in my hard-won freedom to promenade about town, in and out of gay clubs, I no longer had to worry that I'd be spotted by a work colleague, Penn classmate, or someone who knew my father.

20   THE I-BEAM

IN THOSE heady days of my new life, all the traffic lights turned green, promising me freedom and gay liberation. I had a brand-new, highly evocative city to explore, and its exceptional features—the wind-blown fog on the pastel-colored hills, the cable cars, the landmarks of Coit Tower, Twin Peaks, and the bold red Golden Gate Bridge—were all so much more exciting and cinematic than prosaic, flat, red-brick Philly.

In every neighborhood, gay men could be seen out walking singly or hand in hand. In North Beach and Russian Hill, I spotted a few here and there, but larger numbers joined the commercial river on Market Street. Even more flowed through Haight-Ashbury, and in the Castro, our numbers turned into a dense, rejoicing crowd. I felt a brotherhood I had never experienced before, a vague sense of belonging to a giant, multifaceted community of men.

It was January 1982, not even four years after America's most charismatic gay leader, Harvey Milk, had been assassinated along with Mayor George Moscone in City Hall. Although I had seen highlights of replacement mayor Dianne Feinstein's press conference about the murders before leaving Philadelphia, the news had seemed like no more than a far-off headline. Still a fresh, agonizing memory for gay men living in San Francisco at the time, the tragic hate crime felt to me like an event from the remote past.

Meanwhile, I had only the dimmest awareness of the freight train that was even then bearing down upon us, its cyclops-like front light no more than a distant dot on the horizon. I had heard hushed and vague snippets of conversation about a "gay cancer," but those rumors seemed scarcely more worrying than concerns about a bad flu season. I didn't realize that I was living in a sunny bubble in time between the violent horror of Dan White's murderous rampage and the dark killing fields of AIDS to come. All I knew was that, for the moment, gay liberation seemed to be winning the battle against hate, intolerance, and violence. The long, cinematic, candlelit protest marches down Market Street were now over, and a new time to party was at hand.

Every Friday, Saturday, and Sunday night were for going out. The first place I discovered was the I-Beam, a gay disco on Haight Street, only a block and a half from my apartment. The best time to go to the I-Beam was for Sunday tea dance. The place was rarely jumping on a Friday or Saturday—Sunday evening was its time in the sun.

Housed in an ordinary-looking wooden building, the I-Beam announced itself with a wide outer stair that led up to the second-floor entrance. Once inside, the club was like a gigantic version of Equus, except that it was all on one level and there was no dry ice fog on the dance floor. And it had one striking innovation: two large video screens above the dance floor played snips from the campiest Hollywood films in a continuous loop. Bar videos were a new feature that year, and it was not possible to visit the I-Beam without witnessing Joan Crawford glaring fiercely as Mildred Pierce or grimacing while wielding an axe in *Strait Jacket*.

The I-Beam boasted new eighties dance music, with a generous sprinkling of Euro-pop. I tolerated Tony Basil's "Hey Mickey," but the DJ played Laura Branigan's "Gloria" so relentlessly that I soon came to detest it. The Human League's "Don't You Want Me Baby" was my favorite song until "Tainted Love" debuted on the Top 40, and I never tired of its odd beat that mimicked the double beep of a streetcar. The colorful city, the vivid gay dance scene, and the heavily amped eighties soundtrack—I loved it all.

Having no friends in town yet, I always went to the I-Beam solo. When I heard a song I liked, which was pretty much every number apart from the histrionic "Gloria," I resumed my practice of trying to find a boyfriend by asking guys to dance. Dancing was an activity, and if a guy said no, technically his "no" referred only to the song, not to me, so it felt less rejecting than when someone brushed me off in a conversation. On the other hand, if he said "yes," most likely he enjoyed the song as much as I did, generating a tiny thread of common enthusiasm from which to weave a conversation.

Once the dancing started, I studied the guy's movements and facial expressions. If he smiled broadly, snapped his fingers, and threw his head back while he bopped, that meant he was having a good time, which was a win. It was even better if he reached over to grasp my waist, and it felt like a score if he grabbed my butt.

By contrast, sometimes the guy danced too well, which was a bad sign. It wasn't that I didn't admire good dancers—I very much did; I could spend hours watching their sexy moves—but I had learned that, if they were too showy, it meant their lives had no discernable meaning outside the nightclub. Never was this truer than when I clocked a guy watching himself dance, not only in the mirror, but via his stealthy habit of gauging the reaction in all the pairs of eyes tracking him on the floor while he assiduously ignored me.

Another unsuitable type was the exact opposite, the guy who appeared so immensely bored by the music that he was only going through the motions. If dancing to the hits made those men yawn, then most likely nothing else interested them either, which was not a good foundation on which to build a relationship. Regardless of whether it was unconscious or strategic, being blasé was an unappealing pose.

One Sunday night at the I-Beam, I met a guy who became my first new friend in San Francisco. Jesse was a husky African American with a tall flattop that he pulled straight up with the pick comb that lived in the back pocket of his jeans. He smiled and laughed easily, effortlessly expressing the joie de vivre that so appealed to me in men. When I asked him to dance, I was pleased to note that he was just the right type of dancer, the kind who danced enthusiastically but without trying to win a prize on *Soul Train*.

After a couple of dances, Jesse and I repaired to the side lounge, with its TV screens displaying the same campy videos that appeared on the dance floor. Once we were far enough away from the speakers to hear ourselves talk, he asked, "Have you ever been out to Sutro Heights?"

"No," I said.

"Come on, I'll show you," he continued, grabbing my hand in his large palm and leading me toward the front stairs.

"I don't have a car," I protested.

"Don't worry, I do," Jesse said, already halfway down the steps. The next thing I knew, we were heading west toward the ocean, headlights beaming under the night sky. When we reached the end of Geary Boulevard, Jesse turned right onto a narrow lane overlooking the Cliff House and Seal Rock.

"Follow me," he said. Jumping out of the car, he led me between a couple of tall bushes to a small, sandy spot on top of a high bluff overlooking the Pacific. The sky was black, the moon was full, and a corkscrew of white moonlight wriggled over the waves crashing below as Jesse began to kiss me. It was the most romantic moment I had ever experienced in my entire life, except for one small problem. I wanted to feel red hearts pouring out of my chest and into Jesse's face when he kissed me, while matching hearts emanated from his lips and flowed directly into my soul. Was it even possible for male-on-male encounters to rise to that highest standard of romantic love, the standard my grad school housemate, Birgyte, so adored on-screen between Elizabeth Taylor and Richard Burton? I very much hoped so, but I didn't really know.

Still, no matter how much I craved romance, and crave it I did, I wasn't feeling it with Jesse. Of course, that was no reason not to go to bed with him. Like the rest of my generation, I came prepared to obey Stephen Still's anthem urging listeners to love the one you're with if your true love is nowhere in sight. Plus, it was easy to rationalize. Who knew how many months would go by before I fell in love with someone new or before I could convince Chad to come live with me? I had felt those red hearts, Valentine's Day card emotions with him, but they hadn't been strong enough to prevent me from moving to San Francisco without him. Nor had we ever discussed our long-term commitment to one another. Were we each expecting the other to be faithful? I wasn't sure, but either way it seemed irrelevant from twenty-five hundred miles away.

Until that almost perfect moment with Jesse, I hadn't fully realized what a romantic I was. Sex was just sex, that's what all the guys implied by constantly switching partners on the dance floor, and even more so by quickly "doing it" with one man in the bushes, only to shove him aside and move on to the next. That was not what I wanted. I wanted chocolate, a dozen red roses, and deep, tender kisses. I wanted to resurrect the memories of Ken's caresses. I wanted his lips on my neck and the bristles of his goatee tickling my cheek. Most of all, I wanted to hear his soft whisperings again.

Although I didn't feel romance blossoming with Jesse, the experience of moving so rapidly from the exciting, noisy dance scene at the I-Beam to the serene beauty of moonlight over the Pacific taught me something important about San Francisco that was to reoccur to me many times over the years to come: San Francisco was the City of the Sacred and the Profane. It was a city where you could, in the space of only ten minutes, experience the profoundest beauty that nature has to offer—the sublime spirituality of the sun, the moon, the wind-blown ocean waves, and the lion-like flanks of the golden Marin hillsides—and in the next moment be swept up in the most hedonistic ecstasies of dance, Dionysian parties, and of course, sex.

As if to underscore that point one day a few weeks later, Jesse and I were tooling around the Richmond District, not far from Seal Rock, when he stopped at a small house to say hi to a white friend whom he had spotted outside washing his car. We got out of Jesse's Toyota Corolla to talk to him, and within seconds, the conversation turned to gay pickups.

"How many men have you been to bed with?" Jesse asked the guy, who was deeply tanned and beginning to display fans of tiny wrinkles at the corners of his eyes.

"Oh, I don't know," he said. "Thousands . . . it's been thousands."

"Really?" I asked, more to myself than to him. This was a huge eye-opener to me. People in high school had always said that I was hopelessly naive, and maybe this proved their point. Still, it was hard for me to imagine having sex with that many guys. Truthfully, I could scarcely imagine my count rising to one hundred, let alone a thousand.

Pondering this in some tiny corner of my brain, I remembered those hushed murmurs, the quiet whispers about a gay cancer spreading like wildfire through Manhattan. I took note, although I wasn't sure what to make of it. No rule book had been published for what was not yet called AIDS. All I knew was that, in the two years since I had come out of the closet, a whole secret and beautiful world had opened up for my exclusive pleasure. It was unbearable to think that it might be about to close again.

IN SAN Francisco, I was as free as the seagulls that swarmed the Embarcadero piers. The cords that bound me to Chad slackened more and more every day we were apart, and nobody had yet appeared who even slightly resembled Ken. Apart from my inhibitions, there was nothing preventing me from hitting the gay pickup scene in a big way.

On Friday and Saturday evenings, I invariably engaged in the ritual I had learned from Ken—trying on four or five faded T-shirts before settling on the right one. I never thought of myself as getting fierce—that was a higher calling that only hip guys like Ken could pull off—but I knew that if I at least *felt* cute, I might get lucky.

Still, I hesitated on many of those evenings, hand on the doorknob, before heading out to the Castro. Once again, I found myself struggling with my all-too-familiar anxiety of having a divided self, my lingering conviction that I was a stand-up professional and therefore not a slutty whore. On those occasions, I turned back into my room and observed myself critically in front of the mirror. Taking a deep breath as I approved my latest cruising outfit, I willfully banished the thought, told myself it was time to seize the night, and headed quickly out the door.

No matter when I arrived, the intersection of Castro and Market thrummed with the palpable excitement of thousands of young men coming alive after a week of office drudgery. Each and every one was ready to let loose, have fun, and hook up. The scene was even more electric under a full moon, which the revelers loved to point out. "Look, the moon is full!" they'd yell excitedly to one another, pointing at the silver orb as if predicting an orgy. Each young man's heart beat with the not-so-secret desire to meet Mister Right, although we were all horny enough that, by common agreement, Mister Almost-Right would do just fine.

Crossing Market Street, I headed down the sensuous incline of Castro to 18th—the beating heart of the gay village. On that corner stood the Elephant Walk, a convenient landmark and a great place to meet up with your friends. Down 18th to the left was the Midnight Sun, where all the guys stood packed inside like sardines, each neck bent backward to gaze at a multitude of TV screens mounted from the ceiling. I rarely went there because how could I hope for eye contact with a guy staring up at music videos?

Happily, two more suitable bars were located uphill on 18th: Badlands and the Pendulum. Badlands was an everyman's bar for an army called the Castro Clones, whose universal look paired a bushy, dark moustache and clean-shaven cleft chin with a flannel shirt and jeans, as if every one of them were the handsome, Olympic-gold-medalist swimmer Mark Spitz. Large and roomy inside, the wall behind the bar was packed to the ceiling with personalized vanity license plates from every state and Canadian province. Each one bore a tantalizing, coded gay phrase. One plate read CAL BEAR, meaning that the owner was a hirsute brute from California. Another said 4 SIR, meaning that the driver was the top in an S&M relationship, and his boy had generously bought him the car. It was an impressive, highly varied collection of double entendres, and I probably spent more time staring at the license plates than cruising the men.

Like most of the other bars, Badlands was where you went to pick up a Castro Clone. Although I loved its Eurotrash soundtrack, the joint was too white-bread for me. Invariably, the mostly white men at Badlands engaged in what everybody called standing and modeling. Adopting a posture of leaning against one of the walls while squinting abstractedly over my head at the opposite wall, they attempted to project allure by throwing attitude, but succeeded only in looking unattainable. Exactly how were you expected to cut through their insolence to talk to them?

Fortunately, across the street and a tad uphill, stood the Pendulum, whose large sign hung over the sidewalk. In black linework against a white background, it featured an abstract image of a pendulum in a clock, except that the clock face was missing. Consisting of a long and narrow vertical rectangle engaged with a small circle at its base, the logo cleverly doubled as a stylized phallus. The meaning was obvious: this was a place for swingers, although the swingers were not so much seesawing between women and men as they were men swinging between races.

As a white guy with an Ivy League education, someone on the beaten track to professional success, marriage to a white woman, and kids, I felt at least as subversive entering the Pendulum as I had when I first opened the door to Equus. Inside, the welcoming, diverse crowd was more or less evenly divided between Black and white men, though at times it was majority Black. There, I encountered little of the posing that I had learned to expect in the white bars, where so many men stood and preened, judging you by looking through you as if you were invisible.

Every time I visited the Pendulum, I soaked in the convivial atmosphere as if I were sunbathing on a beach towel. Many of the Black patrons were jolly extroverts, quick to laugh, joke, or sing along to Rick James, James Brown, Chaka Khan, or the white soul singer Teena Marie, whose nickname was Vanilla Choc. There was always a party in progress, so refreshingly unlike the buttoned-up intellectual atmosphere of my upbringing or the alienating atmosphere at Badlands.

One night at the Pendulum, while standing in my usual cruising position, my back to the wall, I met my second new friend in San Francisco, a short and roly-poly young Black man named Jimmy. Well educated both at college and at an integrated high school in Ohio, Jimmy had a dazzling smile and an almost hysterical laugh. When he first caught my eye, he came right up to me.

"Are you Predator or are you Prey?" he asked in a breathless voice, capitalizing the terms as if they were allegorical figures. This, of all things, was his campy opening line. A naughty smile crept from the side of his mouth as he placed one hand on his hip, teapot style, awaiting my reply.

"Um, I guess I don't know?" I said, which prompted more laughter from Jimmy, the sly, worldly note in his chuckle climbing all the way up the harmonic scale to unabashed wickedness. Truthfully, his question had never occurred to me. Was it really as simple as that? Was the queer world neatly divided into tops and bottoms—predators and prey? The campy question amused, titillated, and confused me all at once, but it didn't help me understand who I was or what I wanted to project to the world.

You're overthinking it, Brooks, I said to myself. *Just relax and go with the flow. Why is it so hard for you to just take things as they come and have fun with it?*

After that unforgettable opener, Jimmy and I wasted little time before jumping into bed, but as with Jesse, I was immediately aware that I was not going to fall in love with him. One bright Sunday morning we were strolling through trendy Noe Valley, the neighborhood on the hilltop above the Castro, looking for a place to have brunch, when we spied another interracial gay couple walking down the opposite side of the street. Recognizing both of them from the bars, my eyes drilled a hole into the Black guy. Both men halted on the spot to flirt back.

"Do you want to *trade*?" Jimmy asked histrionically, gazing up at me.

"Of course not," I said, but I was covering up because I had already started fantasizing about the guy. Ashamed to be caught in such a brazen act, I turned all shades of red, so I was relieved when Jimmy started laughing again, as amused as ever. We both knew that, much as we liked each other, Romeo and Romeo we were not. Instead, I was a kid in a candy store, just beginning to flex my newfound cruising muscles.

Over the next couple of years, I scored with more than a few men at the Pendulum, usually bringing them home to 1763 Page Street, but occasionally going to their place. While one-night stands were not, deep down, what I craved—I still yearned for real, long-term love—the excitement of the game gradually became so enticing that I nearly forgot why I was playing it.

Although my cruising skills were improving, my come-on lines were still amateurish.

"Hi, I'm Brooks," I said one night to an especially handsome young man.

"I'm Mickey," he said, his face opening into a broad smile.

"What do you do for work?"

This was a holdover from my college years, when on meeting one another for the first time, students would invariably ask, "What's your major?"

"I work for PG&E," Mickey said, referring to Pacific Gas and Electric.

I was lucky that he had answered the question openly, because I often received a frown or a puzzled expression when I asked men at the Pendulum about their work. Many were guys whose jobs meant little to them, and I had to remind myself that, for as long as I could remember, I had wanted to move outside my ivory tower to socialize with a diverse group of people.

"Wanna come to my place?" I asked. "I share a nice flat in the Haight."

"Sure," Mickey said, squeezing my thigh and moving in for a kiss. When we arrived at Page Street, we had climbed only a few of the endless steps up to the flat when Mickey grabbed me from above and began kissing me passionately. In no time, he was unbuttoning my 501s, and I was rock-hard. What made it so hot was his impatience to have me before we even made it up to my room. His haste left no time to doubt that he wanted me. No way did I have to beg for it, and for once, I was the prey.

The true answer to Jimmy's pickup question, I later began to realize, was that I was a top by expedience because I was actually natural prey—a bottom who had waited too long to be preyed upon. Normally, I hit on guys because I was too impatient to wait passively for someone to hit on me. I found it was easy to score with the guys at the Pendulum, but rare were the occasions when, as with Mickey, one of them expressed such an urgent need for me. When that did happen, I was in heaven, but I had learned not to expect it.

On another evening, I met a debonair Black man named Matt.

"Why don't you join me for dinner at the Neon Chicken?" he asked, referring to the well-known, elegant gay restaurant just a few doors down the street from the Midnight Sun. In his navy blazer and slacks, Matt looked sharp and fit.

"I've only been in San Francisco for a couple of months," I said, once we were seated at our candlelit table, "but I already love it."

"Oh, let me tell you about all the great clubs!" Matt said, with relish, and he proceeded to map out all the gay clubs and venues in the entire city for my exclusive enjoyment, as if he were my personal tour guide to our giant but semisecret underworld.

Matt seemed to be everything I was looking for in a man: self-confident, sophisticated, and worldly. So far, it looked like he was that mythical, mystical Mister Right, my number ten, but when I tried to phone him over the next few days, he never picked up. Finally, I reached him, but when I suggested another date, he replied almost caustically, "I've shown you everything there is to know, and now it's all on you. You're on your own."

Having delivered that Delphic oration, he hung up as abruptly as he had deftly rolled out the charm a few nights earlier. I felt a lump in my throat and began to cry. What had I done to deserve this put-down, and why did he think our date was about nothing more than him showing me the ropes? Most of all, why did so many of my encounters have to end in sadness? In my rush to seize Matt and hand him the trophy of Mister Right, it had never occurred to me that, for him, I might have been just a stopgap, someone to hang out and kill time with until *his* Mister Right came along.

Whatever the case, I was so crushed that I confided in my roommates, Lyle and Stuart.

"What's the matter?" they asked in chorus, seeing how glum I looked after getting off the phone.

"So, I went on a hot date a few nights ago with this guy named Matt. He acted like he wanted to show me around town, and now he doesn't want to have anything to do with me," I blurted, bursting into tears.

"Shh, Brooks, it's okay," Lyle said, embracing me in a big hug. "It's unfortunate and regrettable that things like that happen but you shouldn't let it get you down."

It took a few days, but with their sound advice, I recovered, ready to prowl for the next hot guy.

Many more one-night stands later, I came to understand something essential: the hunt was more exciting than the consummation. The real climax occurred not with orgasm but with a guy's infinitely sexy nod "yes," when I suggested we grab a cab home from the Pendulum. After a number of those cab rides, I finally realized that my obsession was more of an addiction to the momentary high of being *chosen*, of being singled out as sexy and desirable, than to the sex itself. I still wanted so much to find a long-term relationship, but if I was being honest with myself, I could no longer deny that I relished the chase for its own sake.

Ruminating on this conflict between my lust and my romantic disposition, I was determined not to forget that I still had a boyfriend in Philadelphia—or was he already an ex-boyfriend? I wasn't sure, but I kept telling myself that I wasn't ready to give up on a future with Chad. At least two or three times a week, I faithfully phoned him after 8:00 p.m., when the rates went down. At first, our calls were full of enthusiasm and spontaneity, but as our weeks of separation lengthened into months, they declined into a strained ritual, a well-worn and repetitive script in which I left out more and more details of my personal life. I knew I was playing it both ways, leading Chad on while cruising as much as I dared, but I didn't know how to stop. I had never ceased loving him, but I felt disconnected from him, and we were inevitably growing apart.

In San Francisco, the cruising never stopped. That's what the parks were for—Golden Gate Park and, especially, hilly, foggy Buena Vista Park. At any hour, it seemed as if almost every Monterey cypress in its majestic groves concealed at least one guy on the make. Although I sometimes fantasized about surprising a hot guy behind a tree, I could never get beyond the idea that anonymous sex was sordid. Before having sex, I felt that it was important to make an introduction, exchange names, and acquire at least a vague idea of what a guy's life was about. My faltering inner compass reminded me that I was romantically inclined, and my obsessive cruising was just a temporary game. It was the means to achieving a particular and preordained end: the longer, less addictive high of long-term love. That was what I really coveted.

The ubiquitous temptation of anonymous sex underscored my growing awareness that San Francisco's libertine, all-accepting spirit forced every young queer man and woman to construct his or her own personal moral code from whole cloth. That was because we categorically refused to cede any Mormon, Baptist, or Catholic Church the power to dictate one for us. They had aggressively done as much as they could to cast us out of the fold, and we militantly rejected them right back.

By extension, I realized, it was equally incumbent on me not to judge others for their differing moral standards. Just because I was a romantic didn't mean I had the right to judge men who wanted anonymous sex. I remembered the guy washing his car who said he had been with thousands of men. My first reaction had been to think, *How could you? How could you be such a slut?* Part of me still felt that way, but I blamed myself for it. Assuming that I had the right to judge him meant I was no better than the homophobes who condemned me for being attracted to men in the first place, regardless of how many guys I went to bed with.

But a more fundamental conflict than the straightforward struggle between lust and romance was running in the background like an unseen computer program or a muffled drumbeat. The zeitgeist of queer San Francisco in that period elevated promiscuity to a place on a sort of altar. The knowledge we all had that mainstream society, with its complacent, self-satisfied churches, had condemned us, had declared us to be perverts, made the crowds of gay men in the Castro thumb their collective noses at our hetero overlords. What better way was there to do that than to dismiss our straight brothers as mere breeders?

They—the churches and society at-large—insisted that we were different and undesirable. Since they went to such great lengths to ostracize us, we would *claim* our difference. The best way to do that was to reject marriage as no more than a hetero norm having nothing to do with us. Along with turning our back on marriage, we would reject having kids. And if we were going to reject breeders and marriage, why restrict ourselves to monogamy? What was the point? No, we were a different breed, a tribe that rejoiced in the diverse flavors of all the men any one of us could seduce in a lifetime.

That was the Castro zeitgeist, but I was confused. I didn't know what it had to do with me or my romantic dreams of finding Mister Right. Did it mean they were simply illusions? That I could never find true love? It didn't occur to me that this iconoclastic vision of gay liberation would, within a few years, give way to the long political struggle for gay marriage. Decades later, when gay couples started adopting children or having children of their own, I was even more surprised. When that happened, my dreams were unexpectedly vindicated: I was not the only gay man who questioned the activists' negative view of those hetero norms of monogamy, marriage, and family, after all. Nor was I presumably the only one who questioned using our defiance to justify sleeping around more than any of us really needed to.

My first six months in San Francisco went by in a flash, and when the end of June arrived, it was time for the Gay Freedom Day Parade, which Pride was then still called. There was a new electricity in the air, a heady feeling as every gay man and lesbian made plans to meet up with friends and celebrate. I donned my black leather bar vest and a black cowboy hat and smiled at myself in the mirror. This time I was not going to miss a perfect opportunity to make up for my earlier failure to wear my cowboy gear with pride.

Once properly attired, I set out on foot to Castro and Market. When I arrived at Market Street, battalions of young revelers were already flooding up Castro, rounding the corner and flowing downtown in a giant river. At that moment, I encountered an entire troop of Brownies heading for one of the vintage street cars that plied a slow route downtown. I squinted at them, thinking I was seeing things. These were not little girls; they were all grown men in wigs and lipstick, dressed in matching Brownie uniforms with red bandannas around their necks. Joking and blowing kisses at the crowd, their joy was so infectious that I couldn't help following them onto the streetcar, where I leaned on a post and laughed at their antics all the way to Montgomery Street.

My first Pride did not disappoint. The waves and waves of young people lining both sides of Market Street astonished me. Only a few years earlier, I had honestly believed that there were just a handful of homosexuals in the world. Nothing had prepared me for the *armies* of young men and women sitting, standing, and filling every available square foot of space. Harvey Milk had exhorted us to come out, and come out we did. What a joy there was in our huge numbers!

Suddenly, the crowd yelled in response to the distant rumble of dozens of motorcycles, and in a flash, the Dykes on Bikes roared past in intricate figure eights, Pride flags waving. Later, I was awestruck by the high-stepping African American male baton twirlers in shorts with rainbow fringes that shone like tinsel. I had never seen anyone drum and twirl with so much rhythm and pride!

Several hours later, the last float in the parade turned up Market Street. It was the I-Beam truck, playing all the dance hits. As it swept along, heading back toward Castro, the crowd poured onto the street, merging into a giant wake behind it, and I joined a sea of young, queer men and women dancing our way up to the Civic Center, where the rallies were held.

I knew my freedom depended on our leaders, the young men and women who were brave enough to stand tall on a makeshift stage, challenging our homophobic enemies with their bullhorns. Their solidarity boycotting Florida orange juice to protest Anita Bryant's hateful rhetoric and their refusal to let Harvey Milk's assassination stop us from advancing our rights in the state legislature were inspirational. But standing still to listen to their reverberating exhortations after dancing in the streets? That was too much of a mood-killer. My first Pride had exceeded all my expectations, and now I was ready to party. Delighting in my euphoria, I had no reason to expect that the time to party was not destined to last.

ONE NIGHT in the Castro, I met a ruggedly handsome African American man and quickly fell into his orbit. Dan loved to unwind with a bottle of wine, a good joint, and mellow music, savoring the ambiance and laughing at the exploits of his two roommates, who were both at least as sexy as he was. Being with him felt completely different than being with Chad. Where Chad was boyish and fun-loving, Dan was wise and mature; he was all man. I could sidle up to him and feel like he was in charge, as if he were my protector, and it was a sensation I had never experienced before. Although in bed we were "versatile," in our relationship he was every bit the top, and I couldn't help but enjoy that.

After we had gone out a couple of times, Dan unexpectedly asked, "Wanna go to the Russian River?" I had never been to the consummate gay resort in the woods less than two hours north of San Francisco, but I had heard enough about it to pique my curiosity.

"Yes," I said. "When do you want to go?"

"I'll pick you up in the morning," he replied.

Dan loved German cars, so I shouldn't have been surprised when he pulled up in a classic Mercedes Benz 280 SE coupe, painted a gleaming shade of burgundy.

"My friend Kat lent it to me," he explained, as I jumped into the caramel leather passenger seat, with its wide, rounded pleats.

We immediately took off for the Golden Gate Bridge, and on the drive up Highway 101, the Mercedes's powerful engine hummed contentedly while we talked and laughed. I liked Dan a lot, but I was falling in love with the car.

"We *so deserve* this," Dan kept saying, referring to the good time that was in store for us. I was quick to agree, although truthfully I wasn't sure if I had done anything to merit celebrating. In my straightlaced universe, pleasure was doled out in small capsules as a reward for some laudatory academic or professional achievement, and at the moment I couldn't find anything on my report card to boast about.

Just north of Santa Rosa, we exited onto River Road. Soon the parched, flat fields gave way to scenic vineyards, and the topography began undulating. Somewhere between the tiny hamlet of Hacienda and the Korbel Champagne winery, where the vineyards dissolved into isolated clumps and then large groves of redwoods, Dan pulled a joint from his pocket and lit it.

"We deserve this too," he said, taking a hit and passing it to me.

I inhaled deeply, and within minutes I was as high as I had ever been. *I so deserve this*, I repeated to myself. Who was I to dispute it? Why did I have to make pleasure contingent on some concrete achievement? Wasn't I just being uptight? We were both blessed to be young, healthy, and alive on God's sunny earth. Wasn't our gratitude for that sufficient reason to embrace pleasure and celebrate? *Of course it is*, I said to myself. *Of course it is!*

Music was playing on the car's recently renovated sound system: a cassette of my new favorite album, which Dan had introduced me to, Quincy Jones's *The Dude*. As the ecstatic choruses of the song "Ai No Corrida" washed over me with the enhanced hearing that comes only from smoking weed, I glanced at the steering wheel, with its iconic, three-pointed star in the center. Behind the wheel, the speedometer glowed under a flattened dome of faux leather that swept up from the dashboard. Unlike the usual dial gauges, it took the form of a vertical red line that rose as the speed increased. Dan put his foot on the gas, the red thermometer climbed, Quincy Jones's jazzy soul music flooded my ears, and I was in heaven. *I so deserve this,* I thought again, and this time the weed left no room for doubt. I wanted Dan to drive faster and faster until the red line climbed through its vinyl roof and up into the sky, but he was slowing down and turning off the road.

"Time for our picnic," he explained. We had reached the romantically named village of Rio Nido, in the heart of Russian River country, and we both already had the munchies. Dan maneuvered the Mercedes off the blacktop onto a gravel road that soon petered out into a grassy parking area. I had no idea how he had found this place, nor had I noticed where he had turned off the road.

"Here's a good spot," he said. "It's the nude cruising area."

The nude cruising area, I said to myself. How could this be? I knew there were plenty of cruising areas in the San Francisco parks, but it had never occurred to me that there would be one of them up here in actual *nature.*

Before I could analyze it too thoroughly, I gazed out the windshield at the perfect bucolic scene under the cloudless California sky. Tall grass stretched in its fresh, spring-green phase, low-slung grape vines crept here and there, noble, dark-green redwoods marched around, and the hazy outline of distant hills filled the background. It was a distinctly western landscape, hinting at ruggedness, but with a pinch of the tamed, sensual quality of Tuscany.

There was not a building in sight, and as I adjusted to the scene moment by moment, the way we do when we're stoned, my eye caught something moving. What was it? I focused on the source of movement and then, *Bam*, suddenly a naked young man appeared in my line of sight, far enough away that I almost inadvertently reached for binoculars. Slim and well-muscled, he was certainly appealing.

Then, what was that off to the left? Oh my God, it's another naked man. One after another they appeared, each beautiful young man moving slowly and languidly, some from left to right, and others from right to left, as if onstage under God's blue sky. I felt like I was a tourist in a Land Rover in the Serengeti, watching exotic, sexy animals on safari. How I wanted to run after them, but I was horrified that I might actually do so. Fortunately, Dan reached over at that exact moment, planted a big wet kiss on my lips, and saved me from myself.

I don't remember anything about our lunch.

Sometime later, we made it to the resort town of Guerneville, where we pulled up at the Willows, a picturesque, gay inn nestled on the riverbank under dark redwood groves. I loved its dusty, old-lodge character, its dark wall paneling, and its large living room full of overstuffed wood armchairs arranged around a massive fireplace built of giant tumbled rocks from the river. The nostalgic quality of the place was thick enough that it could have been bottled and labeled Rustic Inn. This, too, was something we deserved, I reflected—to be accepted unquestioningly as a Black and white gay couple, fully entitled to the resort's hospitality.

After dropping off our bags, Dan and I walked down the road toward the center of town. Passing a scenic, girder-framed bridge over the river, we arrived at the main street, which served up a tidy and pleasant line of shops. These included a small bookshop and the sort of manly general store that I suppose every American small town used to have. It dispensed camping gear and fishing rods, lures and Weber grills—just the sort of thing any visitor to this resort country would want, except that all the gays made a beeline for the flannel shirts, each of us jockeying to look more butch than the next. We basically ignored all the other offerings, which, to our eyes, were mere props in a play, amounting to nothing more than pure atmosphere.

Once Dan and I passed the long line of shops, the redwood trees began again in earnest, and River Road wound on, eventually to reach the coast. Let's stop right there, though, because the most famous and fabulous of all the gay resorts stood on this spot, nestled in the redwoods just beyond the shops. Although officially named Fifes, naturally all the queens called it Fifi's, referring to the most famous of French maids, not to mention an entire flotilla of moppy-haired, four-legged little French bitches. Fifi's had a full bar and a restaurant, and we enjoyed a good margarita while we watched the last rays of the sun reflecting on the river, silhouetting the deep forest on the opposite bank.

Over our drinks, Dan gestured outside toward the rest of the resort. Off to one side of the bar was a swimming pool, lit to a warm, glowing blue by submerged lights, and arranged around the pool were little log cabins in the woods. Just beyond the pool and its cabins was a larger log cabin called Drums. (Get it? Fifes and Drums, bitch!) The sun went down, the night was young, and Fifes came alive. In a flash, a relentless *boom boom boom* of amped-up bass cranked up from inside Drums, signifying that the DJ was at his station. At this siren call, the doors of all the cabins flew open, and gaggles of scantily clad gay men rushed out as if on cue. All of them flocked to the disco except that, first, a big splash went up as one or two men pushed their buddies into the pool with butch, Boy Scouts–style affection.

Much as I loved disco dancing, for once this hedonistic scene repelled me. Not only did I like a little melody with my bass rhythm, but I had dreamed of coming up to the country to relax, not to party until dawn. All the noise and revelry seemed like an affront to the lovely peacefulness of the redwood groves. It dawned on me that this was the first time since coming out that I felt alienated from the gay party scene. Until that moment, it had not revealed its essential shallowness to me. I took a deep breath and sighed. Did being gay always have to be about dancing and partying? Couldn't it ever be about making love at a leisurely pace, a soulful slow jam?

Suddenly, I remembered something my father had told me in private years before, when I was going through puberty. He had summoned me to his window-walled studio on the third floor of our Modernist house, where I assumed that he was going to tell me about the birds and the bees.

Instead, Dad unexpectedly said, "Brooks, the love between a man and a woman is a sacrament. Cheating ruptures love; it's like polluting a sacred stream. Don't do it."

I have no memory of my reply. In my adolescent embarrassment, I must have just nodded and cringed.

Now, not only did I very much hope that Dad could look upon the love between a man and a man as equally sacred, but I knew in my heart that, however intoxicating I found the chase,

I wanted above all to meet Mister Right and settle down. While my incessant cruising could appear mindless, it had a clear goal. I wanted to prove the homophobes wrong. I wanted to overturn their unspoken contention that queer love was at worst meaningless and at best insignificant or unenduring. What I cared more about than anything else was finding a man whose passion and commitment would demonstrate that the love between a man and a man could be as meaningful and deep as that between a man and a woman.

"Dan," I said, "I'm not in the mood to dance in the middle of the woods. Can't we just go back to the Willows and snuggle?" I looked at him, worried that he would be irritated because I was the only man in the whole resort with those misgivings.

"Sure," he said, ever the perfect gentleman. "Let's go."

We returned to the welcome firelight of the Willows, where snuggle we did. I was so grateful to him for that. *I'm not sure whether or not he's Mister Right*, I thought, as I drifted off to sleep, *but he's definitely Mister Almost Right.*

In the coming days, Dan and I continued to spend most every night together, either at his place or at mine. Sometimes our relationship glowed bright and passionate, but at other times Dan retreated into himself, becoming taciturn and aloof. Ruminating on this painful reality, it occurred to me that the gay male condition—or maybe just the plain old male condition —presents an unresolvable paradox. Lust inevitably leads us to hope for some sort of connection with its latest object. When we confirm that the connection is undeniably there, we long for it to blossom into an affair of the heart, but when the affair matures into a true relationship, we grow complacent, and, consciously or unconsciously, we hunger for the enticement of the old free-floating lust. Never satisfied, we fall into an endless whirlpool of lust and love, love and lust.

Perhaps this circularity explained my growing ambivalence to the still-absent Chad. Either way, it appeared to shed light on why the more intimate Dan became during an evening, drawing me close, the more forcefully he would retreat early the next morning, dressing quickly and wordlessly to go off to work. Watching him run out the door without so much as a glance back at me left me almost as empty inside as I had felt after all my one-night stands.

This push-pull was already tugging at my heart when, a few weeks into our affair, Dan announced that he had been accepted into the MBA program at MIT and was moving to Boston. I felt my sails furling, knowing that he would soon depart for the other coast, the one I had just left, abandoning me to the loneliness of being single again. Still, I reprimanded myself. Hadn't I done exactly the same thing to Chad? Of course, there was an important difference: Dan never invited me to accompany him across the country, whereas I had enthusiastically extended that invitation to Chad.

A REUNION WITH CHAD

AFTER TEN long months, I finally convinced Chad to join me in San Francisco. But now that his arrival was imminent, I came close to panicking. Part of me wasn't ready to give up the intoxicating singles scene, even though I knew full well that its pleasures were ephemeral and hollow. The other part, the part of me that still longed for Chad, made me nervous. He and I had never had a conversation about whether we expected one another to be faithful during our long separation, but I assumed we had made a tacit agreement that, just as we had been monogamous in Philly, we would once again be monogamous in California. Now that we were about to be reunited, how could I possibly hide from him the signs of the promiscuous life I had led for nearly a year? That was the problem, and the clues were imprinted on my heart. What if we ran into one of my tricks? What would I tell Chad? Never a good liar, I doubted that I could avoid slipping up and revealing my all-too-recent enthusiasm for cruising.

With a mixture of excitement and trepidation, I took the Super Shuttle out to the airport to meet Chad at the gate. When he stepped off the jetway, his smile lit up his face and he batted his eyelashes with his usual panache.

"Is that mah baybe?" he gushed, opening his arms in a wide embrace. Although I rushed to hug and kiss him enthusiastically, something about our reunion felt false, off-balance.

"Welcome to San Francisco," I remember saying. "Your troubles are over!"

Why would I say such an inane thing? Partly, I was still in my honeymoon phase with the Bay Area, and there was nothing about San Francisco that did not delight me. Another part was that, remembering the bitter cold of Philadelphia's winters and the unbearable humidity of its summers, I wanted Chad to delight in the balmy weather of his new home. But there was a third factor: San Francisco was so liberal, so accepting of gay men, that I naively assumed it would be equally free of the racism Chad had experienced in Philadelphia. My asshole landlord had refused to lease my apartment to him. Surely that would never happen in San Francisco!

After collecting his bags, I conducted Chad on a tour of San Francisco's greatest sights while assiduously avoiding the Pendulum. Over the next few weeks, we gave the project of living together our best shot. He had little trouble landing a secretarial job at Chevron's downtown headquarters, but not long after his arrival, he came down with Hepatitis A. It didn't occur to me to stop and ask him how, or why, he had contracted it. In those days, gay men were always coming down with one disease or another. I myself had recently recovered from a bout with mononucleosis. If he had caught it from a lover, I had no right to ask, having myself been with so many men in his absence.

When Chad got sick, I was working long hours at Omi Lang, still plotting those intersecting underground utilities, which meant that every day I had to leave him jaundiced and bedridden in the apartment. Was I treating him with the same indifference that Dan had shown me on those mornings when he left for work? I hoped not; that was not my intention. Fortunately, I had brought my portable TV from Philadelphia, which helped Chad pass the time, but being the extrovert he was, it must have been doubly painful for him to be confined to the apartment with no friends of his own.

One day, when I came home with Chinese takeout, Chad said, "I'm getting the cold shoulder from Lyle. He barely speaks to me."

"What? That's terrible," I said.

"I don't think he wants me around."

"Are you sure? I thought he welcomed you."

"No, it's pretty clear he doesn't like Black people."

Lyle's racist attitude shocked me because I had blithely assumed that he treated everybody fairly and equally, just as he had always treated me, despite our tiff over my radio. Still, there was no point in trying to get Lyle to make friends with Chad.

"Okay, I'm sorry to hear that," I said. "Let's look for a place of our own!"

Chad nodded, and I hugged him. Consulting the want ads, we found a newly renovated place high above the corner of Castro and Market, on 17th Street. Inside lay a symphony in beige: beige walls and brand-new, beige, wall-to-wall carpet with a pleasant new carpet smell. What saved it from unbearable blandness was that sunlight flooded in from windows on three sides. I loved to gaze out the living-room window at the enticing Castro scene: the butter cream confection of the Castro Theater held down the foreground, while Monterey cypress trees climbed the hill to Noe Valley. The effect was like a Wayne Thiebaud streetscape chopped into horizontal bands by the half-open blades of our stylish new Levolor blinds. Now that Chad had recovered fully from his illness, it was the perfect pad from which to launch a fresh start.

When the holidays arrived, Omi Lang threw a Christmas party, and we were encouraged to bring our husbands, wives, or significant others. All my colleagues accepted Chad unquestioningly, which was a definite win, especially as I had always kept him hidden in Philly. Then came the party's climax: a Secret Santa gift exchange, in which we all drew playing cards to determine which gift we would take home. When Chad's turn came, the card he drew was the queen of spades. I quickly inhaled and held my breath, worried that the card's racist and homophobic double entendre would humiliate him, but he reacted with aplomb, laughing heartily, and holding the card up high, the better for all to see. I exhaled with relief, impressed by his unruffled poise.

"You handled that really well," I said, when the party was over. "How *are* you?"

"Aww, it was kind of funny," he said, with another little chuckle. It was hard, if not impossible, to embarrass him, as self-confident as he was.

Chad liked to jog, and sometimes I joined him. One evening, we took off uphill on 17th. At the summit, we turned right onto Clayton Street and ran downhill toward the Haight.

Night fell, and as we made a circuit of the Panhandle, I said to him, "It's so nice having you running by my side." I really meant it—I very much liked having him as my boyfriend, despite the demonic temptations that kept urging me to sneak another visit to the Pendulum.

"Is you is, or is you ain't . . . mah baby?" he responded, with a chuckle, not breaking his stride.

As we turned off the Panhandle for the grueling return climb back up Clayton, I smiled inwardly at this beam of sunshine. It was perhaps the closest moment we had shared outside the sheets since he had moved to San Francisco.

Shortly afterward, our troubles began. When I said something that Chad disagreed with, he waved his hands in protest, drowning out my voice with his classic exclamation, "Aaahh, Aauuugh!" Not a scream, exactly, it was more like a roar, the roar of Leo the Lion, his astrological sign. How could I fight fairly with a guy who merely covered his ears with his hands and drowned me out in a wall of noise? The result was that I never knew why he disagreed or what exactly he objected to. Maybe the simplest explanation was that we were both used to living alone and unaccustomed to our new roles as partners.

We also had a basic incompatibility that I had scarcely been aware of. Although I had never seen him put on a wig and lipstick, Chad could have been a hit as a drag performer. He hardly needed eyeliner. At Chevron, he had a female secretary buddy whose impish sense of humor rivaled his own. Enlisting her as his comedy partner during one lunch hour, he related how he had proceeded to run laps around a conference table, arms in the air, fingernails raised to the ceiling, yelling, "Help! Help! Sexual harassment! Sexual harassment!"

"I'm gonna getcha!" cried his workmate, chasing him in hot pursuit.

Meanwhile, in a city full of hot guys in motorcycle jackets, boots, and jeans, I had discovered that I had a leather fetish. One day I spotted the *Castro Times* in a bar. On its glossy cover, a full-page photo flaunted the sexiest male image I had ever seen. A shirtless, young Black guy in a leather jockstrap leaned back against a wall, pelvis thrust forward. A motorcycle cap with a shiny visor was pulled down low over his eyes. He wore a black leather chest harness with stainless steel rings and clutched a leather motorcycle jacket between his thumb and forefinger, casually draping it over one shoulder. This was the precise image of my Number Ten, the guy I most wanted.

That night, I brought Chad a gift.

"What's this?" he asked, ripping open the plain cardboard box. "I hope you don't expect me to wear it in bed," he said disdainfully, holding up the beautiful black leather jockstrap I had bought him.

"But you'd look so hot in it," I said hopefully.

"Nope," Chad said, closing the lid as firmly as Dad had boxed up my childhood cowboy outfit, spiriting it away to an upper shelf in a neglected closet.

If we had been more creative or adaptable, like so many experimental San Francisco couples I was hearing about, maybe we could have managed to bridge the fetish gap between drag and leather, but unfortunately we were not equipped with that kind of maturity or wisdom.

Chad also had a jealous streak. We were living in the Castro, and we could not avoid flirting with other guys even if we tried. The temptations came fast and furious. On Friday nights, we often walked to a little Middle Eastern bistro called La Méditerranée, just down Market Street at Noe. Traversing the one long block from Castro Street to the restaurant felt like crossing a minefield of flirtatious glances, multiple pairs of eyes sweeping our faces from all directions. I congratulated myself for controlling my desires as well as could be expected, but Chad didn't share my assessment. When he caught me looking at someone, he angrily pulled me away.

"Keep your eyes to yourself. You don't have to drill them into that guy with the leather vest!"

"I wasn't looking at him!" I lied.

I suppose that, had we been more evolved, we could have discussed the matter, and reassured one another that looking was not cheating. Either that or we might have arranged to have an open relationship, which was one of the thorny solutions that San Francisco's hypersexual scene threw out to gay couples, like a bone to a dog. In a city where everything goes, where there was no universally accepted moral code, we might have plumbed our hearts and tapped our creativity to fashion an unconventional relationship tailored precisely to our unique personal needs. Instead, we merely bickered, failing to reassure one another or to make either of us feel secure in the other one's arms. Deep down, it always felt as if we were each trying the other one on for size, never quite sure if we were a proper fit.

One night, Chad said, "Let's go dancing at the I-Beam."

"Sure," I said, always enjoying my disco nights.

When we got there, I headed for the dance floor, but Chad grabbed me by the arm, holding me back.

"Wait a minute," he said, as we stood in the slightly quieter video room. He pulled a little plastic-wrapped package out of his back pocket and held it up to me. "Here, take a hit of crystal," he said, dabbing his finger into the white powder and touching my nostril with it.

"Okay," I said compliantly, snorting deeply. Chad then took my hand and led me to the dance floor, where he wrapped an arm around my shoulder and pulled me toward him. "Hey, bo-fre," he said, opening his eyes as wide as they would go and batting his famous lashes.

"Hey, back," I said, kissing him, and we began to dance. The music sounded more vivid than usual, and all at once I found myself surfing a tall wave of energy. I danced faster and faster, making ever more wild gyrations. Never had I enjoyed dancing so much and never had Sylvester's high-energy beats, his sensual, gospel-inflected voice, sounded more heartbreakingly beautiful. Chad was beautiful, I was beautiful, and life was amazing. I wanted to grab onto it and never let go.

When we got home, though, kaleidoscopic visions swirled through my head at an unbearably rapid clip. Chad quickly fell asleep, but my brain was still a giddy merry-go-round. Sleep eluded me until the early hours of the morning, and since I often suffered from insomnia, I swore to myself that I would never take crystal again. Meanwhile, Chad was eager to try it again and again, which worried me. I didn't know how to dissuade him, but I didn't want to live with a meth addict.

Then, one Friday night, he and I went out to dinner at Letitia's, a stylish Mexican restaurant on Market near Church, which was popular with the Castro Clones.

We had just clinked our margarita glasses when Chad unexpectedly said, "Brooks, I'm leaving you."

"What?" I asked, not sure if I had heard him right.

"I'm breaking up with you. You and I—it's over."

Having delivered this pronouncement, he lowered his beautiful eyelids and stared at his plate before looking up again, ready to gauge my reaction. Despite all the warning signs leading up to this moment, I felt like he had dropped a bowling ball into my lap.

"You can't be serious," I said. I had just dug into my chicken enchilada, and now I lowered my fork to the table.

"Yes, I am."

"But why? What's wrong?"

"It's time you learned how it feels when your lover leaves you," he said, as if he were a strict parent or a municipal court judge intent on teaching me a lesson.

"What? Why?" I asked. This was yet another curveball, and so far he had given me no concrete reason for why he wanted to break up with me.

"It's happened to me before, more than once," he said cryptically. "It happens to all of us. And now it's your turn."

I looked across the table at him, and in that moment his expressive face appeared more handsome than ever before. Was I a masochist? Did I really think he was more beautiful because of the seismic fault of pain I felt cracking open inside me?

"So, that's the reason, and there's really no other? It's not because of something I did?"

But Chad just nodded, waving his hand dismissively, as if to suggest that the conversation was over. I suppose I should not have been surprised, since he always played a secret hand, holding his emotions to his chest like so many poker cards. After all, he had left me hanging for months when I had invited him to join me in San Francisco in the first place.

I took a bite of my enchilada in silence. I couldn't think of anything more to say beyond begging him once more to tell me why he was *really* breaking up with me. In my imagination, I knew the scene called for me to burst into tears and go running out into the street, but so legendary is my appetite that I didn't let the bad news prevent me from finishing my dinner. Probably, a part of me didn't believe what he was saying. Instead, the pain hit me later, back in the apartment, after Chad went to bed. I so wanted to make love with him just then, but he had placed himself beyond my reach.

Kneeling on the floor in our sparsely furnished living room, I bent down until my forehead brushed the pristine, beige, carpet fibers, and then I did burst into tears. Had he been planning this for a long time? I had no idea. No matter how charismatic he was, he was equally obtuse and enigmatic, and there were parts of him he was clearly unwilling to share.

The next day, I got up before him, and waited until he yawned, stretched, and sat up in bed.

"We're not really breaking up, are we? I hope you were kidding last night because I don't want to break up with you. Please don't leave me," I said.

Chad frowned and stared at me. "Brooks, we're over. I'm moving out today," he said, as if that put an end to the subject.

"But where will you go?"

"I'll stay with my friend at the top of the hill until I find a new apartment," he said. This was the friend, I realized now, who had supplied him with meth. Drugs or not, though, I didn't understand why he was convinced that we needed to break up, why he kept insisting that it happened to all of us gay men and now it had to happen to me. Couldn't one couple buck the trend, I wondered, simply by resolving to stay with each other? But I didn't mention any of these thoughts to him.

24 BLACK AND WHITE MEN TOGETHER

NEITHER OF us could afford to keep the apartment on his own, and in any case, the landlady had informed us that it was soon going to be converted into a condo, so we had no choice but to look for two new places. Chad took an apartment near Market and Van Ness, and I found a studio at 101 Broderick, in a blocky mid-century apartment building at the corner of Haight Street. On fogless nights, if I craned my neck out the picture window to the left, I could catch the orange-and-red glories of a San Francisco sunset. Turning to the right, stars opened in a midnight-blue sky, and the moon shone on the twinkling wedding cake of a giant Art Deco building across the street.

When I walked the neighborhood alone and single again, the image of Chad in my mind's eye became more and more burnished until he appeared so handsome and desirable that he ascended to a perfect Number Ten, the very template of Mister Right, and all because I had lost him forever. One night, he came around to Broderick Street, and later that evening we made love at his place near Van Ness. It was one of our hottest sessions ever, so I dared to hope that we were making up, but the next morning he explained that it was no more than what Sarah Jessica Parker, playing Carrie Bradshaw in *Sex and the City*, later so memorably dubbed "consolation sex."

I saw Chad only a few more times after that day. At one point, he told me he had found a new boyfriend, another white Philadelphia transplant whom I had met a few times at the Pendulum. Later, he moved into an apartment up the hill toward Twin Peaks, which he shared with a housemate who smoked so much meth that he stayed awake for days on end, narrowly avoiding accidents when he drove with one eye open and one eye shut.

Several years later, I saw Chad at a party in Oakland, and then he was gone, disappeared forever from my life. Maybe he moved back to Philly; maybe he remained in San Francisco. There was no one around who could tell me.

Whatever happened to Chad? It's a question I still ask myself to this day.

I never did find out the real reason he broke up with me. It was not in his nature to explain things, so he left it completely to my imagination. I could only try to fill in the details. What had I seemed like to him? I was undeniably a privileged white guy, but did he also see me as a racist? The worrisome question left me neurotic, always fretting over "maybe," never knowing what was true. The one fact I clung to was that our relationship had always revolved around play, the shared pleasures of dancing, clubbing, and sex. Somehow, we had lacked the tools to communicate at a deeper level, to express what each of us most needed from the other.

Looking back after all these years, I assume he left me because, above all, I left him first by moving to San Francisco. Then we grew apart, and when at last we reunited, he found himself sick and alone on Page Street, where his suffering was compounded by Lyle's racial snubs. Later, we were surrounded by all those lustful eyes, those relentless Castro cruisers. He was no dummy; he couldn't help but sense my lingering desire to flirt with them. Maybe I had unwittingly transmitted my ambivalence toward him, an ambivalence that had only grown when I found myself enjoying Dan's more mature company, the way he emanated a manly authority. Beyond that, I was a white guy with a distinguished architect father; Chad was a Black man from a working-class family in a small Pennsylvania town. We had done our best to connect across the gulf of our contrasting racial and cultural backgrounds. Maybe our relationship had simply collapsed under the weight of our attempt.

My relationship with Chad had elapsed in three short phases—ten months in Philadelphia, ten months apart, and ten months reunited in San Francisco. Now it was over—I had lost Chad. Brooding and tearful, I returned to my apartment, where I played my favorite sad record and had a good, long cry. The song was Deniece Williams's ballad "Silly," with its devastating chorus about how silly Deniece was to assume she could ever have the man of her dreams. It never failed to bring forth my tears.

As the days and weeks went by, the I-Beam and the Pendulum lost some of their allure, and I felt more and more rootless in the big, anonymous city. The most appealing thing about San Francisco, I was finding, was also the most challenging. The complete freedom that she bestowed on all her young, queer children, the freedom to invent a new life from scratch with scarcely any boundaries, was a sort of litmus test that led more often to loneliness than to fulfillment. In my heart I desperately yearned to belong to something bigger than myself, but when I went out to the bars, I encountered conviviality without finding community.

Adding to my unease were the daily reports in the *San Francisco Chronicle* concerning promiscuity among the "cohort" of young gay men who were already coming down with full-blown AIDS. A rivulet of cases in New York, San Francisco, and Los Angeles had become a river; now the river was rising fast and entering the flood stage of a true pandemic. Scanning the newspaper in the bus on the way to work every morning, I obsessively familiarized myself with the latest pronouncements from Dr. Anthony Fauci of the National Institutes of Health, the leading national authority on AIDS. Accompanying Fauci's articles came occasional bulletins from the surgeon general, C. Everett Koop, who courageously countered President Ronald Reagan's willful inaction by publishing safe sex advice.

"Wear a condom" became a sort of mantra, but beyond that, Fauci and Koop offered little practical advice regarding the mechanics of how one could avoid getting infected. It scared me because the Centers for Disease Control vaguely labeled nearly all sexual practices only as "safer" or "less safe." Unprotected anal sex was flat-out unsafe, but when "entirely safe" was a nonexistent category, what should we do? The AIDS ward at San Francisco General Hospital was overflowing; men were getting infected and dying every day. The one thing I knew for sure was that I didn't want to be the next one.

Due to my abstinence from anonymous sex and the relatively small number of men I had slept with, I assumed I was perhaps a bit less at risk than other men like my apartment manager, a supernumerary in the San Francisco opera, who had professed to me how much he enjoyed his afternoon romps in Buena Vista Park. However, my count was growing, and I knew that every new encounter was a roll of the roulette wheel. Later, when AIDS testing became available, guys began telling one another whether they were positive or negative, but just because someone said he was negative, that didn't mean he was telling the truth. What incentive was there for being truthful if it meant you'd be turned down for a score? Facing this new, frightening reality, I took a deep breath, decided I wasn't ready to give up sex, and stocked up on condoms.

As I coped with my loneliness and my fear about AIDS, I heard guys talking about an organization called Black and White Men Together (BWMT), and I took note. Originally formed in San Francisco by a white man named Mike Smith, I learned that BWMT was part social club, part civil rights advocacy organization, and part group therapy institute. This intrigued me because attending BWMT meetings seemed like a better way to meet men interested in long-term relationships than going to the bars. But I quickly realized that my interest ran deeper than that. My persistent attraction to Black men was something as fundamental about me as being gay in the first place, but what did it mean? I had no idea where it came from. It just *was*. It occurred to me that nobody would ever ask a white, blond, blue-eyed man why he was attracted to a white, blond, blue-eyed woman, but why did that mean it was incumbent upon me to explain or defend my contrasting sexual attraction?

Still, was it really as simple as that? Until then I hadn't given much thought to what my strong attraction to African American men meant. Was it something basic and normal about me, something to be honored and celebrated? Or was it unusual and socially detrimental, something to be analyzed and derided? So far, I had not experienced any pushback from Black men, any overt skepticism about the motivations behind my attraction. Even so, I felt I needed to learn how to tread cautiously through the minefield of racist bombs that threatened to go off whenever and wherever Black and white guys shared a conversation, let alone a bed. Maybe BWMT's members could help me find those safe pathways.

Meanwhile, I kept returning to one thought. My relationship with Chad, no matter what it had signified, no matter its highs and lows, had been fundamentally different than a relationship between any two white people or any two Black people, whether gay or straight. When I searched my memories, it seemed that scarcely a day had gone by when Chad or I did not have to confront our racial differences in one way or another. It was impossible to ignore the truth and horror of America's racist history, which arguably infected or polluted every contemporary encounter between any two persons of different races.

For Chad and me, this manifested as a vague mutual mistrust. It was a constant radio static, a scratchy background noise of anxiety, barely noticed and rarely acknowledged. Like AIDS-infected cells multiplying on a microscope slide, every little disagreement, no matter how small, bore at least the suspicion that it had metastasized from a racial origin, whether real or imagined. When Chad flashed with jealousy and anger because he saw me gazing at another man, was the thorniest part for him that the guy was another *Black* man? I could never be sure, but I could never discount it. No matter how hard we had tried to engage with each other as equals, was that even possible given the crushing weight of America's history? I hoped that attending BWMT meetings could teach me better ways to confront this invisible elephant in the room, the curtain of anxiety that America's racist past had pulled over Chad and me. And if I were to get involved in another interracial relationship one day, I further hoped I could learn how to yank that curtain aside, opening the window of understanding.

Serendipitously, the San Francisco chapter of BWMT met just around the corner from my apartment. How could I not go? When I arrived for my first Thursday evening meeting, I entered a former Masonic ballroom with a basketball-ready polished wood floor covered by battalions of those standard-issue, tan metal folding chairs found in nearly every church basement. Dressed in flannel shirts and jeans, little knots of men, some white, some Black, stood laughing and chatting. Others draped themselves casually across the chairs before the meeting began.

I soon learned that BWMT's ingenious bylaws required two co-chairs, one white and one Black. Standing at the lectern, the co-chairs launched into the night's agenda, which was to be followed by a potluck. Jim Ivory, the Black co-chair, had the floor first. Not to be confused with the movie producer James Ivory, the ironic appropriateness of his surname amused me. Jim was round, spectacled, and balding, while George, the younger white co-chair, was thin and pale, with dirty-blond hair and a matching moustache.

"Racism is prejudice plus power," Jim was saying from the podium. That made a lot of sense to me. Given that white Americans enjoy the power of their privilege, it followed that white people are likely to be racists unless they can be proven not to perpetuate those prejudices. I recalled how my father had once referred to a Black woman as a "handsome Negress," a careless phrase that emphasized her otherness. Had that planted a seed of prejudice in my heart, a seed that might later prompt me to commit racist acts? Even though I was fairly sure Dad did not intend to be racist, I wondered if, in similar fashion, each generation of American whites unconsciously passes the seed of racism on to the next.

This raised another disturbing question: Were my interracial attractions, while ostensibly positive, actually an inverted form of racism? Just as straight men were criticized for objectifying women, turning them into mere sex symbols, was it equally wrong for a white man to sexualize a Black man? Did we gay white men differ from garden-variety racists only in that we objectified Black men for our shared pleasure, rather than out of raw racial fear? It seemed to me that the answer was no, if only because the Black guys at the meetings liked us white men back, but these questions and others simmered in the background of my conversations with the BWMT members. All the discussions left me wondering what racist acts I might have committed, however unintentionally. I didn't really know, but I hoped I could learn how to avoid them in the future.

After several Thursday night sessions in the Masonic ball-room, I learned that beneath all the layers of analysis lay the radioactive stereotype that men of color have big dicks. This was the thorniest issue of all. A lot of the Black guys cynically suspected that white men were attracted to them exclusively for their rumored endowments. That was not true in my case. I liked the whole package, from head to toe—for me, so many Black men reached unparalleled heights of desirability even while fully dressed. I loved their colorful figures of speech—the way they leaned hard on a word or a vowel to emphasize the emotional content of the point they were making. Most of all, I was won over by the refreshing candor, good humor, and hearty hospitality that

I found among them. Taking a deep and honest look, maybe I did objectify Black men, and yet, doesn't forming *any* sexual attraction, whether gay or straight, depend on objectifying the stimulus of one's attraction in one fashion or another?

If my tendency to perceive Black men as a cohesive social group made me a racist, I knew that was wrong-headed, and I would have to confront it. Either way, it felt deliciously subversive to show up at the meetings and engage with a group that was at once iconoclastic and idealistic enough to break the racial taboos against Black and white men socializing with one another, let alone sleeping together. Soon I was attending the meetings every week, getting to know the members, and even going so far as to become the newsletter editor.

The most memorable of all the regulars was an expressive African American named Reggie Williams. Reggie had a long nose and an elongated jaw that gave him an almost equine appearance. Smiling and laughing readily, he gesticulated like a dancer, moving with a lithe grace that I had rarely seen in a man. Hands in the air, wrists twirling inward or outward as the occasion demanded, he was always articulating one point or another. Female and male beauty seemed so effortlessly intertwined in him that I was fascinated to discover, to my surprise, that I could be just as drawn toward effeminate men as to butch ones.

Reggie was among the first to sound the alarm that HIV was striking gay men of color in greater numbers than whites; alarming numbers. He raised a new standard to march behind, striving to empower Black and brown men to educate and arm themselves against the disease. Slowly, he began to establish a national reputation, traveling all over America to rally men of color in their self-defense, and he marshaled the BWMT chapters in the cause.

While I admired him for his commitment, part of me was still in denial about the hurricane force of the epidemic. Now that BWMT was suddenly and necessarily being transformed into an AIDS service organization dedicated to saving lives, I grieved for the organization that I had signed up for, the club whose primary goal was to empower Black and white men's relationships by helping us heal the unique, deep, and painful wounds between the races. AIDS appeared to be steamrolling all our useful work, and I was dismayed that BWMT's small but vital role was disappearing, perhaps never to be reclaimed.

The first member of our little circle to die was an affable, quiet-spoken Black man named Kalu. When I showed up at a small meeting hall in the Fillmore district for his memorial service, two dozen men sat tearfully on folding chairs, whispering among themselves. Taking my seat, I glanced up the aisle at a heavy wooden coffin resting on a folding table covered in bouquets of white gladiolas. I took a deep breath—the sight unquestionably made AIDS real to me for the first time. If it could claim Kalu, it could just as well claim me.

But I quickly recalibrated. *He must have slept with a lot more men than I have,* I told myself, remembering the man Jesse had introduced me to who had gone to bed with thousands of partners. Of course I was rationalizing, trying desperately to cloak myself in a protective coping mechanism by willing logic to fit the dire situation. Just as for years I had told myself I was not gay, now I eagerly told myself a myth that I must be safe, resisting the notion that *anybody* could get infected. Whether he had been promiscuous or not, it was easier to judge Kalu for his conduct than to admit that AIDS did not discriminate among its victims.

25 A ROCK

MORE AND more often, I found myself venturing down to the Folsom District, where I liked to barhop among the many butch bars, from the Stud to the Brig. The Ambush had a small but well-stocked leather shop, off to one side of the main room, where I gazed admiringly at the array of studded and spiked jock straps hanging from a pegboard, each with the heady smell of new leather. If a hot guy ventured in to check out the wares, the scene was even more erotic, and if we managed to establish eye contact, who knew what might happen?

The Eagle was quite simply an institution. Located under a spaghetti of freeway ramps, it announced its presence by a flotilla of Harley Davidsons parked at the curb. If there were at least five of them, you knew a party was going on inside. It was intoxicating to part the heavy black leather curtains that filled the doorway, a fitting portal into the dark underworld that lay beyond.

Inside, a red laser beam pierced the gloom overhead, shooting across the entire length of the room into the pulsing red eye of a painted eagle head on the near wall. Half-naked men in leather moved about in the noisy din of rock music and conversation, the thick air pierced with the pungent smell of their cigar smoke.

On Friday and Saturday nights, the Eagle was all business—pickups, hookups, and sexual transactions. Guys were always standing and modeling against the walls, so careful to keep up a macho facade that if you asked them something, most often they'd respond with no more than a grunt or a growl.

But at around 4:00 p.m. on Sunday afternoons, the Eagle transformed itself into a place of Dionysian joy. At the Sunday beer busts, it was standing room only on the sunny patio. A disc jockey spun records, and the Sisters of Perpetual Indulgence or the San Francisco Gay Men's Chorus would often perform on a narrow, raised stage that backed up against the adjoining town-house. Whatever the entertainment, the guys all laughed and joked, pouring beer into red plastic cups from shared pitchers. When the noisy buzz of joyful banter rose to a climax, beer spilled on the ground or sloshed over someone's bare shoulder until a hoppy aroma rose like mist from the hard pavement underfoot.

Much as the South of Market leather and fetish scene turned me on, I found it impersonal and disorienting except during the Eagle's Sunday beer busts. Being verbally oriented, I enjoyed a good conversation and liked to speak in more than grunts, so it was a relief to return to the convivial atmosphere of the Pendulum, where I picked up a short, well-built Black guy. Taye was the closest I ever came to hooking up with the hoodlums or hard-knock guys that everyone called rough trade. Soon, I began spending more and more time at his place, which was a large, spare apartment in the Fillmore, a nondescript neighborhood just a tad more respectable than the Tenderloin. The only con-cession to decor on its bare walls was the large and impressive collection of jean jackets that he displayed, tacked above his bed. Torn and threadbare, sporting long fringes, or studded up the sleeves and onto the shoulders with glittering rhinestones and spikes, the jackets were a stunning visual reminder of the fabu-lous disco past.

On one thrilling occasion, Taye fluffed me, as they say about the handlers who prepare porn stars for the camera. Once he was sure that I was good and hard, instead of leading me into the bedroom, he outfitted me in one of his festive shirts and insisted that we go out to a party. The experience of sporting another man's clothes, feeling horny while meeting queer strangers in an unfamiliar house, temporarily liberated me from my own identity, as if I could be anything I wanted. It was an exciting rush. I wanted to hold on to that oddly exhilarating moment, even though it was no more substantial than a soap bubble blown aloft by a child. But it was not enough just to dress for the part—I had to act the role of my new identity, and acting was never my strong suit. I sighed, realizing that, like Cinderella at midnight, I would have to go back to being myself.

On another evening, Taye implored me to come over right after work. When I got to the apartment, he drew me a bath, even though it was only 5:30 p.m. and I had showered that morning. I did as I was told because I was finding that I liked being bossed around. After my bath, we shared a dinner of spicy beef cubes and rice, then repaired to the living room, where Taye lit up a bong.

"Ever freebased?" he asked.

"No," I said. I had snorted cocaine a few times with Birgyte, but I had only the vaguest idea of what freebasing was.

"Well, it's never too late to start," Taye said.

In the bottom of the bong was a little white rock from which milky vapors rose while we inhaled. I quickly felt an oddly metallic high that seemed to have nothing in common with the natural leaf of a tropical plant. It felt forced, and even before coming down from it, I knew that the high would be as brief and fleeting as the excitement I had felt at the party. I didn't like it, and I didn't want to try it again, but Taye announced, "Hold on, I'm going out for more."

Apparently, we had already smoked the entire rock. "I don't want any more," I said, but he was already rushing out the door. I heard it click shut, then I heard his key turn the deadbolt, then the sound of his footsteps pounding down the stairs. One flight below, the street door slammed shut as he ran out. I felt nervous, as if I were caged. Why had he bolted the door? I got up and walked to it, my metallic high already fading, and sure enough, my suspicions were right. The door was locked from both sides, and I was trapped.

Already paranoid, I wondered how long Taye would be gone. Maybe I should just let myself out by the window and go home, but moving to the window, I confirmed what I already knew. It looked down into a small, enclosed courtyard, illuminated by the last golden rays of sunshine. I was on the second floor, and the ground seemed dizzyingly far below. There was no point in trying to lower myself with a sheet: there were no exits from the court-yard, only the windows of the other apartments. Returning to the sofa, I prayed that Taye would come back before the building went up in flames. I had never felt so vulnerable.

Fortunately, I soon heard a turn in the lock, and Taye came back in, bearing another rock of what, within a few months, everyone was calling crack. I knew where this was headed—the next time, I'd be abandoned in the apartment again, or worse, asked to pay for the drugs.

While he lit up, he sent me down to the corner store to buy some dish detergent. Fishing in my pocket, I discovered that I had only two bucks and change. That was supposed to last until my next paycheck, but now I would have to blow it on the most miniature bottle of detergent they sold. How had it come to this? I fretted. I normally didn't run out of money before the end of the month, but it was shocking to think how chronically broke I would become if Taye asked me to buy the rocks the next time, and the time after that. I could think of a thousand things I'd rather spend my money on.

Sure enough, when I returned to the apartment, the second rock had already gone up in smoke. I didn't stick around long enough to find out if he would go out again for a third.

The next day was one of those overcast San Francisco days when the fog stops moving and the sky turns white. I was riding the bus back from a doctor's appointment when an unaccustomed wave of hopelessness flooded over me. My self-esteem spiraled down a drain, and I felt completely ungrounded, without any useful purpose, belonging to nothing and nobody. Loathing myself for ending up at this lowest point of my cruising days, I was too weak to break it off with Taye, even though the last thing I needed was to date a crack addict. Fearing that it would lead inexorably to my becoming a junkie as well, the oppressive feeling continued to hover over me.

A couple of nights later, Taye and I went dancing at the Eagle Creek, a little African American gay nightclub on Market Street, near the San Francisco Mint, where they played all the latest R&B hits. As we exited the dance floor, the crowd parted, and out of nowhere, who should appear but the best friend of a sweet man named Darrell, whom I had briefly dated before breaking it off to go with Taye, and why? Only because I had decided that sex with Darrell was too "vanilla."

Staring at me with an exaggerated look of feigned surprise, the best friend delivered his verdict with a derisive twist of his head.

"Didn't I see you at Darrell's?" he asked in a high, nasal voice, as if to imply that I was a whore who had had the audacity to cheat on his friend. Then he frowned at me, waiting aggressively for what he rightly assumed would be my lame reply.

When I could think of nothing to say, he quickly swiveled his hips, spun around, and returned to the dance floor.

How had it come to this? Had I really sunk so low that I was no more than just another duplicitous queen, after having long prided myself for being honest with my partners? What's more, was I now so hopelessly caught up in the merry-go-round of cruising that I had lost sight of what I was doing it for, to find the wonderful long-term love that had always eluded me? I hoped not, but I could see how others might perceive it that way, and that hurt. Exiting the club with Taye, I glanced back at Darrell's friend, who was now dancing energetically. When I saw him turn to give his boyfriend a big, sincere kiss on the lips, I felt that overcast sky moving in and pressing down on me all over again.

THE BLEAK bigger picture was that moving to San Francisco had not cured my fragmented sense of self, the feeling that two warring personas were trapped inside me—an ambitious conformist clashing with an iconoclastic gay adventurer. Until then, I had assumed that residing in the City by the Bay would be sufficient to clear all the obstacles from my path, allowing me to unite my respectable work identity with my chaotic personal life, which in turn would make me feel balanced and whole. Why had that not happened? I still felt like one person at work and an entirely different person in the evening; I still kept my personal life in a box marked "private," invisible to my workmates.

Part of the problem was that, apart from attending the BWMT meetings, I had not found a new community to belong to. I had moved out west to embrace San Francisco's large, diverse gay population, but I was learning that our masses did not necessarily add up to a shared identity. If anything, they splintered like so many random images in a kaleidoscope, slicing and dicing into a myriad of specialized gay subcultures. Drag queens convened in one bar, leather daddies in another. Lesbians congregated at Amelia's. There was even a bar called the Triangle Tavern that sponsored an annual drag tricycle race up Market Street.

Where could I go to enjoy all the colors of the rainbow flag flying in one room? In San Francisco, the only time I had witnessed that was at the annual Pride parade, yet on a short trip to San Diego, I had visited a bar where all the flavors of our gay, lesbian, and trans identities were on view, assembled together under one roof. Was it any wonder that I had a better time at that bar, relishing its diversity and obvious pride, than at most of the specialized San Francisco clubs?

Regardless of our large numbers, or perhaps because of them, each of us was left to navigate his lonely journey. No matter where we came from, how "out" we were at work or with our straight friends, what types of relationships we were seeking, what fears we had, and what rules, if any, we followed, all of those were up to each individual to work out on his own. I had felt vulnerable before, but my struggle to mold a new identity in San Francisco seemed like a futile attempt to impose structure on a town that, in its passion for freedom, never ceased to rebuff it.

Another part of my ennui had to do with work. While I liked my colleagues at Omi Lang well enough, they were no match for my quirky old cronies at Hanna/Olin, and I missed the intense comradeship and pride that I had felt as part of that dynamic team. Bored of working on Chevron Park's endless underground utilities, I gave notice at Omi Lang and found a new job at an architecture and urban design firm called Hall, Goodhue, Haisley, Barker (HGHB).

At first, "Hugga-Bugga," as we called it, seemed promising. Owing to lead partner Gordon Hall's reputation as a preeminent urban designer, the firm had recently been hired by the Santa Fe Railroad to prepare a master plan for a massive mixed-use urban redevelopment on prime, unused railroad land along the Berkeley waterfront. The gigantic project involved building what amounted to an entirely new city along four miles of the East Bay shoreline, across the I-80 freeway from Berkeley's established neighborhoods. I welcomed the opportunity to plan for this exciting urbanist confection, which would be arranged around parks and open spaces commanding views of the Golden Gate Bridge.

After spending hours illustrating the grand scheme, with its hotels, office buildings, courtyards, and tree-lined streets, I was assigned to prepare a giant color rendering of the new city that we could pin up at town hall–style meetings to sell the concept to key stakeholders. Day after day, I stood in the office spraying the blue waters of San Francisco Bay onto a thick sheet of paper with an airbrush. The chrome device resembled a hair dryer but, when I pressed the trigger, a high-velocity mist of ink shot out. Like Laurie Olin's nighttime scene of the Pitney Bowes Park, it took hours to saturate the four-foot-by-five-foot sheet of paper with enough spray dots to render the dark aqua tint of the Bay. Unfortunately, the plan was bitterly opposed by Berkeley's left-leaning citizens who wanted to claim the entire acreage for a waterfront park. Now the future of our project was in jeopardy.

One of the business partners' wives was French, so the Hugga-Bugga Christmas party was held at a fancy French restaurant on a Saturday night. I wanted to dress up, but I rebelled against our preppy uniform of sport jacket, tie, and slacks that my bosses promoted as part of their brand. After some hesitation, I finally chose to wear my black leather pants with a crisp, latte-colored shirt and a narrow 1980s-style black leather tie. While conceding that it was not quite right for the occasion, I decided that my outfit was dressy enough for the restaurant, while being edgy enough to honestly express who I was outside the office.

At the restaurant, we were seated in a sumptuous leather booth around a large, round dining table with a linen tablecloth and ranks of wine glasses. Just as the waiter placed an impressive platter of rack of lamb on the center of the table, lifting its sterling silver lid with a flourish, my boss glared at me from across the table.

"That was nervy of you to wear your leather pants," my friendly coworker, Dave, whispered from his place on my left, with a little wink of conspiratorial approval.

"Thanks," I whispered nervously. I appreciated his solidarity, knowing that he felt the firm was as stodgy as I did. Still, my boss's cold stare hurt, and it hurt again one Sunday afternoon, a few weeks later, when I was walking down the street near the Civic Center, hand in hand with my latest boyfriend. Suddenly, my boss appeared, as if he had been lying in wait for me.

"Hi, Brad," I said, taking the initiative.

"Oh, hello," Brad responded coldly, glaring at me once more and giving my boyfriend a critical head-to-toe body scan before quickly moving on without another word. When Brad had hired me, he had assumed he was getting a straight-laced, clean-cut Ivy League star, and I had assumed I was joining a firm with a dash of Hanna/Olin's panache and can-do spirit. We were both mistaken. How ironic it was that I had moved to the most liberal city in the world, only to be ostracized for revealing my sexual orientation to my work colleagues. Granted, San Francisco embraced the gay community more heartily than Philly, but I still felt like I had to be two different persons, one at work and one at home.

To make matters worse, I had recently received a phone call from Bob Hanna.

"Brooks, there's an opening for a teaching position in the landscape architecture department at Penn," Bob said. "Why don't you apply?"

"Um, that's wonderful, Bob, thanks for telling me," I said. "Let me think about it and I'll let you know." This was a real surprise. I hung up knowing I should be overjoyed that he still thought highly enough of me to propose such an honor, so why did it feel like a thorny dilemma? Why did it leave me cold? I tortured myself about it. There was nothing holding me in San Francisco, so why not let this be my next big career move? On the other hand, I still had so much left to explore in California. The conundrum forced me to ask myself which part of me was more important, anyway? The career landscape architect or the gay clubber, the sexual explorer? And why did I always have to choose between those two conflicting halves of myself?

After two miserable days of futile inner debate and over-thinking, I dialed Hanna/Olin's well-known phone number, and Bob answered. "I'm sorry, Bob," I said. "It's a great honor, but I just don't want to leave San Francisco."

"I understand," Bob said. But when I got off the line, I didn't feel relieved. I knew I had just closed the door on a potentially rewarding teaching career when there was no guarantee that I would ever find what I was seeking in the Bay Area. I took a deep breath, realizing that I wasn't ready to leave my beloved San Francisco, no matter how disillusioned it had recently made me. I had come to the city for a reason—to search for lasting love and an accepting, creative community of like-minded gay people. Even though I hadn't found them yet, I felt sure that one or the other must be right over the horizon.

I was right.

GLANCING ACROSS the polished floor at a BWMT meeting one night, I spied a beautiful young man standing between two of his friends, grinning with merriment. Tall and thin, with caramel skin and a pair of the most beautiful light-brown eyes I had ever seen, he wore an olive-drab butch cap and matching army fatigues. His long moustache turned up and then down again at both ends, framing his radiant smile. I was sure that I detected something special reflected in his eyes, a vulnerability and an unguarded openness that I had never before encountered in another man. Something told me that, if I could just get to know him, he might prove to be more than just a date.

Over the next couple of weeks, I thought of him often. I was disappointed when he skipped the next couple of meetings, but when he came to the one after that, I sauntered up to him with my usual bluntness.

"Hi, I'm Brooks," I said, extending my hand. "Nice to meet you."

"Same here," he responded, enveloping me in a hug. "My name is James—James Draper," he said shyly.

"Would you like to go out sometime?"

"Sure, we can go out," he said. "Why don't you meet me next Sunday afternoon at the Japanese Garden in Golden Gate Park?"

In San Francisco's hypersexual gay scene, this was an unusual suggestion, which made it all the more enticing. It had to mean that he wanted more than a hookup. What's more, I loved spending my Sunday afternoons in the park. How could he possibly know that?

"I'd love to," I said.

The next Sunday was our first date, and I marked it on the calendar: April 8. When I walked up, James was already standing in front of the ornate wood gate gracing the entrance to the Japanese Garden, dressed in a white sweatshirt and his little army cap. When he saw me, his face lit up in a big smile. "Hi, Brooks," he said.

"Hi, yourself!" And I leaned forward to kiss him on the lips. "Shall we go in?" Turning to stroll through the verdant garden with its cloud-pruned pine trees and the dazzling accents of its many azaleas, we climbed the steep arch of the little red bridge at its center. I instantly felt relaxed with James; there was none of the tension I had experienced around the other men I had dated. It was as if we were already at home with one another.

As we descended from the bridge, James recounted charming stories about his friends, often breaking into an elf-like laugh. Immediately engaged in these incidents, I noticed he seemed to derive endless amusement from the foibles of the people he knew, without judging them.

"So, where do you live?" I asked.

"East Oakland."

"Why there, and not in San Francisco?" I asked.

"I just moved back in with my parents," he explained. "I lived for a year in San Francisco with a boyfriend, but we just broke up."

"I can't imagine moving in with my parents!" I said. "Why did you break up with your boyfriend?" Naturally, I was glad he was single, but I wondered what the guy had done to lose such a kind and gentle person as James, with his appealingly mischievous sense of humor.

"We were platonic," James said. "He didn't want to have sex, so I haven't had sex in a year."

"That's hard to imagine," I said, all my recent sexual encounters flashing through my mind like images in a kaleidoscope. It had been my most promiscuous year to date, and I struggled to picture how James could have been celibate for that entire time. But did that mean I was a whore? And did James's celibacy mean he was being smart and taking AIDS more seriously than I was? Both conjectures worried me, but I couldn't think what to say about them.

"Where do you work?" I finally asked, changing the subject.

"Mother's Cookies," he said. "I work on the production line—the factory is near my parents' house."

"Oh, my goodness—I never met anybody who works at a cookie factory before!"

"A friend of mine is throwing a party in Oakland, near Lake Merritt, next Saturday," he said, changing the subject again. "Why don't you come?"

"I'd love to," I said, and James explained which bus I should take.

The party was held in a Craftsman bungalow, and a few steps into the noisy, convivial living room, I glimpsed James's smiling face floating above a crowd of gay men mixed with a sprinkling of women. Catching my eye, he detached himself from his friends and stepped forward to enfold me in a long hug. Then he pulled back to hold me at arm's length. The noise of the room receded around us, and as I gazed into his lovely, light-brown eyes, I beheld a deep well of generosity, kindness, and yes, love. It didn't take any longer than that one fleeting moment for me to fall in love with him. I knew in an instant that what I felt was something deeper than I had ever experienced before, and I yearned for another enveloping embrace.

When I left the party, though, a tiny seed of doubt planted itself in my brain. I had had so many rejections and disappointments in the dating scene . . . wasn't it too soon to be sure about him? But after a few dates, my doubts completely evaporated. I had never met anyone at all like James.

Soon he began taking a bus over the Bay Bridge to meet me in San Francisco, arriving in the late evening or the early morning depending on the time of his shift at Mother's Cookies. Each time I opened the door to him, he was still in his white apron, which was invariably coated in thick, sticky layers of baked white sugar, as if he were one giant cookie just emerging from the oven, ready to be eaten. It was not long before I gave him a key to the place.

A few months went by, and after returning from a Christmas visit home to Seattle, I arrived at the apartment, surprised to find James opening the door for me. Dressed all in white—clean white slacks and a white Cossack shirt with flouncy sleeves, not his dirty cookie uniform—he grinned at the sight of me before returning to the pots and pans bubbling on my tiny stove. Yes, he had prepared dinner for me. As he lit a candle on the kitchen table and gestured for me to sit down, I felt it was the nicest, most romantic gesture that anyone had ever done for me. After all the times that it had felt wrong with other men, it felt exactly right, and my heart burned bright with love for him.

"I've really missed you, sweetheart," I said, kissing him. "It's been too long since I've held you in my arms, and it's been too long since we made love!"

"Ah," he said. "I know what you mean. You've been dormant."

Early the next year, James began imploring me to move to Oakland, where we could find a place together. At first, I resisted, being stubbornly committed to living in San Francisco, which I still regarded as the gay mecca. But James was quietly persistent.

"You'll like Oakland," he kept saying. "It's a real community, and life is a lot easier there. And you can get to work across the Bay Bridge on AC Transit faster than it takes you to ride the Seven Haight downtown."

"Really?" I asked, genuinely surprised that the intercity bus might be faster than my local Seven.

After weeks of his prodding, I finally admitted that it wouldn't hurt to at least look at some apartments. When we did, it was an eye-opener to see how much more space we could have in Oakland for comparable or lower rent than in San Francisco. Eventually, we settled on a large, sunny, two-bedroom apartment at 377 Santa Clara Avenue, in Oakland's Grand Lake district. With its winding avenues, wide sidewalks, and picturesque palm trees, the neighborhood was named for the Grand Lake Theater, a charming Mission-style landmark on the shores of nearby Lake Merritt, where tiny skiffs sailed by, pursued by couples in pedal boats.

Located in a large, mid-century building, our apartment had south-facing windows looking out over the neighborhood. It tickled me that one of the cream-colored bedroom walls was angled to the other, matching the bend of the street outside. The best part was our generous covered balcony, which was enclosed by an iron railing in an undulating wave pattern. Since San Francisco's chilling winds and fog rarely penetrated across the Bay, we could actually use it. I couldn't wait to set out some potted plants and join James outside for a drink. Soon we had a lovely large jade plant to accompany our cocktail hours.

Until I moved across the Bay to Oakland, I didn't realize how oddly painful and alienating my life had been over the previous three years. No matter how beautiful, unique, and seductive San Francisco was, I now saw that it came with a huge dollop of big-city indifference. There was abundant freedom in its aloof anonymity, but little warmth. The freedom I had thought I craved thrives on anonymity, but I also wanted to belong to a community, and anonymity is the antithesis of community.

Reinforcing its anonymity, San Francisco's residents were divided into big but separate tribes with their own distinct neighborhoods—Latinos in the Mission District, Chinese in Chinatown and the Richmond; a small cluster of African Americans in the Fillmore; and our own gay tribe in Polk Gulch, the Folsom, and of course the Castro. My oddly segregated life there had been a daily shuttle between the mainstream, almost entirely straight and white world of work and the gay but almost equally white world of the city's nightlife.

By contrast, James was right about Oakland—it was a real community, and I quickly fit in. We both did. While plenty of single people lived in our Grand Lake neighborhood, they didn't dominate the way they did in San Francisco. Like Center City, Philadelphia, it was a mixing bowl of races and ages, with large numbers of Blacks, Latinos, and Asians, as well as a judicious mix of families and gay couples. Everybody flowed in and out of the appealing neighborhood bookstores, cafes, and shoe repair shops, which were enjoyable and useful without being preciously hip and trendy. Pulsing with life and vitality, our neighborhood was an eclectic place where it did not take long for people to recognize me as a neighbor.

Beyond the bigger apartment buildings, we strolled down residential streets to admire the single-family stucco houses with their Mediterranean gardens. A few blocks in the other direction lay beautiful Lake Merritt, where joggers and cyclists passed by as we walked the shoreline trail. Best of all, it turned out that James and I were even more compatible living together than when we had merely been dating. We were an item, we were in love, and I assumed that we were going to live happily ever after.

When life with James settled into a pleasant routine, I began to feel genuinely connected to a person and a place for the first time since moving to the Bay Area. Every night after work in downtown San Francisco, I took a bus across the Bay, where most often I spent the evening alone because James was working the swing shift. After calling me on his break at 9:00 p.m., he usually arrived home before midnight, just in time to say good night. Because our work schedules were out of sync in this way, we saw little of each other except on weekends. Although I would have loved to spend more time with him, I found this arrangement infinitely preferable to the rootless singles life I had been leading in San Francisco.

Sunshine streamed through the windows on Sunday mornings when we read the *Chronicle* and the *Oakland Tribune* in bed. In the afternoons, we went for long walks in the East Bay regional parks or we took a picnic to the Berkeley Botanical Garden, high in the hills above the UC campus, where we spread a blanket and hung out for hours, sharing anecdotes and laughing at the eccentric behavior of our friends. Often, we headed over the Bay Bridge to Fisherman's Wharf, where we loved to sit on the grass at Aquatic Park, watching the panorama of sailboats drifting rapidly past Alcatraz. As their sails blew nearly horizontal against the wind, a chorus of conga drummers beat out endless hypnotic rhythms from the bleachers behind us. Across the Bay, the legendary and romantic prison rose up in front of us, resembling an ancient castle rendered with daubs of white and yellow-ochre paint.

Returning to Oakland, we shopped for dinner at the Piedmont Market, an upscale grocery store with an outstanding butcher shop. Our favorite Piedmont offering was veal paupiettes, sausage-shaped cuts of veal, wrapped in prosciutto, which were delicious sautéed in olive oil with a pungent blend of garlic, rosemary, and wine. No matter what we did or where we went, we were an item, and I felt safe and secure in James's company. Whether we were holding hands or not, I was sure that everybody perceived us as a couple, and I was proud of that. There was a new kind of openness, a new sort of freedom in it, and it felt exactly right.

The oldest child in a large family, James dearly loved his mother, Charlene, his two brothers and three sisters, and a number of cousins, nephews, and nieces who lived nearby. Accordingly, we nearly always spent Sunday afternoons at the Draper home in East Oakland. At first, I was afraid to meet James's relatives, worried that the Drapers would reject me, this highfalutin white college boy who had come out of nowhere to grab their oldest son away from them.

My fears were needless. James's mother and siblings welcomed me with open arms. When they saw that I had staying power, that I was not just a fly-by-night boyfriend, they generously inducted me into the family. Years later, to my great pleasure and honor, Charlene even fondly confided that she was my "second mother."

"Damn. How 'bout them A's!" shouted James's brother, Shawn, one spring afternoon as James and I came in the door of the Drapers' modest wood frame house with its front porch and California fan palm.

"Canseco. He always gets 'em!" James responded, as we watched Jose slide into home plate.

"You know they say he's on those steroids," Shawn said.

"Aren't they all? Seems like you can't watch a game these days where at least one of 'em ain't juiced."

"Damn shame," Shawn said.

"Hey, Daretta!" James turned toward his little sister, who had just come in the door. "You're over the hill, you know." This was a reference to the fact that she'd just turned thirty.

"Shut *up*," Daretta said.

Hanging out with the Drapers, where the ongoing conversation was nearly always about family, sports, and local current events, was so different from being in Seattle with my parents and brother—not better or worse, just different, and I enjoyed the contrast. Apart from the obvious racial difference, they were a large, extended family. This meant that the flow of time and activities was so much more fluid than at Mom and Dad's, where mealtimes were always carefully pinned to the clock. Weekend afternoons at the Drapers were a sort of open house. Family members came and went on their own time, and there were nearly always hot links and ribs on the grill, ready whenever anyone felt hungry. Growing up in Seattle's rainy climate, we had never barbecued, but it didn't take me long to anticipate the savory fumes of the wood smoke as it curled up into the bright-blue California sky from the Drapers' backyard.

During those Sunday barbecues, I noticed how much less emphasis the Drapers placed on career advancement than Mom and Dad did. While this must have been due in no small part to a relative lack of opportunity, they rarely spoke of it that way. Instead, they seemed content with decent jobs that were not what most people would call careers . . . jobs that paid them well enough while leaving plenty of time off for the large family gatherings they so prized and prioritized.

Although mild-mannered, James got a kick out of performing harmless practical jokes. One day, his friend Minnie came to visit. An African American former factory worker, Minnie was confined to a wheelchair after an industrial accident. As soon as she arrived, James steered her chair directly under the ceiling-mounted smoke detector. "Sit here," he said, stepping back to take a seat on the sofa. Minnie immediately pulled a book of matches out of her handbag and lit up. Lifting her cigarette to her lips, she took a deep drag, then exhaled. As soon as the smoke rose to the ceiling, a loud alarm screamed through the apartment, reverberating against the walls of the buildings across the street. Minnie nearly jumped out of her chair—the shock of the alarm momentarily appeared to have restored the use of her legs, curing her paralysis.

"Motherfucker!" she yelled. "What the fuck?"

"Looks like you can walk again!" James said, and I gasped while he collapsed into a torrent of mischievous giggles. Minnie continued to scream and cuss picturesquely, waving her cigarette for emphasis, and several minutes passed before she regained her composure.

Like me, James loved to travel, which set him apart from the rest of his family members, who seldom left Northern California. He and I bonded over our love of France because, only a couple of years earlier, he had spent a year in Antibes and the city of Nancy with a French boyfriend. He also shared his enthusiasm for female jazz singers, introducing me to Etta James and Susannah McCorkle. One night, we went to Yoshi's, a celebrated jazz club on the Oakland/Berkeley city line, to hear the legendary Carmen McRae. There was nothing feminine about the figure she cut onstage. With her tank of a body, she was built like a furnace, but when she sat on a stool and grabbed the microphone, she turned into a nightingale.

Partway through her first set, James suddenly yelled "Look Out Now!" loud enough for the entire club to hear. With my polite, white-boy upbringing, often attending hushed performances of the Seattle Symphony where we were careful to applaud only at the end of each piece, I was worried that Carmen would take offense. Instead, she smiled broadly, nodding her large, square head at James without pausing to interrupt her perfect musical phrase. I admired the easy communion that James so effortlessly shared with her.

Already happy with my newly stable and mostly stress-free life, I was happier still when Mom came down from Seattle to meet James in April, soon after we moved into our Oakland apartment and one year after we started dating. For the short time that Mom was willing to be away from Dad, the three of us enjoyed playing tourists on both sides of the Bay.

"Do you like him?" I asked her, when I had a chance to take her aside.

"James is a dear," she said with a little smile.

As measured and diplomatic as ever, she didn't seem willing to express more detail about her thoughts and feelings. Still, it was clear from their quiet conversations that she was letting him into her heart. James's gentle nature matched hers, and I was delighted to observe him return the favor.

A month or two after Mom's visit, having grown weary of Brad's hostility, I managed to leave Hugga-Bugga after interviewing at MPA Design, the firm of a well-regarded San Francisco landscape architect named Michael Painter. Although my new fellow staffers lacked the quirky, oversized personalities of my colleagues at Hanna/Olin, they were cohesive, friendly, and professional, and I was pleased to discover that Michael's designs were innovative and creative. Working on any number of Silicon Valley corporate campuses and suburban open spaces, I was eventually assigned to lead the planning of IBM's new office park in San Jose, where I designed a large plaza shaded by a bosque of leafy Chinese elm trees. The plaza provided a major employee gathering space near the entrance to the campus, achieving my long-term goal of designing a park for use by multitudes of people, if not technically by the public at large.

The next Christmas, I brought James home to Seattle to meet Dad for the first time.

Dad rose to the occasion with aplomb. "Welcome to our home," he said. "Brooks has told us so much about you."

"Thanks! It's nice to meet you," James said.

"Come upstairs with me, James. I want to show you the view of Mount Rainier from my studio," Dad said.

"Are you working on any buildings these days?" James asked innocently as we climbed the stairs to Dad's third-floor, glassed-in studio.

"I'd be happy to show you one or two projects. Right now, I'm doing the working drawings for the Puget Sound Blood Center."

Oh boy, I told myself, *here we go.* I would have to find a way to rescue James from Dad's monologue, which was sure to run on too long.

For his part, James seemed completely at ease with both Mom and Dad, and it was the first of many happy holidays we spent together in Seattle.

For the first time since relocating to the Bay Area, I felt I could concentrate on my career without neglecting my personal life. Until moving in with James, I hadn't realized what an enormous toll of time and psychic energy my cruising had taken, forcing me to ricochet back and forth between two distinct personas, one at work and one at home.

Now it seemed as if my life was finally falling into place, becoming whole at last. I had a boyfriend I loved, and we were building our future together with the approval of both his family and mine, along with the embrace of our Oakland community. What's more, my job was creative and stimulating without requiring me to work all weekend or into the night.

THE ONLY pall hanging over the happiness James and I shared was the ever-present threat of AIDS. In April 1984, the very month I met him, San Francisco's Board of Supervisors passed an ordinance banning unsafe sex in the city's gay bathhouses. Soon, Mayor Dianne Feinstein began sending police officer "spies" into the baths to enforce the rule, and a few months later, Public Health Director Dr. Mervyn Silverman shut them down completely. The closure engendered a furious debate in the pages of the *Chronicle* and *The Bay Area Reporter*. While a few gay leaders supported the move as a public health necessity, most felt that it was a missed opportunity. Since the baths were vibrant community meeting places as well as sex clubs, they argued that keeping the baths open would allow volunteers to staff tables giving out free condoms and pamphlets promoting safer sex practices.

Although I had never visited a bathhouse, I knew all too well that closing them represented a powerful metric for how serious the disease had become. With every passing day, James and I became more worried about contracting AIDS. All we could do to avoid it was to stock up on condoms, so that's what we did, but our fear lingered right up to the point of every orgasm, infecting the joy of our lovemaking.

By the mid-1980s, HIV testing was widely available, but we were both afraid of getting tested. As long as we didn't know our

HIV status, we could cling to the hope that we were both nega-tive, whereas getting tested amounted to deliberately rolling the dice. With any luck, they would land on the jackpot—virus-free status for both of us—but if our luck failed, it almost certainly meant a death sentence.

Four years into our relationship, there still were no effective medications for AIDS, but I was optimistic that there soon would be. Maybe the CDC would even come up with a vaccine. For those reasons, no matter how scary testing was, I began to think it was crazy for us not to know our HIV status.

"Let's get tested," I said one morning.

"I don't know . . . I don't think I want to," James responded.

"But they're learning more about the virus every day," I said. "If one of us—or both of us—is positive, we need to know so that if they come up with some good meds, we can take them."

"I'm not sure. And besides, right now there aren't any meds."

"Oh, come on," I said, gazing out the window at the gauzy clouds floating by. "Well, please at least think about it and let me know what you decide."

Eventually, James came around. One random morning we found ourselves at the Castro Free Clinic, sitting side by side on metal chairs upholstered in a bureaucratic shade of mint-green vinyl. The sun was hiding but the famous San Francisco fog had yet to propel its chilling winds down the street outside. Behind us, tall windows flooded the waiting room in a neutral white light, illuminating the handful of other faces who no doubt shared both our fear and the courage it had taken us, first to make an appoint-ment, and then to follow through by actually showing up for it.

After a few minutes, a door opened across the room and a white-coated clinician appeared, carrying a clipboard.

"Brooks?" she inquired, eyes searching for me across the ranks of chairs. "Right this way." I stood up, clasped James's hand briefly, and followed the woman into a small examination room. James remained behind.

"Have a seat," the clinician said, gesturing toward a chair. "Which arm do you prefer?"

"Right arm, please." I sat down, placed my elbow on the armrest, turned my palm up, and curled my fingers outward. With my free hand, I slowly rolled up my shirtsleeve.

"This will sting a bit," she continued, pulling on the end of a hypodermic needle and probing for my best vein. I felt the soothing moisture of a cotton swab soaked in rubbing alcohol, then the sharp prick in my forearm.

"That's it," she said with a smile, opening the door. "We'll be in touch."

"Thanks," I said, pulling my sleeve down and glancing back at her as I left the room. Her neutral expression masked anything it might have revealed about what the future held for me.

Back in the waiting room, another door opened and another clinician appeared.

"James?" she asked.

James grimaced and rose from his chair, following her obediently across the room. As the door closed behind him, I noticed how thin he looked.

For some undecipherable reason, the results of our blood tests were not ready at the same time. When I received a note in the mail two weeks later, I returned to the clinic by myself. Once again, I found myself in the little room, with its chair, its armrest, and its blood-pressure cuff hanging on the wall. A different nurse sat in her white coat behind a small desk. Her wavy black hair cascaded down both sides of her round face—she must have been a Latina in her late thirties. A small piece of paper sat in front of her, the only object on the table.

"Are you ready?" she asked.

"Yes."

"Good. Let's see what we have here." Lowering her eyelids, she turned the paper over and frowned at it briefly. If I hadn't been so nervous, I would have laughed at how much she reminded me of a celebrity presenter on Oscar night. Then she raised her eyes and smiled.

"Negative," she said. "Congratulations!"

I stood up, feeling my body relax for the first time in two weeks. "Thank you," I said.

"You should get tested again if you stay sexually active, especially if you have multiple partners."

"I know," I said, but my hands were already on the doorknob. "Thanks again."

As I left the clinic, the sun pierced through the clouds, shining brightly on the pastel Victorians across 17th Street. At first, I felt like doing a little dance. Then I remembered that James had not yet received his results—it was not yet time to celebrate. I sighed, resolved to restrain my extreme relief, my rush of joy, until we were both off the hook.

After work a few evenings later, I returned to our airy apartment to find James sitting glumly on the sofa, his head slumped forward, his eyes fixed on the brown shag of our wall-to-wall carpet. When I closed the door as gently and quietly as possible, he did not look up.

"What's wrong?"

"They called me," he said, without lifting his eyes from the floor. I didn't have to ask who "they" were.

"And?"

"I'm positive. I have HIV."

"Oh, darling," I said, rushing to sit down and hold him in my arms. "I'm so sorry! But we'll get through this. We'll pull through." I don't know if I believed what I heard myself saying. I was merely on automatic pilot, mouthing my hope for the future. Truthfully, the news frightened me to the core, but I didn't want to make James feel worse by sharing my fear with him.

James remained mute, and I knew then that nothing I could possibly say would soothe him. Even so, my active brain was already at work trying to fix it.

"You know, many people don't get symptoms for years after testing positive. By then, for sure there will be a cure, or . . ." My voice trailed off. "At least some good meds." Did I even believe that? I wasn't sure.

James said nothing, and his body sank even deeper into the couch.

"Did they give you any counseling?" I was suddenly horrified that the nurse had reached him by phone. Everyone knew—it was common knowledge—that the protocol dictated in-person disclosures. At those appointments, clinicians pushed brochures toward you and offered therapy sessions, hugs, or even a shoulder to cry on. They were never supposed to just call you, blurt out your test results, and then hang up. That was the worst thing they could do—people could become suicidal.

"No," he said. "No *counseling*," he added, pronouncing the word as scornfully as possible.

I was appalled. How had the nurse had the gall to telephone my beloved, my deserving, my innocent James with the heartbreaking news? For four carefree years, we had lived our life together as equals, sharing a bright future together, but now it was as if an iron spike had been driven between us, cleaving us in two. From that moment forward, our destinies were fated to unfold in different, even opposite directions. And from that moment onward, I could no longer delude myself that HIV happened only to other people.

Until we got tested, I had lain awake at night afraid I was HIV-positive because of the promiscuous life I had led before meeting James. By contrast, I was fairly confident that he would test negative due to the chaste year he had spent with his former boyfriend. Now, reality turned out to be the exact opposite, and James was inconsolable. Nothing could raise the cloak of depression that settled over him like a blanket of San Francisco's damp fog. The reality was just too stark—AIDS spared nobody in those days, and how could I sugarcoat that?

When James sobbed, all I could do was to hold him and rock him, but how long could I do that? The situation was scary, and not least because I didn't know how I was going to find the inner strength to love him, soothe him, and care for him over the coming years. Sometimes I thought of something I could say that might help lift the dark cloud over him, but often nothing came to mind. When I couldn't think of anything to say or do, I escaped for a few hours on the long bike rides that increasingly reassured and sustained me. With the wind on my back and the ocean waves in my eyes, the wide-open feeling of space in motion consoled me. My emotions were already becoming a roller coaster of fear, anguish, and anticipatory grieving, and my bike rides helped flatten them into a more manageable baseline of quiet sadness.

My initial euphoria over my own good health evaporated, replaced by angst. There was no way I could know how this was going to play out, but I feared that things were just going to get worse. Our situation was deeply unfair. Why, on top of my foundation of white privilege, should I be permitted the inestimably greater privilege of a renewed lease on life at James's expense?

I'm not proud to admit this, but even before we were tested, James and I made a conscious decision not to befriend other gay couples because we wanted to shield ourselves from the pain we would feel when one or both of them sickened and died. We had heard the devastating numbers from friends and acquaintances across the Bay in San Francisco—we knew guys who had lost dozens, if not hundreds, of lovers and friends.

It was not unusual for a man to break down and say, "Everybody I knew and loved is dead. There is literally no one left."

Partly because there were fewer gay people in our Oakland neighborhood, we were lucky enough to count the number of friends who had died on the fingers of one hand, and we wanted to keep it that way. Our diversion tactic—trying to run away from the disease by absenting ourselves from its victims—backfired. It did nothing to prevent AIDS from breaking right through our front door.

Instead of turning toward other gay men, we deliberately surrounded ourselves with straight friends like the diminutive Vicky, whom I had originally met when she worked next door to Omi Lang's office in San Francisco. She and her boyfriend,

Luke, lived nearby, and over time she became our closest friend and confidant, assisting James through his illnesses and helping me cope. Until we got tested, there had been no scientific consensus as to whether a positive test meant that you would inevitably progress to disease. However, only a few months afterward, blaring headlines in the *Chronicle* proclaimed that a positive test meant near certainty that you would contract full-blown AIDS. When those newspaper stories appeared, the three of us had no choice but to confront the probability that James's days must be numbered unless Big Pharma could come up with some effective drugs.

After a few more months went by, James began coming home from his shifts at Mother's Cookies looking increasingly tired. He had always been skinny, but when he was tired, he looked thinner than ever, and it worried me. One evening, fighting back a cold, he took a little nap before dutifully rising at 11:00 p.m. to start the graveyard shift. I implored him to call in sick, but he insisted on soldiering on. Dragging himself out of bed, he washed his face in cold water and headed out the door. He would not be home until 8:00 a.m., when I was due to leave for work, and I felt so deeply sorry for him. His bout of fatigue was soon over, but the painful memory of it haunted me. I couldn't talk myself out of the impression that it might mark the beginning of his AIDS symptoms.

Although James's depression never completely lifted, after a few weeks he managed to start enjoying life again, at least a little. A welcome distraction arose when we decided to buy a car. I needed one increasingly for work, due to all the trips I made to construction sites in San Jose and other far-flung places. In the end, we settled on an Acura Integra. Our brand-new silver coupe was sporty and youthful, and we both loved how the retractable headlights made a satisfying *zoop* sound when we pressed a button to raise them.

Then something more significant came along to buoy James's mood: he learned of a job opportunity greeting tourists on Alcatraz and decided to apply. Quickly hired, James loved his new role handing visitors a Sony Walkman with a recorded, self-guided tour through the storied prison, and every night he came home full of hilarious stories about that day's crop of crazy tourists. Smiling and laughing, James delighted in the new lease on life that job gave to him. It was fun for him to join a team of friendly coworkers on the island, with its fresh air and sea breezes, away from the oppressive fluorescent lights and clanging machinery of Mother's Cookies.

"Today, Whitey got in a brawl with one of the other authors!" James said one evening, breaking into a laugh as he came in the door.

"What are you talking about?" I asked. I knew that Whitey was one of the former inmates whose memoirs about their time on Alcatraz were stocked in the prison's bookstore, but I didn't know any more than that.

"Well, the head office that arranges author appearances in the bookstore screwed up big time and scheduled two authors at the same time—Whitey and Jim Quillen. They almost came to blows!"

"What for?"

"Each one was trying to grab sales off the other. That's why the office bends over backward to make sure only one author is scheduled to appear in the store at any one time."

"So what happened then?" I asked, alarmed.

"My boss and one of the cashiers had to pry them apart," James said, clearly amused.

I witnessed the conflict myself one afternoon when I visited the store to buy a copy of our new friend Jolene Babyak's book, *Eyewitness on Alcatraz*. On that day, Whitey was the author in residence. Before I could reach the shelf bearing Jolene's memoir of growing up on the island as the daughter of a guard, Whitey jumped in front of me, pushing his book into my face. It was all I could do to sidestep him as I rushed to the cashier to claim Jolene's volume. I chuckled, imagining how much more fraught the occasion would have been had she walked in just then.

I had a big surprise planned for James's next birthday, making one of his most fervent dreams come true. It was on a Sunday, and I told him to be home from his parents' house by 4:00 p.m.

"So, what's the big secret?" he asked, rushing into the apartment on the stroke of four.

"You'll see," I responded. A moment later, there was a knock at the door, and Vicky and Luke came in, dressed in festive attire.

"Happy birthday, James!" they chorused.

"Thank you!" he said, rushing to hug them.

"We're going on a ride," I said.

"What, all four of us are getting in our little car?" James asked.

"You'll see," I said, opening the door, and heading out.

Just as we reached the bottom of the front steps, a long, black limousine pulled up and idled at the curb.

"That's for us?" James asked excitedly, a big smile lighting up his face. Dressed in a tuxedo, the chauffeur got out and graciously opened the back door for James. Inside, we were enveloped in a black leather cocoon, lit only by runway lights that ran the length of the center aisle. A bottle of champagne sat chilling in a bucket of ice between the two back seats, and four glasses appeared in the fold-down armrest. I popped the bottle open, filled the glasses, and we toasted James as the black steel caterpillar pulled out from the curb. Over the sound system, the Steve Miller Band's song "Abracadabra" began playing, striking exactly the right chord of exhilaration mixed with cheesiness. As we crossed the Bay Bridge, the sun began setting over the Bay, and when we continued across the Golden Gate, it glowed deep orange over the whitecaps on the Pacific. We weren't going anywhere in particular, we were just out for a ride, and James's face lit up, grinning at the pleasure of it.

Now that he was working daytime hours, we were together on weekday evenings for the first time since we met, and that brought both of us a new measure of happiness. On the mornings when he left for work before me, I walked out onto the balcony to wave goodbye to him. While he descended the long slope of our street, I watched him turn to wave back at me, blowing kisses at him until he disappeared around the corner. After he vanished, his smile lingered in the air like the Cheshire Cat's, as if he were blessing me. We kept up this daily routine until it became an ever more poignant demonstration of our love. Each time, we tried our best to ignore the two laborers who stood laughing at us from across the street, where they leaned on shovels in front of an eternal apartment construction project they appeared to be too lazy to ever finish. We could practically hear them saying, "Look at those crazy faggots," but we didn't care.

After James traded his sugar-crusted smock for the opportunity to greet the public at Alcatraz, his self-esteem shot up, and he began holding his head high, a big smile on his face. No longer a mere cog in a machine, he was a flesh-and-blood hospitality clerk, and the extroverted job elated him. Never was his professional pride more joyously flattered than early one fine morning, when, as usual, he boarded the employee-only shuttle to the Island. As he stood in the open door, one foot in the boat, the other on the pier, a glamorous figure approached, and it was not one of his coworkers.

"Hi, Cher, welcome to Alcatraz!" yelled James, and he took great pleasure in extending the greeting to her boyfriend and her twelve-year-old son Elijah, whose names he knew by heart. We had both been aware that Cher was in town because the *Chronicle* had fawned over her visit to Macy's, the day before, to peddle Uninhibited, her new perfume. But what James could not have known was that, as Cher now explained, Elijah had to write a school assignment on the history of Alcatraz. Stepping onto the boat, she planted a kiss on James's cheek.

That evening, I was reading a magazine in our apartment when James rushed in. "You'll never believe this, Brooks!"

"What?"

"Cher kissed me this morning! I'm never going to wash my face again!"

LATE ON the afternoon of October 17, 1989, I caught a bus across the Bay Bridge to a client meeting at Berkeley City Hall. Working for MPA Design in San Francisco, I had two projects in Berkeley, both for the Parks Department. One was the Aquatic Park Master Plan, a grand reimagining of a ninety-acre, narrow, dagger-shaped lagoon sandwiched between the East Bay shoreline and the waterborne causeway of the I-80 freeway. Our Aquatic Park plan promised hiking trails on new tall berms that would block the noise and sight of all the cars and trucks screaming by at top speed, mere feet away.

Called Berkeley Omnibus Parks, the other project was an extremely modest venture to repair crumbling steps and install new bathrooms in three or four small city parks. We called this a "bread and butter project" because, while it paid our salaries, its humble scope and budget prevented us from demonstrating the sort of design panache that could win an award for a distinguished landscape architecture firm.

About twenty minutes into my meeting with city officials, the room suddenly began shaking violently.

"Earthquake!" yelled a Berkeley city official. "Get under the table!"

In my haste to dive under the giant oak conference table, I knocked over someone's mug, which rolled across the table, spilling coffee. Knees and elbows flew everywhere as we all rushed to get down on our hands and knees. The last thing I saw before taking refuge under the table was a large lightning-shaped crack opening in the sheetrock of the nearest wall.

"Yikes!" cried someone as we all huddled in fear under the table, which seemed massive and heavy enough to withstand a nuclear blast. The tremors still had not stopped, and I couldn't recall experiencing any quake that even nearly approached this one. I had lived through countless small earthquakes in the Bay Area, not to mention a fairly large quake in Seattle, in 1965, when the stair hall in our house had slid back and forth as if on tracks while I descended it. But nothing had prepared me for this.

After nightmarishly prolonged shaking, an unreliable calm returned, and we emerged cautiously from beneath the table. Nobody had to inform me that the rest of the meeting was canceled as we staggered unsteadily out the door. The time was just after 5:00 p.m., the sky was already darkening, and I could see that many buildings had lost power. Puffs of dark gray smoke rose from distant buildings while a few cars advanced slowly down the street. Sirens sounded from all directions as I stumbled to a bus stop, hoping that the buses were still running. *So, this is the big one,* I said to myself, brushing plaster dust off my shirt that must have fallen from the ceiling.

After a long wait, a bus rumbled up, shuddering to a halt. Relieved by its mundane familiarity, its welcome evidence that civilization was still functioning, I was grateful to find a seat for the slow journey it plied back to Oakland over city streets. A few riders were distributed sparsely throughout the bus, nearly all of them rendered mute by the quake. While I was too preoccupied to size them up, it appeared that most of them were riding solo, as alone as I was. Only a couple of young guys in the back of the bus were nervously talking.

"I'm worried about my sister," I heard one of them mutter to the other. "By now she should be on BART on her way home from San Francisco."

I shuddered at the thought. We all knew that the BART line tunneled deep under the floor of San Francisco Bay. Had the earthquake squeezed the tunnel shut, or worse, opened a big crack in it, allowing water to rush in?

When I reached home, all I could think to do was to draw a bath to calm myself down. The power was out but the tap water was still tepid, and I lay bobbing in the darkness with only a flashlight for company. I had no idea what had happened to James. In my worry and anxiety, I wondered if the employees' boat from Alcatraz had capsized in a tidal wave on its way back to the pier. Then a tiny, uninvited voice in the back of my mind whispered that it might actually be good if the boat had overturned because it would spare James the horrific litany of opportunistic infections that surely lay ahead of him, each more debilitating than the last.

Chiding myself for what amounted to a selfish fantasy, I confronted my suspicion that I was more concerned with saving myself from witnessing James's coming AIDS trauma than I was with relieving him from it. I was always sabotaging myself in that way—experiencing a genuine moment of empathy, only to follow up, one moment later, by believing the worst of myself. My biggest fear was that my will to survive and thrive, paired with my desire to shield myself from pain, would block me from becoming a compassionate caregiver.

After what seemed like an eternity, James finally burst into the apartment at 10:30 p.m., and I sighed with relief. He was laughing a little as he made a beeline for the bathroom. When he finally emerged, he explained what had happened.

"The trans-Bay buses aren't running, and BART is closed. I had to take a bus across the Golden Gate Bridge to Marin County. Then I had to take another bus across the San Rafael Bridge to get to the East Bay!"

"Oh, my goodness—where did you get on the San Rafael bus?" I asked, marveling at what a circuitous route he had been required to take.

"You pick it up next to San Quentin," he said. It occurred to me how odd it was that he had left one prison—Alcatraz—only to travel to another notorious one.

"The bus driver refused to stop to let us pee!" he added indignantly. "Can you imagine? All those passengers, each and every one of them dislocated, and the driver wouldn't make any accommodations for them!" Shaking my head disapprovingly, I hugged him tight. It was such a relief to have him home safe and alive. At least for the time being, life's unpredictable events had conquered my fears about his fate and my place in it.

When the power came back on, news reports informed us that a section of the Bay Bridge's upper deck had collapsed and fallen onto the lower deck, scarcely one hour after I had crossed it. Later, I learned that a young landscape architect I had only recently met died when the car she drove was crushed by the collapsing upper deck of Oakland's double-decker Cypress Structure freeway. I took a deep breath and said a silent prayer of gratitude. Due to no more than great timing, I had narrowly evaded death that day on the bridge.

The next morning, I got up with a vague sense that maybe I should go out on the front lines and help excavate stranded people from the rubble, but it appeared that everyone who had been caught in the earthquake was either safe, dead, or already in the hospital. Television news reports were beginning to call it the Loma Prieta quake, named for the remote peak in the Santa Cruz mountains that served as its epicenter. Most of the damage was confined to the low-lying, squishy liquefaction zones of West Oakland and San Francisco's Marina District— flat shorelands that were inherently unstable due to their lack of bedrock.

But the most sensational disruption was to the Bay Bridge World Series, which at that very moment was being fought between the Oakland A's and the San Francisco Giants. It seemed extraordinary that a major earthquake could have occurred at the exact moment of this historic and unprecedented cross-Bay matchup, severing their two home stadiums. When the Series resumed, ten days later, James was delighted that his beloved A's won, becoming world champions. As to the Bay Bridge, it remained closed for a month, although BART service was quickly restored. The well-engineered tunnels had survived the earthquake with no damage. To replace the interrupted trans-Bay buses, temporary ferry service to San Francisco opened at Oakland's Jack London Square, and it was an unexpected delight to take a boat to work across the waves, with the sun and wind in my face.

Despite my jitters about the substantial aftershocks that followed, I assumed that the big quake had bought us plenty of time until the next one rolled in. After all, eighty-three whole years had passed since the previous big one, the famous San Francisco earthquake of 1906. Still, between the scourge of AIDS and the ever-present seismic threat, Northern California was beginning to feel like a dangerous place in which to live.

Early one Friday evening, a week or two after the quake, there was a knock at the door. James and I opened it to the beaming face of Delia, our neighbor in the apartment building.

"Hey, guys," she said, nodding her head at the gorgeous Black guy who stood next to her, hand in hand. It was not the first time this had happened. Forever serially dating Black men, Delia never bored of presenting us with her newest "friend" before going off on a date. Apart from the fact that her olive skin revealed her Portuguese heritage, she reminded me of Nola Darling in Spike Lee's *She's Gotta Have It*.

Delia took it for granted that my admiration for the guy would register on my face, but this time even James rose to the bait. As soon as we shut the door behind her, he exclaimed, "Mmmmm-*mmmmm*!"

One of the things I loved about James was that, unlike Chad, he didn't mind when I was attracted to another guy, as long as I made no moves in his direction. Nor was James shy at sharing his own attractions with me. Flirting with Delia's boyfriends was a welcome diversion for both of us, taking our minds off James's condition by rekindling our desire for one another.

30 A THREESOME

AS DIVERTING as the earthquake and Delia's sexy boyfriends were for us, they could do nothing to stop the inexorable progress of the HIV time-bomb in James's bloodstream. Not long after we first met, Ashford and Simpson had released a new duet called "Solid," and we quickly agreed to call it our song because its refrain about how the singing couple's love was rock solid aptly evoked the strong bond of our love. In the beginning, we played it regularly, singing along with enthusiasm. But if our love was a rock, now a narrow but lethal crack was beginning to form in it, threatening to wedge it apart.

When James's AIDS symptoms first manifested, I began to fantasize that there were three of us living together in a ménage à trois: James, me, and an uninvited guest—a mysterious disease with a scary personality all its own. Previously, James and I had made all our decisions together as a couple, but now Mister HIV had to be consulted on everything. His quirks demanded to be respected, and not least when James and I negotiated the roulette wheel of safer sex options. There was the downright risky option—unprotected anal sex—followed by an à-la-carte menu of somewhat more-to-less-risky options, from using a condom, to sucking with or without swallowing pre-cum, to kissing. Reduced to printed text on bulletins from the local health department, the choices all sounded so mechanical and clinical, so unlike what the corresponding sexual activities actually felt like.

No matter which safer sex options we chose—no matter how we chose to make love—the virus climbed into bed with us. I soon developed a grotesque fantasy that James was having an affair with his sinister boyfriend, AIDS. As absurd as the thought was, it made me jealous—I wanted James to myself—but the bottom line was that the virus had claimed him, and now my gut said it wanted to possess me too. At the same time, I knew that James was begging to escape the third man's clutches. He wanted desperately to return to me, even as I was trying to run away from our uninvited guest.

One morning, James woke up with a bad cough, and when I went to make the bed, the sheets were soaking wet. By that afternoon, it was time to take him to the emergency room, and he was admitted to the hospital with what turned out to be pneumocystis. There he remained for several nights. At first, I stayed overnight with him, lying fully dressed in a cot, but I scarcely slept. It was the first of five hospitalizations for pneumocystis, each one lasting three or four nights.

After his first bout, James's doctor prescribed AZT, which was effectively the only available AIDS treatment at that time. Like chemotherapy, it was a highly toxic medication, and one of its side effects was peripheral neuropathy, which manifested as severe numbness and pain in James's feet. There was no way to soothe him without taking him off AZT, but that choice would have led to certain death.

Sitting on the sofa one night, he implored me, "Would ja rub ma feet? Would ja rub ma feet?"

His voice was the plaintive voice of a child. Of course, I willingly complied, hoping against hope that massaging his feet would miraculously cure him, but I could never rub them long enough to assuage his pain. Every night, I massaged his feet, and the following day they were painful all over again.

"Would ja rub ma feet?" he said, again and again. I can still hear that beseeching voice in the back of my head.

After each hospital stay, an endless round of doctor's appointments ensued. Some involved crossing the Bay Bridge into San Francisco, while others took place at Kaiser Permanente in Oakland. Each appointment meant long delays in the waiting room, sitting among tattered magazines, until at last his name was called. Each one led to lab tests, and each test led to the next appointment, in a perpetual round-robin. James's body was continually poked and prodded; his blood constantly analyzed for his viral load, the number of his helper T cells, and a thousand other things. With transportation time, the appointments could easily take up more than half a day, becoming almost as much of a source of misery as the symptoms themselves. I came to think of them as Med World: James had entered Med World, and there was no more escape from it than for a prisoner on Alcatraz.

"I'm not a science project!" he exclaimed angrily, after one particularly grueling round of tests.

Our friend Vicky was a frequent visitor and a great helpmate. She and James kept each other company while I was away at work or on a bike ride, relishing the wind and sun on my face, the respite they brought from stress. Many times, I returned to the apartment to find the drapes pulled shut in broad daylight while Vicky and James huddled closely together, giggling and gasping as a horror movie flashed by on the VCR in lurid hues of red and black. At other times, I found Delia sitting on the couch watching an Oakland A's game with James. Delia loved sports as much as Vicky loved horror flicks.

As the months dragged on, James alternated between bouts of pneumocystis and periods of relative health, progressing through four of the five stages of grief described by Elisabeth Kübler-Ross. Mostly skipping the denial phase, he zigzagged between periods of bargaining and anger. Naturally, he directed his anger toward me, since along with his mother, Charlene, I was the person he was closest to.

One Sunday afternoon, Vicky invited me to attend a service at an African American congregation where a friend of hers was singing. Since James was working that day, I agreed to go. Sitting next to Vicky in a raised pew, I admired all the gospel singers and the heavenly voice of a nine-year-old girl prodigy. But when I returned home after the service to find James sitting on the living room sofa, I instantly knew that he was furious.

"What's wrong?" I asked.

"Nothing—I'm *fine!*" he said, glaring at me briefly before returning his gaze to the TV set.

"Oh, come on—what's the matter?"

But he only frowned and continued staring resolutely at the television. I shouldn't have been surprised. I knew well that he had a passive-aggressive streak that led him to give me the silent treatment when he got angry, and it was only getting worse. Often, it took days to coax him into explaining what I had done wrong.

I sighed, retreating to the bedroom. This time there was no need to press James because I already knew what I had done or, rather, not done: I had attended Vicky's friend's church service, when I had never cared enough to make time to hear Charlene sing in her Southern Baptist church choir. He had repeatedly asked me to accompany him to her church, but I had always declined because I lived for my regular Sunday lap swim and the service conflicted with the pool schedule.

Just because the timing of Vicky's church service was more convenient for me was no excuse for my failure to accompany James to his mother's church. I knew that. The incident only amplified the ever-present background noise of mistrust that I had learned nearly always characterizes interracial relationships. Did my hesitation to attend Charlene's service mean that James felt I devalued her, his Black mother, or that I devalued her church, which was such a pivotal beacon for Oakland's Black community? I didn't know, but since I had never bothered to hear her sing in the choir, those questions were destined to remain hanging in the air.

From the moment we first met, James had expressed his fear of abandonment, and of course his illness only reinforced it. Every day he asked me to hold him, just hold him. I did it willingly and with all my love, but I could never hold him often enough or long enough to soothe him. While he coped as well as he could, I rushed to embrace my instinct for self-preservation. Every day, I looked in the mirror, confirmed my well-being, and felt grateful for what I assumed was the fortress of my good health. Perversely, the sicker James got, the healthier I felt. As time went by, that fundamental distinction became the wedge of ice in the rock of our love.

We knew of other gay couples who had broken up when one or the other got sick, and I realized it could happen to us.

Fortunately, James agreed to go to couples counseling, and our therapist, Marly, implored me to remain faithful to him, no matter how bumpy the journey. Even though my sex drive raged insanely on, oblivious to all that was happening around me, I managed to do so right up until the end. To this day, I am proud of that.

There was no winning in this situation, so I threw myself into an irrational and futile effort to mitigate loss, as if I could reduce it to the bare minimum through an act of sheer will. I began to erect a force field, a hard, transparent shell, to protect myself from my rawest emotions. The truth was that I was experiencing anticipatory grieving, already positioning myself for what life would be like after James died. I knew that I was going to grieve, and the first stage was an apprehension of the flood of emotions to come.

When we feel a lump in our throat at the thought of our loved one dying, it's a proof of our love, which is something to celebrate. But, at the same time, since we are grieving only the *idea* of our loved one's death, it must mean that part of us has already given up on the beloved's life force. That part has yielded to disease and fate.

I felt guilty not only for expecting to survive James but also for lacking faith in his longevity. Burdened by this conflict, I began attending caregiver support groups at Kairos House, in San Francisco, near the corner of Castro and Market. Named for the Greek word meaning "the time when things come to a head," Kairos was a terrific shelter against the AIDS tsunami, a safe place for caregivers to check in for peer support, guided by group therapists. It was a wonder how the counselors soldiered on. Burned out by all the grief around them, they somehow managed to rally their spirits, giving even more of themselves as they passed the "talking feather" from one participant to the next. To my immense relief, at Kairos I learned that all of my complicated feelings of guilt and anticipatory grief were normal.

In the group sessions, I was horrified by the stories of caregivers who had been at it pretty much full blast for seven, eight, or nine years. Their loved ones had repeatedly approached the brink of death, only to rally one more time, granted a few blessed weeks of remission to prepare for the next debilitating onslaught. James had been sick for not much longer than a year, but he had already had four hospitalizations, and I wondered how long his battle could last. Of course, we both wanted him to live as long as possible, but wasn't it an awful fate to hang on for years, oscillating from one opportunistic infection to the next, each time returning to relative health at a lower ebb than before? All the while, AZT was still the only viable treatment, and it was imperfect at best.

Life became an exhausting round of leaving for work, coming home, doing the grocery shopping, and going to Kentucky Fried Chicken to get James's favorite treat, extra crispy wings. On my regular trips to our local Walgreens to pick up his prescriptions, the lines were long and the employees poorly trained. Standing in line sometimes for over half an hour, I grew increasingly tired and frustrated. Far from being apologetic when a medication was not yet ready, despite having been ordered days ahead, the pharmacy assistants only shrugged and beckoned to the next customer. Could it be disgust for AIDS sufferers that registered on their dismissive faces? It was maddening. Once I finally got home, I would find James curled up on the sofa watching TV, covered by his favorite blanket. He was beginning to look like no more than the shell of the enthusiastic, funny, and passionate man I had fallen in love with.

As exhausting as life was for me, James was the one in the eye of the storm, and I tried my best to be his lifeline. On the occasions when he had enough energy, we continued our joyful weekend walks.

One afternoon, while we were walking down the street on our way to Lake Merritt, he suddenly said, "It's so hard dying like this."

"I can imagine," I quickly responded.

"No, you can't—you can't possibly imagine!" he shouted angrily, thrusting his hands into his jacket pockets.

We walked on in silence—there was nothing I could say. He had said it all. I tried my best to put myself in his place, to visualize what he was going through, but it was true that I couldn't actually feel it.

Along with my survivor's guilt came a resurgent sense of guilt about being gay in the first place. There were small but toxic antigay protests at the San Francisco Pride parades and the Castro Halloween celebrations, and it felt as if the power of the entire religious right were levied against us, channeled through the hatred of Anita Bryant and North Carolina's viciously homophobic senator, Jesse Helms. Now that these powerful dragons were on the warpath, I began to fear that maybe Ronald Reagan's indifference was right, that AIDS was a moral judgment visited on me and my kind by the wrath of God. No other disease came with the same pariah status—no politician ever claimed that God punished sinful people by giving them cancer or diabetes. The root cause of their judgment relied on the fact that HIV is transmitted sexually. To break down their argument, it was that contracting the disease amounted to a direct punishment for what they viewed as our deviant sexual behavior. My brain rejected that proposition, but on a deeper, subconscious level, I found it harder to shake off.

The power and reach of the San Francisco gay community, ravaged though it was by AIDS, worked hard to impress on me and my queer brothers that AIDS was not a moral judgment; it was simply a disease like any other, no matter how deadly. At the Pride parades, I never felt more empowered than when we yelled, "Hey, Hey, Ho, Ho, Jesse Helms has got to go!" while flinging coins onto a giant rainbow flag held aloft like a hammock by eight or ten young men and women. As the flag slowly made its way down Market Street, sagging lower and lower under the weight of all our anti-Helms campaign contributions, each coin seemed to represent one more dead man tossed into a mass coffin propelled forward by pallbearers.

Still, no matter how strong the chanting made me feel, no matter how wholeheartedly I embraced Pride at the parades and rallies, when I left the rejoicing crowds and returned to the quiet privacy of home, my gay tribe's transfusion of strength wore off and I was once again reduced to a weak and vulnerable state, to the guilty sense of being impure. But why? When I was honest with myself, I couldn't say that I truly believed that God was angry at me and my kind. Instead, I felt the weight of an enormous social pressure that condemned me for my refusal to conform, for my insistence on owning my sexuality and claiming my freedom.

James wanted very much for us to get married. Gay men and women were enacting commitment ceremonies, and the City of Berkeley had passed a proclamation recognizing these as equivalent to marriages, although the ordinance had no legal standing.

While I would have enthusiastically married him a couple of years before, HIV had strained our relationship enough that I was hesitant. I loved him still, very much, but it saddened me to think of marrying while we were often at odds, quarreling about such things as his mother's church. Of course, marriages were all about committing to one another in sickness and in health, and I was already doing that to the best of my ability. But the wedding itself? I wanted it to be a joyous occasion, with champagne, cake, smiles on our faces, and lots of laughing, dancing guests. Shouldn't weddings happen when both partners are in radiant health, fully ready to embrace the joyful moment?

Still, if it was what James wanted, I was up for it.

"I suppose we could go to Berkeley and get married…" I said one evening. My voice trailed a bit, inadvertently revealing my reluctance.

"No," James said defiantly. "I want to get married in Oakland."

He loved Oakland and desperately wanted the city council to issue a marriage proclamation equivalent to Berkeley's. When Oakland did not comply, that put an end to the matter, and we never got married.

Whatever the incident revealed about me, it showed how James was becoming rigid and stubborn. One evening, when I came home sporting a new pair of glasses, he was incensed.

"What are you doing with those new glasses?" he asked dismissively.

"I had to get a new prescription," I explained, already on the defensive.

"Why couldn't you just keep the old frame?" Clearly bitter, it was obvious that he wanted me to keep the old frame so that I would look exactly the same as I always had. He must have felt that if he could freeze time, if he could eradicate all the changes it inevitably brought, no matter how small, maybe he wouldn't have to die a young man.

Not long after, James's inner barometer shifted from anger toward acceptance. One day, he brought home Eric Carle's little children's book, *The Very Hungry Caterpillar*, about a caterpillar who turns into a butterfly. It managed to soothe his anxiety about dying, as if the butterfly represented the heavenly body we earthly caterpillars might all hope to inhabit after death. Illustrated with graceful drawings, its promise of redemptive transformation and rebirth was inspirational.

"What do you think of this?" James asked, slowly turning the pages in front of me.

"It's a nice message," I said brusquely, "but I wish the author could have expressed it in a more sophisticated, adult way."

Tears of frustration immediately welled in James's eyes, and he turned away angrily, leaving the room without another word. I was devastated. Why had I been so callous, so dismissive and unsupportive? I could have said the book was beautiful. Instead, I had to get all analytical, which I have a bad habit of doing at the wrong moment. I knew he felt that I had rejected him, dashing his newfound hope of finding inner peace.

It was all a mistake, a misunderstanding of what we were each trying to communicate, and I wished with all my heart that I could take back my words. The last thing I wanted was to hurt him, and to this day, I don't know what possessed me to say something that must have sounded so arrogant. After all, the book poetically expressed my own belief in reincarnation and my faith in the potential we all have of attaining enlightenment. Just because I wanted it formulated in a more sophisticated manner didn't make it any less legitimate or meaningful. Every time I think of that incident, a new wave of sorrow washes over me.

One day, a few weeks after our impasse over the butterfly, we were both sitting on the living room sofa. I was rubbing James's feet when he covered his face with his hands and said softly, "I just want to go home."

"What do you mean? You *are* home," I said, but I knew exactly what he meant. He wanted to go back to the place where the butterflies fly free.

31 A PSYCHIC

NOT LONG before James's first bout with pneumocystis, Saddam Hussein invaded Kuwait and America was plunged into a recession. My work at MPA Design, where I continued to design Silicon Valley corporate landscapes, ground to a near halt. While I was not immediately threatened with being laid off, I was afraid that I'd lose my hard-won rank in the firm, so I interviewed for a new job at a small landscape architecture firm in Berkeley called Andrea Lucas Associates. Although the projects were not particularly inspiring, this turned out to be the right decision because the office was close by. When James got sick, it was only a short drive home or to the hospital to care for him, and Andrea could not have been more understanding and supportive.

Meanwhile, after several hospital stays, James was forced to go on medical leave from Alcatraz. It was a huge blow—he loved that job and wanted to return to work more than anything other than survival itself. When he was released from one hospitalization, Vicky and I tied a bouquet of colorful helium balloons to his wheelchair while we escorted him out to the car. Returning home, we affixed the balloons to a dining room chair, where they rose to the ceiling, becoming a powerful symbol of our prayers for his recovery, his return to a full life.

On our ninth anniversary, we sat down on the sofa to exchange cards. James was beaming as he handed his to me. Quickly tearing open the envelope and pulling out his card, I found a stylized picture of shooting stars and comets against a sunset sky, bearing the words, "You came, falling like a miracle into my life, filling my heart with beautiful dreams and wishes." On the inside, in a small and shaky hand, James had written a note that I will always treasure:

My Darling,

Life has not been very easy for us lately. With the illness and tears, we have been through so much. But through it all my love for you has not changed one bit. We had so many hopes and dreams for the future. But fate has changed all of that. We can dream about the future, but let's think more about the great memories. After nine years, we have collected a lot of wonderful memories. You have really made my last nine years the most treasured in my life. That will be the best gift that you could give me. Don't doubt my love. I thank you for the strength you have given me. I can face anything with you at my side. Let's enjoy the time we have left. And collect a few more memories. Happy ninth.

I love you, J.

Tears sprang to my eyes as I reached over to hug him and hold him tight.

"I love you too," I said. "I love you so much, and I treasure our time together."

I was filled with relief to have received this proof of his love, of his continuing trust in me. It meant that he had forgiven me for everything . . . even my failure to listen to his mother sing in church, even my callous words about the butterfly book. It meant that, despite all my faults and my shortcomings as a caregiver, I had given him the gift of love and stability, the two things that both of us valued most. It also meant that James's emotions were progressing from anger to acceptance. His death still seemed inevitable, but now when it happened, I felt sure that he would be able to pass away in peace.

"Oh, and there's something else I want to tell you," James said.

"What is it?"

"When I'm gone, I want you to move back to Seattle. You need to be closer to your mom and dad, and I think they're going to need you."

This was so unexpected that I didn't know what to say, but it touched me deeply and started me thinking. Everybody loved my parents, and James was no exception. They appeared to everyone like the very model of a loving and supportive elderly couple, and few people guessed at how I had sparred with Dad over the years. I did miss them a lot, and what made it more pressing was that Mom was beginning to exhibit the first signs of heart disease. I had to admit that if James were to pass, there would be little left to hold me in the Bay Area.

My restless mind had already begun to ruminate about what shape my life might take after James's death. Even though our couples' counselor, Marly, urged me to be alive in the present moment, I couldn't help daydreaming about the future. She must have known I was troubled about it, but she certainly didn't bring it up in front of James. Instead, one day, she unexpectedly referred me to a psychic who she said had helped her a lot.

"What's the point of going to a psychic?" I asked. "Isn't that just a cop-out—an illusory short-cut from the hard work of therapy?"

Marly had a ready answer. "I'm here to help you cope with your day-to-day life, but Stan will have insight into the long view, into what the past portends for your future," she said.

Her words made a lot of sense to me, allowing me to overcome the reservations cooked up by the rational side of my brain. I decided to make an appointment with him. This was San Francisco, where any and every type of spiritual healing was embraced with near universal enthusiasm.

On the day of my appointment, I parked on upper Market Street, high on the hillside leading up to Twin Peaks. Presaging the long view that Marly had promised, a panorama of the Bay Area unfolded before me, from the crystal-sharp point of the Transamerica Pyramid to the majestic Bay Bridge, and across the turquoise Bay to the golden Berkeley hills. After drinking my fill of the spectacular view, I rang the doorbell at Stan's flat.

"Nice to meet you, Brooks—come on up," Stan said, opening the door.

With his green eyes and tousled brown hair, he looked like a friendly gay man only a tad older than me. I felt at ease as he guided me up a stairway. At the top, he gestured toward the small room where he conducted his readings. Sitting down across from me, Stan placed his elbows on a small bistro table, clasped his head between his hands, and closed his eyes. A moment of silence passed, and I wondered if he was just being theatrical. But then he spoke.

"I'm getting lots of vibrations," he said, pointing this way and that, his eyes still closed. "Yes. There's one over there, and another one over there—Brooks, is your father's name Joseph?" he abruptly asked, interrupting himself.

"No," I answered, wondering if I had made a mistake in coming.

"Hmm, I'm getting the name Joseph. Maybe your grandfather . . . was he named Joseph?"

I felt myself becoming irritable; there was nobody in my family named Joseph, but then it hit me.

"No," I said. "But my grandmother's name was Josephine. I called her Nana."

"That's it," said Stan. "She wants you to know that everything's fine and she's gone back to having long hair."

I was astonished because this disclosure could mean only one thing—Stan was the real thing, a legitimate psychic. My father's mother had died earlier that same year, but there was no way Stan could have known that. One of my earliest memories was of watching Nana sit down at her vanity at the end of the day, when she would gently remove the decorative combs in her hair. Loosening her giant salt-and-pepper bun, she tossed her head vigorously, letting her hair down. When she brushed it out, I saw that it extended all the way down to the small of her back. I could never think of Nana without picturing her long, lustrous tresses, yet in recent years she had shorn her now white hair into a short, practical cut. At these vivid recollections, I leaned forward, eagerly awaiting what Stan would tell me next.

"Whenever you go through an emotional crisis," he was saying, "there are five negative A's and five positive A's. It's up to you whether to give in to the negative A's, such as apprehension and anger, or whether you're ready to embrace the five positive

A's—awareness, acknowledgment, acceptance, affirmation, and finally, action. You might be aware that you desire a change in your life, but you're not ready to acknowledge what is at first an unwelcome thought." Stan placed his forefinger on the back of his neck. Then he moved it sequentially upward and over his head, briefly touching four points before stopping at his frontal cortex.

"Every thought leading you toward change begins at the back of your head," he explained. "It begins with awareness, then gradually moves up over your head until you're finally ready to affirm it. When you reach affirmation, you can proceed to action, and it will be *positive* action," he concluded, touching his frontal lobe again.

I didn't realize it at first, but we were talking about an embryonic thought already gestating in the back of my mind.

"What do you see if I move back to Seattle?" I asked.

"I see quality people," he said. "You will meet quality people."

Leaving Stan's apartment after the reading, I wondered what he meant about meeting quality people. Did it mean that the people I knew and loved in the Bay Area were not valuable? Of course not, but nevertheless, the phrase intrigued me. "Quality people." Didn't that mean people who might understand me better—the whole me, and not just my career persona or my gay identity? The more I thought about it, the more I wondered if that's what Stan meant. In the Bay Area, my friends and acquaintances tended to group themselves around either my work or my personal life, but rarely both, just as they had in Philadelphia. Could moving to Seattle mean meeting people who would be equally receptive to both sides of my personality?

Two months after James and I exchanged cards on our ninth anniversary, something happened that made Stan's words even more prescient. I was on a brief visit home to Seattle when my boss, Andrea Lucas, called.

"Hi, Brooks," she said. "I'm sorry to tell you this, but I have to lay you off. Revenues are down and I don't have enough work to keep you employed. I know this is a hard time for you," she added. "But you've got talent and ability. You'll manage."

"Um, okay. . . thanks," I said, hanging up.

What more was there to say? Having never been laid off before, I was stunned. I took a deep breath, letting it sink in. This meant that, over time, there was one less thing holding me to the Bay Area. Sitting in the two-floor high space next to the tall windows in the house Dad had designed for our family, I let my mind wander. Stan had said unequivocally that if I moved back home, I would encounter quality people. Maybe what he really meant was that in Seattle I would at last find the enduring sense of community that had so eluded me in San Francisco? I let that question hang in the air.

Snapping out of my reverie, I was scared to realize that I was suddenly jobless, and I didn't know how James and I would manage financially. Fortunately, only a few days later, I received another unexpected phone call, this time with good news. It was an invitation to come work for a new firm called Befu, Morris, Scardina. Jon Befu, Dan Morris, and Paul Scardina were three former colleagues from my first San Francisco job at Omi Lang Associates. George Omi and Willy Lang had retired, but their high-profile project, the Franklin Delano Roosevelt Memorial, had finally been resurrected by President Bill Clinton after eleven years during which Reagan and George H. W. Bush had blocked funding for it. The preeminent landscape architect, Lawrence Halprin, was once again at work on the memorial, and he had asked Paul, Dan, and Jon to assist him by preparing the construction drawings. Rejoicing at this unexpected second chance to—at last—work on a meaningful project that elevated landscape architecture to a high art form, I accepted the offer enthusiastically, even though it meant driving forty miles every day from Oakland to Redwood City, across the San Mateo Bridge.

When I started my new job, James was healthier than he had been in months, and it even looked as if he could return to work in a few weeks. "I'm planning to march in the San Francisco AIDS Walk, and I'm going to ask my whole family to join me," he said.

"Great—I'll march with you," I said, and James's hands were already on the phone, dialing his mother. After one or two quick calls, his mother, Charlene, his brother, Shawn, and his three sisters all exclaimed, "We're in!"

When the big day arrived in mid-July, all of us crossed the Bay Bridge to meet up in Golden Gate Park along with thousands of young men and women and their families. Everyone wore bright T-shirts, many of them bearing the logos of sponsoring corporations like Chevron, where James's sister Daretta worked. Accented against the emerald backdrop of the park, the colorful and diverse crowd offered up a resplendent display of well-being, a united front of joyous defiance against the tragic pandemic. A drum corps beat out rousing samba rhythms, and drag queens twirled rainbow fans as we began to march.

Beaming and grinning from ear to ear, James proudly held his head high. Slim to begin with, he now looked thinner than ever, and the disease had somehow darkened his skin. As I watched him move, he resembled a weightless marionette propelled by strings from the sky. But James still held the strings. Despite his fragility, the great light of his spirit shone through, and I knew how proud he was to be marching in solidarity with his real and metaphorical brothers and sisters. He was celebrating his survival and his upswing in health, proud to have lived long enough to participate in this joyous march. He was also delighted to be giving back to the community by mingling the individual donations we had received with the crowd's contributions, in a great river of charity.

Martin Luther King Jr. had led his armies of peaceful protesters in the song "We Shall Overcome," and this was James's moment to overcome the plague, no matter how brief was his time left on earth. Although tinged with the shared grief of the marching multitudes, our walk was a great joy. When we crossed the finish line, we felt sure that love and health could somehow triumph against all the odds.

The happiness we felt at the AIDS walk, our sense of joy triumphing, surfaced again during a visit to our local Safeway, of all places. One day, James grabbed a cart and went charging full speed down the aisle, running away from me with his marionette gait. When he reached the end of the aisle, he turned back to face me with a big grin. Then, catching my eye, he affected a theatrical gasp of distress, springing upward on his toes and rounding the corner to run away again up the next aisle. He enjoyed playing this game so much that he repeated it each time we went grocery shopping. I came to love it as well, for it was one of the few times that I once again witnessed the carefree, laughing James I had fallen in love with nearly a decade earlier.

GOODBYE, JAMES

EARLY SEPTEMBER arrived, and I made plans to celebrate my fortieth birthday in Vancouver, British Columbia, with Mom and Dad. I was looking forward to a little getaway after all the months of doctor and hospital visits and the ups and downs of James's moods.

"So, James is not coming?" Mom asked on the phone, her voice flecked with concern.

"No," I said. "I wish he could, but he's finally enjoying a spate of good health, and he doesn't want to jeopardize that."

"Oh, I see, poor baby. Please give him our love, and thank him for loaning you back to us," she concluded. Then Dad got on the phone and chorused Mom's words.

Hanging up, I sighed. While Mom and Dad had not gone out of their way to help us out during my months of caregiving, I didn't blame them for it. There wasn't much they could do from a distance of over eight hundred miles anyway, and they probably felt that it was best not to interfere.

On the outskirts of Vancouver, Mom, Dad, and I visited the Capilano Canyon suspension bridge, a tourist site in a forested gorge, high above a rushing stream. As we got out of the car, a fresh pine scent graced the mountain air. Ranks of conifers rose from the sheer cliff facing us across the creek, reminding me of how much I missed the Pacific Northwest.

Mom and Dad watched from an overlook as I stepped gingerly onto the pedestrian bridge. It immediately began swaying under my feet, unnerving me, but then a group of teenagers came running and jumping, deliberately amplifying its bounce. I froze in fear, tightly grasping the rope rail between two clenched fists. As I looked down at the creek tumbling over the rocks so far below, my stomach twisted and I felt as if the bridge were about to overturn and throw me off.

A moment later, a stout middle-aged matron came along and swept me up, clasping my hand and marching me efficiently across to the other bank. I found that as long as I looked straight in front of me, without pausing to glance from one side to the other or down to the abyss, I could conquer my irrational fear of heights.

The humiliating incident embarrassed me, but when I thought of it afterward, it felt like a parable, like an enactment of the Twenty-third Psalm: "Yea, though I walk through the valley of the shadow of death, I will fear no evil: for Thou *art* with me; Thy rod and Thy staff they comfort me."

Like a guardian angel, the matronly woman had appeared out of nowhere at a moment when I desperately needed faith, if only the faith to continue caring for James with all my heart. Of course, he was the one walking at that moment through the valley of death's shadow—not I—but that did not stop me from feeling weak and inadequate as his caregiver. I needed all the help and faith I could find to get me through.

Returning from Vancouver in time to spend my actual birthday with James, I brought him a dozen red roses. He was surprised and a bit confused. "Why did you bring me roses on your birthday?" he asked.

"I wanted to. I wanted to express how much I love you, how much I admire your courage," I said.

"Oh, that's so sweet of you," he said, enveloping me in a hug. "You really didn't have to, but I love you for it."

A week later, James went to see his doctor, who gave him a flu shot. Although that appeared to be a wise precaution, his condition changed so rapidly afterward that I could never shake the feeling, right or wrong, that it killed him.

A couple of days after his appointment, I was at work in Redwood City when my phone rang.

"I can't walk," James said. "I can't walk and I need something in the fridge."

"Can you crawl?" I asked, and he said yes. "Okay, see if you can crawl to the refrigerator and I'll come home right away," I said, panic rising in my chest. My friend and colleague, Sandra, was sitting next to me, listening to my side of the conversation.

"Go home, Brooks, go home right away," she said, but I hesitated for half an hour. I didn't want to leave the calm and order of the office, which I desperately needed just then, only to return to the chaos, fear, and anxiety that were awaiting me at home.

The drive back to Oakland took an hour. When I finally got home, I found James in bed, still immobile. He looked amazingly weak, especially considering how strong he had appeared on my birthday, less than ten days before.

"Do you think you need to go to the emergency room?"

"No, I don't think so—not yet. And Mom's coming over." Charlene soon arrived and sat with James, comforting him for a few hours, then left to go home. As soon as she departed, he changed his mind. "Take me to the emergency room," he said.

"Okay," I said, reaching for my car keys. Rallying to rise from the bed with almost superhuman energy, he managed not only to walk but to run down the stairs to the parking garage. When he got to the car, though, for some reason he had trouble getting in on the passenger's side, so I had to push him through the driver's door and over the gear shift until he was finally seated. Then we took off, making a beeline for the emergency room. Once there, an attendant came out with a wheelchair, pushing James in while I registered him.

Anxiously standing at the counter, filling out the long forms, I glanced back at him. What I saw was a limp, exhausted, and emaciated figure sitting in a wheelchair like a frayed rag doll. Dressed in my teal-colored windbreaker, hastily pulled on over his pajamas, the sight of him seared itself into my memory, filling me with shock, terror, and compassion. Although he was only thirty feet away, the distance between us seemed insurmountable. I felt a lump rising in my throat, but I quickly pushed it down so that I could answer the intake questions in all their excruciating detail.

What I wanted more than anything at that moment was for God to shoot a beam of pure energy directly at James's chest, curing him instantly and restoring him to the happy, healthy, and vital man I had fallen in love with. But my hope for that joyful outcome had been diminishing for a long time now. The woman on the swaying bridge had helped me redirect my prayers, giving me the courage I needed to get through this ordeal, although not enough to muster the infinitely greater faith I would need to expect miracles.

After what seemed like eternity, we finally got James admitted to the ICU. By now he was highly agitated, thrashing about like a salmon on a hook. Trying desperately to tell us something, it drove him to madness that the nurses and I couldn't understand.

Finally, I said, "Can you write it down?" I handed him a piece of scratch paper and a Bic pen. After several unsuccessful attempts, he managed to write the word "Ice" in a ragged script, the "e" trailing off into a long tail. His mouth was burning with fever and he wanted to cool down with a piece of ice, but the nurse wouldn't allow it, due to his condition, whatever it was.

That was the last communication I ever had with James unless I counted my thoughts and prayers. The next thing I knew, the nurse gave him a shot of a badly needed sedative and he went limp on his gurney. By now it was about 3:00 a.m., so I went home to grab a few hours of sleep. At about 6:00 a.m., I had a call from the ICU.

"Come quickly," they said. "James is in a coma."

My head was pounding as I staggered out of bed for the drive back to the hospital. When I walked into the room, an intubation tube was stuffed down his throat, making an awful groaning noise. As I watched his lungs mechanically inflate, fear, despair, and pity writhed inside me like waves.

"I love you, James," I said. "And I miss you."

Every day over the next week, I came to the hospital and sat by his bed. I told him over and over again how much I loved him and missed him, but he was completely unresponsive. Since he appeared to be beyond any cure, my words were meant more to speed his journey to the other side than to incite his return to me and his family. Much as we all wanted that, I felt in my heart that the radiant white light must have appeared to him by then, bidding him to enter it, and I prayed for him to do so.

As the days went by, his body grew grotesquely bloated. A tube was breathing for him, and the nurses were doing their best to keep him from getting bedsores. There didn't seem to be anything I could do to help him, apart from praying and telling him once again how much I loved him. After a couple of days, a nurse took me aside and told me, "Brooks, all his organs are shutting down."

One day in the ICU, I turned to smile at myself in the mirror. In the caregivers' support group, we had been taught to do that every morning, composing ourselves to ease our passage through the day. Like taking a deep breath, smiling into the mirror helped us carve out a small space for our own well-being, outside the maelstrom of anxiety and grief engulfing us. I was growing a goatee, and when I caught myself admiring my new look, I tried to recognize myself, to identify who I was then, on that day, and who I might become. I was going to be alone again, that I knew, but when I caught my smile in the mirror, I recognized in it a reservoir of continuing energy and vitality. Life was going to be hard, but I would be okay. I would get through this.

When it became clear that James was not going to return to us, I realized that it might be my responsibility as his health care power of attorney to make the decision to withdraw life support. Burdened by the enormity of making such a momentous life-and-death decision on my own, I felt like I was being called upon to become an angel of death. Fortunately, I didn't have to make the decision alone. Everyone in the family was on board except for one sister who hoped against hope that he would have one more comeback. After a grim family conference, she tearfully gave her consent, and I was much relieved that we had all reached consensus. I told a nurse I particularly liked about our decision.

"Oh, that would be a blessing," she said, and her tender words confirmed that we were doing the right thing.

James's doctor took over and all but made the decision for us. After he assured us that there was no chance James could come back, we arranged to convene in the hospital room later that evening, September 30, 1993.

When the time came, Charlene, James's brothers and sisters, and I gathered around his bed, all of us linking hands. Vicky and her boyfriend, Luke, joined us as the doctor disconnected the many wires and tubes that connected James to life support. Praying while the hospital chaplain said a few soothing words, we watched the graph monitoring his vital signs plunge ever so slowly and then flatline. The machine's incessant beeping slowed and stopped. All of us were in tears as we blew kisses and bade James goodbye. He was not even thirty-seven years old.

After James's family departed, Vicky, Luke, and I headed to the nearest bar for a strong drink. As we left the hospital, a black Lincoln Town Car pulled out of a parking space next to the entrance. Headlights glowing, it backed up and turned down the street before disappearing around the corner. All three of us knew instinctively that the driver was James's doctor. After making a special after-hours hospital visit to euthanize James, his work for the day was done. He had lost one more patient, but we had all lost a great love.

In the coming days, moving grief-stricken through the silent, empty apartment, I discovered a cache of tiny scraps of green paper in the unlikeliest hiding places. Each one was marked with a date and a series of little counting bundles: four vertical strokes with a fifth line crossing them horizontally, making a bunch of five. I had often watched James jotting down these little bundles, and I repeatedly asked him what they meant. He always refused to tell me, but now as I glanced at them, I felt sure I knew exactly what they signified. Each date must have represented a future day to which he hoped to live, and each stroke represented one more day lived on the way to that goal. He was counting the rest of his life in days and rejoicing for every five new days God granted him.

THE DAY after James died, I opened the refrigerator to find two little brown lunch bags, ready to be grabbed the next time we ran out the door. One was scribbled with the letter "J" for James; the other with "B" for Brooks. Packed and labeled by James before he went to the hospital for the last time, the humble little bags were so dear to me, so quotidian and normal, that I burst into tears. Never again would he prepare our lunches or write his initials on a bag; never again would we eat lunch together. The apartment was full of little grief-trippers like these, and I was glad for them because I knew I needed to cry.

I cried for a year.

Still working forty miles away in Redwood City, I hardly knew what I was doing, and my days passed by in a fog of confusion. The bouts of anticipatory grieving that I had lived with for almost two years now transformed into real grief, in all its rawness.

Every day, I spent lunch alone at a picnic table in a tiny park near the office. As I ate my sandwich or lay sunbathing on the bright-green grass afterward, the pure, reverberating tones of a wind chime serenaded me from somebody's back porch. The lovely chimes pierced the invisible membrane between the living and the dead, seeming to communicate directly with our departed loved ones. For many weeks, listening to those healing chimes was the high point of my day because, in some mysterious way, they reconnected me with James.

When the day was over, I had plenty of time for more reflection on the long drive home. As I drove, I slid my favorite blues CD into the player. As soon as the weeping guitar riffs cued up, tears sprang to my eyes. I rolled down the window, shouting over and over into the fast-blowing wind, "I love you, James! I love you! I miss you, James! I miss you!"

Many were the times on those drives that I asked God to take me so that I could be reunited with him. In truth, I had not lost my desire to live, but logic dictated that the only way to rejoin James was to follow him in death. The last thing I wanted was to bottle up my emotions. I wanted to move through them like a boat pounding through waves in a storm. I knew that was healthier than forcing them down or shoving them aside. Still, no matter how much I needed to cry, sometimes the tears wouldn't come. When that happened, I resorted to the same catalyst I had used ten years before, when Chad left me: I played Deniece Williams's song "Silly." It never failed to make me cry.

Desperately needing levity and hoping to recapture the excitement of those long-ago days when I sashayed off to the Pendulum to get lucky, I jumped into our little silver Integra on a Friday night and drove across the Bay Bridge. Even though I knew it was crazy to be going out only days after James's death, something spurred me on. Deep below the myriad layers of grief, I yearned to reexperience what it felt like to be single—to be in command of my will, answering to nobody. Claiming my newfound status as a single man seemed like finding a path to survival.

When I got to the Castro, the Elephant Walk, the Midnight Sun, and Badlands were all still present and accounted for. Making my nostalgic tour through the Pendulum, a handful of guys stood around, much like all those years before, but something was different. There was no energy, no electricity in the air. Gazing about, I could see the distorted prism of my grief reflected back at me in the eyes of my gay brothers. Each man was only one of the thousands of men who had watched their lovers die while I was missing from the scene. Although everything looked the same on the surface, underneath lay the smoking ruin of an enormous funeral pyre. We were the widows; we were the ones expected to climb on top and light ourselves on fire. Somehow, I hadn't anticipated this. Despite everything I knew about the statistics of AIDS, I wasn't prepared to witness a Castro that had changed forever. The neighborhood had always danced to the beat of a different drummer, but now the drummer was dead.

After a few furtive circuits through the bars, I decided it was time to go home to bed. On my way back up Castro, who should I run into but Ernie, a young friend and protégé of Chad, whom I hadn't seen in years.

"What are you doing here, Brooks?" he asked, frowning. "Didn't I hear that James died?"

How had Ernie learned so quickly of James's death? Exactly how had the news spread? His judgmental tone stung me, echoing the rebuke that Darrell's friend had given me all those years ago at the Eagle Creek, when I walked off the dance floor with my new squeeze, Taye. Nearly ten years had gone by, but apparently guys were still clocking each other for any sign of duplicity or fickleness. It was the exact opposite of helping or supporting one's gay brothers, which was what we all so desperately needed. More than anything, I still yearned for a community, and where was the belonging in that?

"Yes, he died," I said. "He's gone." There was nothing more to say, so I continued up the street. I never saw Ernie again.

About a week later, James's funeral took place. He had insisted that he wished to be cremated, but because he had no will or testament, Charlene stepped in and arranged for a proper Southern Baptist burial. How could I stop her? The memorial service at the Fouché Funeral Home in Oakland was attended by a handful of my friends and workmates, along with all of James's extended family. I was pleased that my former boss, Michael Painter, came, demonstrating his willingness to show me the same sign of respect that he would have given had I been married to a woman. James's high school choir director arrived from Marysville, California, and when she sang a gospel song in his memory, her searing voice burned into my heart, branding me with the sublime poetry of her grief.

After the service, we stepped into black limousines, riding in procession to Mountain View Cemetery. In the limo, James's friendly sister-in-law held my hand and comforted me. At the cemetery, family and guests assembled on the lawn in front of James's grave. Holding hands, we listened to the uplifting words of the hospital chaplain. As the first shovelful of dirt fell, I looked down at his coffin in tears. It was so final, so painful to think of his body being buried, of being covered by a layer of soil that would soon render even his casket invisible. I whispered my love to him, blew him a kiss, and swore that I would never forget him. All around me I could feel his mother, father, brothers, sisters, and cousins doing the same. But the other people who had once known him? I feared that they might soon forget him.

Afterward, there was a reception at the Draper home, but I was exhausted and had to leave after about an hour. Much as I wanted to share my grief with James's brothers and sisters, the tears would not come in their presence. I had to go home, where I could be alone, to cry.

Every evening, I sat down and wrote a letter to James. I told him what I was doing, how I missed him, and how hard it was to be without him. Somehow, this helped me. To write a letter was an act of hope. The hope was that he was just around a corner, waiting for me, and he was okay. My letters seemed to testify that there is not an unbridgeable chasm between the living and the dead after all.

In an intimate and tender moment, a few months before James's death, when hope for his full recovery already seemed a lost cause, I had curled up with him on the couch and said, "When you're gone and you find your way to the other side, please come to me if you can, however you can, and let me know you're okay."

One or two nights before Halloween, James granted my wish. The apartment was pitch-black when I woke up at around 3:00 a.m. James was standing in our bedroom doorway, smiling, a finger on his lips coaxing me to be quiet. Raising his hand as if to say, "Follow me," he led me to the dining room. It was so great to be with him again, to be in his presence one more time. I was sure that I was not asleep because I could see the walls and ceiling with absolute clarity. I could reach out and touch the rough texture of the brushed silk wallpaper, although my enhanced perception of these physical things had subtly shifted.

In the dining room, James smiled broadly, his loving eyes shining with happiness.

"I can't stay long," he said. "I have to go, but I want you to know that I'm all right."

With that, his head rose like the balloons we had tied to the dining room chair, and his legs curled into the tail of a mermaid.

He was still smiling as he drifted up through the ceiling. When I turned to look out through the balcony door, a giant, orange harvest moon hung in the indigo sky. As I watched, a flotilla of witches' brooms flew upward against the luminous disk of the moon, like the bicyclists in *E.T. the Extraterrestrial.* From one of them, a tiny hand waved back at me. It was James, and he was on his way to heaven. He was too far away for me to see clearly, but even from that distance I could tell that he was grinning broadly, just as he had when we first met and fell in love.

Despite the blessing of this healing visitation, I suffered from a recurring dream.

I'm walking down the street when James suddenly appears out of nowhere. I'm overjoyed to see him, and he's equally glad to see me. He smiles and gives me a light hug, but there's a pensive look on his face. His eyes are asking, *Why did you leave me? Why aren't we still together?* James was always terrified of being abandoned, and according to my dream logic, I left him when I failed to accompany him to the other side. In my dream, I feel intense guilt and pain about leaving him, but we have both moved on. Each of us has a new boyfriend, so we smile furtively at each other one last time before walking sadly off in opposite directions, losing one another all over again. Every time I have that dream, I wake up full of anxiety and sadness.

But this dream was not the only thing that troubled me. Having such an active mind, I couldn't stop analyzing the enormity of what had happened to us from the moment James tested positive and I tested negative, driving a wedge of difference between us. One story I told myself only reinforced my survivor's guilt. I had discovered a book about Edgar Cayce's mystic trances, and I devoured it. When Cayce fell into a trance, many of his psychic readings tell of two souls who consent to be born into a life that they will share, specifically to give one the opportunity to teach a karmic lesson to the other or to relieve the other's karmic debt.

Fascinated, I told myself that perhaps James had subconsciously agreed to prove his love for me by voluntarily donning the robe of a disease that was my rightful karmic burden. In that supreme act of selflessness, he would grant me prolonged life, thereby allowing me to accomplish my own mysterious psychic mission. However painful or absurd, the story had a tiny kernel of logic. It supplied a hypothesis for why James had tested positive, following a year of sexual abstinence, while I had tested negative after the most promiscuous years of my life.

Even my memory of our joyful grocery store excursions had a painful echo in my overly analytical mind. I remembered how James had first smiled broadly, then put on an expression of mock terror at the sight of me following him down the aisle before he turned to push his cart up the next one. It was as if he were acting in a macabre melodrama, donning first the mask of comedy and then the mask of tragedy in quick succession. Could it be that, in those moments looking back at me, he saw me as an avatar for the grim reaper? Was he taunting me because, in his mind, he was thumbing his nose at death? Why else would he be so intent on running away from me? And because I had been part of the family decision to end his life, didn't that too have a tiny kernel of logic?

A month or two went by, and I knew I had to move out of the apartment, which was filled with ghosts and too expensive on my own. I soon found a nearby one-bedroom on the third floor of a mid-century apartment building at 570 Mira Vista. With its parking garage and outdoor swimming pool, it was a nice apartment for a single person, but I didn't belong there because I didn't belong anywhere.

After moving in, I was in a strange mental space, mourning yet craving company, entertainment, and sex. Once again, it felt as if two warring selves were living inside me. Normally, my regular routines comforted and sustained me, but now my fractured emotions sent me spinning into an increasingly manic state. Every day, I tried to cram more and more activity into my waking hours, as if expending all that extra energy could somehow paper over my sadness.

The more blindly I searched for something to fill the emptiness inside me, the more groundless I felt. I began dating again, which was foolish, since it was so premature. None of the guys I dated were a good match—how could they be, only a few months after James's death? Of course, I knew it wasn't possible to meet another great love so soon. And even if I did find someone suitable, wouldn't that reflect a lack of respect for James, for how central he remained in my heart? Still, I pressed on, needing to find some sort of connection, no matter how transitory.

One Saturday night, I drove into San Francisco to meet a date at the Eagle. Worried that I was late, I circled the block, eventually finding a parking space on the other side of the elevated freeway behind the bar. Quickly parking, I jumped out of the car, pushed the door lock down, and closed the door, only to discover that I had left the keys in the ignition with the lights on and the engine running. I suppose this could have happened to anybody, but I was convinced it meant that I was spiraling out of control.

Shit, I thought, *what am I going to do*? Hurrying over to the bar, I found my date waiting and explained the situation. He was very calm about it.

"Don't worry," he said. "I'll call Triple A," and before I could turn around, he was on the pay phone, cradling his ear so he could hear over the noisy sound system. As strange as this may sound, within ten minutes a fire truck arrived in front of the Eagle and a strapping fireman, in uniform, jumped out to assist us.

"Where's your car?" he asked.

"Around the corner on the other side of the freeway over-pass," I said sheepishly.

"Okay, get in—I'll take you there," he said.

We climbed into his cab. I was in full leather and—despite my anxiety—the erotic aspect of the situation did not escape me: two leather men in a truck with a hot fireman. While he revved up the engine and pulled out, the guys lining up to enter the bar gazed back at us with lust and envy. I smiled through the wind-shield, giving them the thumbs-up sign.

We zipped back to my car, where the engine was still running. The fireman gingerly lowered a coat hanger through the crack at the top of the driver's window, expertly disengaging the door lock. We shook hands and I thanked him profusely, but as he roared off, I was supremely embarrassed at having been idiotic enough to leave my keys in the ignition.

A week later, I was no less manic. After I met up with the same guy at the Eagle, he followed me across the Bay to spend the night. Arriving home around midnight, I opened the garage door with my automatic Genie, drove in, and parked. Then I ran up the garage ramp, ducking under the automatic door, which was already lowering. Once reunited with my friend, I was shocked to discover that, although I had my car key this time, I had left my house keys in the car. Now I had no way to get back into the building. How had I once again managed to do something so stupid, and what were we to do? Even more worrisome, the guy must have thought I was a complete flake, but fortunately, he was as calm and accommodating as ever.

Tiptoeing, I glanced over the stucco wall that enclosed the swimming pool from the street. Nearly all the apartment windows were dark, but the pool glowed a dramatic aqua, and yellow light seeped from one first-floor apartment. Gesturing for my friend to follow, I climbed over the wall, walked around the pool, and stood at the sliding glass doors of the lit apartment. The drapes were drawn a few inches, and peering in, I could see a young man and woman reclining on the sofa, languidly making out. My buddy stood next to me as I knocked politely on the door, praying they didn't think we were burglars and shoot at us. Nothing happened, so I gave the door another gentle tap. After a long moment of dead silence, the drape pulled back a few more inches, and we smiled and waved at the young straight couple standing half-dressed in front of us, behind the glass.

"I live here and I left my keys in the garage," I said quickly, as the man cracked open the slider by a hair's width. "Would you mind letting us in through your apartment?"

"Uh—okay," the man said doubtfully, quickly looking me up and down.

Appearing to conclude that there was a better-than-even chance we were not axe murderers, he pushed the slider open, and we gratefully traipsed across the living room to the main hall beyond.

"Thanks," I said. "I really appreciate it!"

The woman's mouth was agape, but both of them grinned as they returned to the sofa. It wasn't every night that they had the chance to observe two homosexuals, clad head to toe in leather, pass through their living room. This was no doubt a night they would remember for a long time, and I hoped it would inspire them to return to their necking with renewed ardor.

After those two embarrassing incidents, I realized that I had to get my manic behavior and mindless cruising under control. This was not who I was—I was a sober, rational, and reliable man, not a ditzy basket case—or so I most fervently hoped. But the things that made me solid and gave my life purpose were falling away one by one: James and his family; Oakland and the community I had built there; even the dream that I could be fully myself as a gay man in San Francisco. Taking wild chances on the dating scene wasn't helping any, but even attempting to impose order on my life by focusing on my routine wasn't enough to ground me. Feeling increasingly unmoored, I wanted to go home, but despite receiving James's blessing to return to Seattle, I didn't know where home was.

Eight months after James died, my temporary job working on the construction drawings for the Roosevelt Memorial abruptly ended on May 8, 1994. The complex set of nearly five hundred drawings was finally complete, ready to be issued for bidding and construction in Washington, DC. To mark the occasion, Larry

Halprin invited our staff to a big celebration at his cavernous warehouse in San Francisco's South of Market district. The party represented another turning point in my life: I had come full circle from yearning to become a landscape architect, to assisting on exciting and meaningful designs at Hanna/Olin, to long years slogging away at a series of firms on mostly undistinguished projects, to now celebrating my small role in the apogee of one of the most nationally significant landscape architectural projects of the 1990s.

The Roosevelt Memorial was nothing like Kedleston Hall or Stourhead, but it was a work of genius, a contemporary expression of what I had so admired in England. It was a three-dimensional, sculptural world that one could move through, experiencing the ephemeral shifts of light and cloud on its red granite walls. More significantly, unlike the English parks, the memorial had been designed with the express intention of inviting the public in.

When I walked in the door of Halprin's office, the large loft was already filling up with people. Hundreds of polaroids of Halprin's family and staff lined one wall, their faces mugging at the arriving guests while servers handed out flutes of champagne and small plates of appetizers. Someone had prepared a video mockumentary lampooning all the people and events that had led up to this moment. Screening in a continuous loop in the conference room, the roast spared no one.

Back in the main room, a gigantic cardboard model of the memorial, bigger than two ping-pong tables, dominated the space. The elaborate scale model depicted a twelve-foot-high zigzagging wall of Carnelian granite, nearly a quarter mile long, that divided the space into four outdoor rooms. Representing one term of Roosevelt's four-term presidency, each room displayed its own unique fountain, beginning with a modest one at the entry, and climaxing with a dramatic waterfall symbolizing the cataclysm of World War II in Roosevelt's final term. Bronze sculptures enacting key scenes from the events of the Roosevelt administration led chronologically from one room to the next, and along the way, visitors could pause to look out over the Tidal Basin, with its iconic flowering cherry trees.

By now, everybody had arrived at the party, the champagne was flowing, and the giant loft echoed with the noisy buzz of excited conversation. Larry Halprin, who had been notably missing, suddenly appeared on the mezzanine above, surveying the crowd as if he were the president of the United States on Inauguration Day.

"Here's to Franklin Delano Roosevelt," he said, raising his glass in a toast.

The clinking of hundreds of champagne glasses resounded from the floor as an army of hands raised in salute. At that signal, Halprin launched into FDR's most famous speech, the "we have nothing to fear but fear itself" speech, in the aristocratic accent of FDR himself. For a brief moment, he actually *became* Roosevelt, and a great cheer rose from the floor.

A day or two later, I left Befu, Morris, Scardina's office in Redwood City for the last time and headed to the Castro, where I repaired to the Pendulum for my own private celebration. Toni Braxton's new hit, "Another Sad Love Song," was playing on the jukebox, filling me with a plethora of mixed emotions—grief over James, the brief excitement of our success with the FDR Memorial, and an unexpected sense of relief at being newly footloose and free again. Torn between anticipation and trepidation at the challenge of my life to come, I knew that I needed a change, but I had no clear sense of what sort of change it might be. All I knew was that I was tired of saying goodbye to everything and everybody I loved.

Fall approached, and with it the one-year anniversary of James's death. To my immense surprise, I was growing weary of the Bay Area's endless sunshine. Although the bright-red leaves of the sweetgums were lovely when the wind blew them along the dry street gutters, I longed to observe them submerged in reflecting puddles of rainwater. It was then that my thoughts turned nostalgically toward my rainy hometown, the city to which James had implored me to return. Pondering it, I remembered how every time I visited Seattle, I felt like I belonged. I belonged to the familiar landmarks, I belonged to my loving family and our extended social network, I even belonged to my group of high school friends, with whom I had not entirely lost touch. Maybe, if I returned to Seattle, I could find a way to feel whole again.

34 THE LESCHI LAKE CAFE

THINGS CAME to a head in July, when Mom had to go in for a heart valve operation. I was not nearly over grieving for James, and on my flight up to Seattle to visit her, I feared that I couldn't handle it if I were to lose her as well. Fortunately, Mom pulled through with panache, smiling up at Dad, Bliss, and me from her hospital bed. I had a few free days, so I decided to set up a handful of informational interviews with landscape architecture offices around town.

One day, I called Bill Talley, a practitioner well-known for his engagement with the professional community, his residential garden designs, and his official role as the campus landscape architect for the University of Washington. Bill could not have been friendlier on the phone.

"May I take you out for coffee . . . or a beer?" I asked.

"That can be arranged. Why don't you meet me Wednesday afternoon, right after work, at the Leschi Lake Cafe?" Bill said. "It's next to my office on the shores of Lake Washington."

"Great," I said. "I'll be there!"

On the lovely summer afternoon of our appointment, the server seated us on the patio under a graceful canopy of ash trees. Raising his beer stein in a toast, Bill turned out to be even friendlier in person. Conversation with him and his younger business partner, Scott Pascoe, flowed naturally, and I noticed with pleasure that it transitioned easily from career topics to our personal lives and back again. I had never felt more at ease talking to an older landscape architect than I did with Bill.

The experience reminded me of how, in my youth, I had always yearned for a mentor. Sometimes I had sought one out, as I did with Bob Hanna, and sometimes one had chosen me, as did Paul Korshin. What I had really needed then was to be mentored as a whole person, not just as a student or a young professional, but both men had stuck relentlessly to the script of academics or shop talk, as if there were something unseemly about discussing our personal lives or outside interests. With Bill it was different. Somehow, I knew I could confide in him about nearly anything, so I told him how I had recently lost my partner, James.

"I'm so sorry to hear that," Bill said. "You know, my stepson, Matt, has AIDS, and it's really up and down with him these days. In and out of the hospital, good days and bad. It's breaking poor Judy's heart," he added, referring to his wife.

"Oh no," I said. "That's so hard. Please give Judy my sympathy." Bill nodded and smiled. After that, he asked me about my parents, whom it turned out he had met through the university. That should not have surprised me because I soon learned that he seemed to know anybody and everybody in Seattle, taking great pleasure in connecting the dots between them. It was a feat he accomplished with admirable ease and humor, as if he saw it as his personal mission to preserve and enhance all that was left of Seattle's small-town character.

"I always found your father a bit doctrinaire," Bill said, unexpectedly. "He can be hard to take, but I love your mother."

"Oh, I know what you mean," I said, smiling inwardly at Bill's refreshingly candid disclosure. It was the first time I could remember that anybody in the professional design community had recognized or vocalized the shortcomings in Dad that I had struggled with my entire life—his stubbornness and ideological bent. Normally, people tended to fall all over themselves in his admittedly well-deserved praise, so when Bill alluded to Dad's abrasiveness it meant that he was observant enough to look below the surface, where he evaluated Dad as a whole person, not just the well-respected professor of architecture.

Soon, Bill had to leave to help Judy fix dinner, but when we shook hands, I knew I had found a new friend. It was all I could think about on the drive back to Mom and Dad's house. In Philadelphia, I had come out of the closet, telling nearly everybody I was gay, but the fast track of my structured career oppressed me, and I had not felt comfortable bringing Chad to our office happy hours. Then, I had moved to San Francisco, craving its greater freedom, but when I brought Chad, and later James, to office parties, it still felt awkward and strained. Even my precious freedom grated because it was so open-ended and boundless that, like a capsized man reaching out to grab a life preserver, I found myself grasping for some new sort of order around which to shape my life.

Despite living in the gay mecca, the place where we were accepted more than anywhere else, I had not really succeeded in finding life-work harmony or inner peace except during those four short years from the time I first met James to when he was diagnosed with HIV. As for the sense of belonging to the larger gay community, I had not experienced it except briefly during the BWMT meetings I attended.

Then AIDS blew everything up. My life returned to being divided into two sharply defined categories. Work and my colleagues were assigned to one box; my personal life and caregiving belonged in the other. After James died, my loneliness prompted me to return to the chaos of the cruising scene, once again pitting my desire for freedom against my need to feel grounded. When that experiment shattered any sense of balance I had achieved to date, I reexperienced the acute sense of being divided into two selves.

Now I wondered, maybe those two selves could finally be united in Seattle? Not only would I be returning to friends and family who knew and accepted me, but if I got a job with Bill, I would be accepted at work as well. I was sure that I had met a kindred spirit in him—someone who both understood and accepted me as a whole person.

About a week later, I was back in Oakland when Dad phoned. "Bill Talley is trying to reach you," he said. "He wants you to come to Seattle and work for him."

"Okay, I'll call him, Dad. Thanks," I said, hanging up. Although that was great news, it left me torn between my desire to move home and my long-running commitment to the Bay Area, with my remaining handful of dear friends. Moving meant admitting that my experiment with becoming an enthusiastic, active member of one of the largest, most influential gay movements in the world had not yet succeeded. In a sense, leaving Oakland also meant leaving James, because our lives and memories were so entwined there. Still, he had blessed my move. Following through with it didn't mean I was running away from him. On the contrary, I would be complying with his explicit wishes.

While I anxiously weighed those two opposing points of view, I realized that, somewhere in the back of my head, acknowledgment had not yet shifted to acceptance, nor had acceptance turned into affirmation. That was how Stan, the psychic, would have put it, and it neatly explained why the decision was torture for me.

Finally, after spending more than half an hour thrashing through thickets of mental thorns, I took a deep breath, called Bill's office and reached Scott Pascoe.

"I've given it a lot of thought," I said. "But the fact is, I'm just not ready to leave my friends—and my life—in Oakland."

"That's fine," Scott said. "I understand, and I'll let Bill know." We hung up, but the next day Bill called me.

"Brooks, if you're having trouble making up your mind, why don't you come up, work with us for a week, and try it out? Then you can decide whether or not you want to make the move."

Bill's invitation was so unexpected, so reasonable and appealing, that I couldn't possibly say no. Not only did it mean he had my back, that he specifically wanted *me* as an employee, but it also meant he had enough insight to understand what I needed better than I did. Bill had been forceful enough to take the matter into his own hands, which was as kind and impressive as it was highly unusual.

Accordingly, in September, I found myself working for a short stint in Bill's tiny waterfront office. Seated at my drafting table, I enjoyed gazing out the large window, where the graceful I-90 bridge floated across choppy whitecaps and deep-blue waves to the forested shoreline of Mercer Island. It felt like the perfect fit, and I knew it was time to pack my bags and move home.

In November, I officially started my new job in Seattle. Within days, Bill and Judy invited me to the first of many wonderful, gourmet dinner parties at their gracious home in the Madison Park neighborhood. Not only were their friends witty and sophisticated, but they were also kind and understanding, never arrogant. By then, Judy's son Matt had died, and several of them came from Judy's Mothers' Group of women who had bonded over the shared loss of their sons to AIDS.

In the presence of Bill and Judy and their friends, I felt that I belonged. It didn't matter that theirs was a small community; what mattered was that it fit me both personally and professionally. It was better than a giant, abstract entity like the gay community because it was real and it was *personal*. I had landed among "quality people"—exactly the type of people Stan had said I would meet.

For now, that was enough. It didn't trouble me that I was single again, that I didn't have someone new to love. I was not ready for a new love. Eventually, I would meet someone special; I was sure of that. When I was ready, he would come sauntering in, a big smile on his lips. In the meantime, I would make a new set of friends. Remembering how much I had enjoyed my sunny bike rides around Tiburon or out to Point Reyes, I resolved to join Different Spokes, the gay cyclists' club. When winter gave way to spring and the days grew longer, I would join their Wednesday evening social rides up Seattle's lovely Burke–Gilman Trail.

Arriving at work early one morning after one of Bill's dinner parties, I was surprised to spot a large panel truck idling across the street in front of the Leschi Market grocery. The cartoon face of an apple-cheeked grandmother with a bun of white hair hovered, smiling, between two giant words emblazoned in whimsical script on the side of the truck. Her face looked just like my grandmother, Nana, before she cut her hair, and the words read *Mother's Cookies*. I had never before seen a Mother's Cookies truck in Seattle, but the message could not have been more clear. With Nana's help, James was blessing me and welcoming me home.

I hadn't left him in Oakland after all. I had brought him home with me.

ACKNOWLEDGMENTS

THIS BOOK has been my dream for the last eight years, but my dream would never have come true without the help and active participation of a whole village of people. Many thanks to Alice Acheson for believing in me, pointing me toward writing conferences, explaining the publishing journey to me, and helping me submit to writing contests and agents.

Bill Kenower continues to inspire me with his *Fearless Writing* classes and his injunction that we all possess the power to write from our heart and our gut. Thank you, Bill, for helping me hone key chapters in your personal essay class at the Pacific Northwest Writers Association Writing Cottage. Thanks also to Corbin Lewars for separating the wheat from the chaff, helping me to mine the themes driving my story while jettisoning reams of irrelevant material.

Chapter 1: Urban Cowboy lacked drama and immediacy until Dorothy Wall guided me in scene building. Brian Giddens, thank you for providing further comments and insight, bringing that first chapter into clearer focus.

I have so much gratitude for Elizabeth Kracht's two complete developmental edits. Without you, Liz, this book would be no more than a draft.

Brooke Warner, I cannot thank you enough for recognizing my manuscript as worthy of publication. Your enthusiasm for hybrid publishing and your praise for the memoir genre have been my lodestar! Thank you for your patience, your organization, and the high degree of professionalism that defines the SparkPress brand. Thank you for connecting me with my amazing developmental and copy editor, Lorraine Fico-White, who helped me polish my manuscript until it shone. Thank you, Brooke, for assigning me my intrepid project manager, Megan Milton and my proofreader, Paula Dragosh. Lastly, thank you to the highly creative team of cover designers at SparkPress!

My acknowledgments would not be complete without a shout-out to the many friends and colleagues who gave me permission to use their real names. Thank you, Dennis McGlade, Alistair McIntosh, Jeff Evans, W. Gary Smith, Anne James, and Judy Talley, among so many others.

Thank you, Birgyte, for loving how I described you and for laughing out loud at the passages I wrote about our unique and deep friendship. Thank you, Leland Shawn Draper and Daretta O'Neil, for blessing me with your approval for the intimate passages I wrote about your deceased brother, James Draper, a man all three of us loved. Thanks so much to my dear friends and alpha readers, Michael Bosnick, Jen McCormick, Molly Davenport, Lynn Pruzan, Bliss Kolb, John Richards, and Jeff Evans for cheering me on, and thanks to Arika Moore Patneaude for her invaluable sensitivity read.

This story would not have been possible without the extraordinary mentorship and teaching I received as a young man from

Paul J. Korshin and Reyner Banham (both now deceased) and as a landscape-architect-in-training from Bob Hanna (also deceased) and Laurie Olin.

Laurie, your generosity in endorsing my chapters about you reveals that your heart is as big as your artistic and design talent. Thank you so much; I am forever grateful to you!

Many thanks to Bill Talley for taking me under your wing when I returned to Seattle and for seeing me as a whole person. I miss you so much! And thank you, Judy Talley, for your quiet and enduring support.

Lastly, thanks to my mother, father, brother, and grandparents for loving me unconditionally. Big thanks to my husband and partner of thirty years, Dennis Mullings, for believing in me and putting up with me while I was in the throes of writing, rewriting, and submitting this book. You are the love of my life!

DISCUSSION QUESTIONS

BASED ON the events and scenes described in this story, what can be gleaned from the following questions?

1. How can any of us move beyond our conflicting professional and personal identities to become our most authentic self?
2. Is it possible to achieve a balance between work life and personal life?
3. What is the relationship between fine art (painting) and landscape design?
4. What invisible or less overt impediments have kept LGBTQIA+ men and women from coming out?
5. Given recent attacks on Diversity, Equity, and Inclusion (DEI) initiatives, is there still a place for LGBTQIA+ support groups such as Black and White Men Together in universities or in the broader community?
6. How does a young person choose between lust and long-term love? Does it have to be a choice?
7. How does racism affect interracial relationships? Can interracial gay relationships overcome racism?
8. Are gay male relationships or marriages as meaningful as straight relationships/marriages?
9. Can gay activism and support systems give us the strength we need to be a loving and effective caregiver to a partner with AIDS or another terminal disease?

10. How are sexual practices affected by having a partner with AIDS?
11. How do anticipatory grief and survivor guilt affect the grieving process?
12. Can it be said that love endures from beyond the grave?
13. How does one move on after losing a partner to AIDS or, by extension, to death in general?

ABOUT THE AUTHOR

BROOKS KOLB was educated at the American College in Paris, University College London, and the University of Pennsylvania. At Penn he trained under Ian McHarg, famed author of *Design With Nature*, and with Laurie Olin, subject of the 2024 documentary *Sitting Still*. After coming out of the closet, he moved to San Francisco, where he witnessed two key periods of gay history: the post-Stonewall era of sexual liberation and the tragic AIDS epoch. The principal of Brooks Kolb LLC Landscape Architecture, Brooks has a practice devoted to residential garden design. A long-term park preservation advocate and founding member of Seattle's Volunteer Park Trust, he currently serves on the boards of Allied Arts of Seattle and the Allied Arts Foundation. An avid swimmer, Brooks lives in Seattle with his husband, Dennis, and their miniature schnauzer, Stella.

Looking for your next great read?

We can help!

Visit www.shewritespress.com/next-read
or scan the QR code below for a list
of our recommended titles.

She Writes Press is an award-winning
independent publishing company founded to
serve women writers everywhere.